GREAT BRITAIN

Discarded

Rhonda Carrier, Belinda Dixon, Lucy Dodsworth, Stuart Forster,
Kay Gillespie, Tharik Hussain, Emily Luxton, Mike MacEacheran,
James March, Amy Pay, Kerry Walker

Meet our writers

Rhonda Carrier
@rhondacarriertravels

Based in Manchester since 2006, Rhonda feels instantly at home in the world-class cities of the north but also adores escaping to the troughs, dales, moors, forests and beaches of northern England whenever her schedule allows.

Belinda Dixon
@BelDixon

A travel writer for the past 25 years, Belinda always loves coming home to southwest England. Partly because it means she can get back to kayaking, running, sea swimming and generally exploring the moors and shores.

Lucy Dodsworth
@lucydodsworth

Lucy's favourite experience is discovering the southeast's WWII secret 'underground tunnels, spy stations and mysterious military bases' (p72). Based in the Cotswolds, she can't resist a honey-stone village, scenic viewpoint or country pub.

Stuart Forster
@goeatdo

Born in Sunderland and now a resident of Tyneside after living in both Germany and India, Stuart loves the sense of freedom brought by hiking in Northumberland National Park. His favourite experience is walking alongside Hadrian's Wall with friends.

Kay Gillespie
@thechaoticscot

Kay's happiness lies in the Scottish islands: indulging in fresh seafood, peaty whisky and home baking, taking windswept selfies, and wild swimming from bonnie beaches (p229). 'The best adventures begin on tartan-tailed planes or the outside deck of a ferry.'

Man
IRISH SEA
Blackpool
York
Leeds
Hull
Manchester
ENGLAND
Liverpool
DUBLIN
IRELAND
Anglesey
Bangor
Peak District National Park
Lincoln
Snowdonia National Park
Birmingham & the Midlands 112
Nottingham
Norfolk Broads National Park
Wales 160
Leicester
Shrewsbury
Norwich
WALES
Birmingham
Aberystwyth
Northampton
Cambridge
The Broads
Pembrokeshire Coast National Park
Brecon Beacons National Park
Stratford-upon-Avon
Ipswich
St George's Channel
Gloucester
Oxford
Pembroke
Swansea
Bristol
Windsor
LONDON
London 38
CARDIFF
Bath
Canterbury
Strait of Dover
Ilfracombe
South Downs National Park
Dover
Salisbury
Southampton
Brighton
Calais
Southwest England 82
Dartmoor National Park
Exeter
Bournemouth
Portsmouth
Southeast England 64
Lille
Plymouth
ENGLISH CHANNEL
Land's End
Penzance
Isles of Scilly
Amiens
Guernsey
Caen
Jersey
PARIS

Stand in ancient, mystical stone circles. Down a pint of craft beer. Don your boots and explore spectacular natural beauty. Experience a night of adrenaline-fuelled live music. Be awe-struck by world-class art and architecture. Question imperial legacies at enlightened institutes. Enjoy a Michelin-starred dish or an authentic curry in a hip, urban neighbourhood. Raise a glass of award-winning English wine. Lose yourself in the richness of Britain's cultural diversity. Swim wild in a loch.

This is Great Britain.

TURN THE PAGE AND START PLANNING YOUR NEXT BEST TRIP →

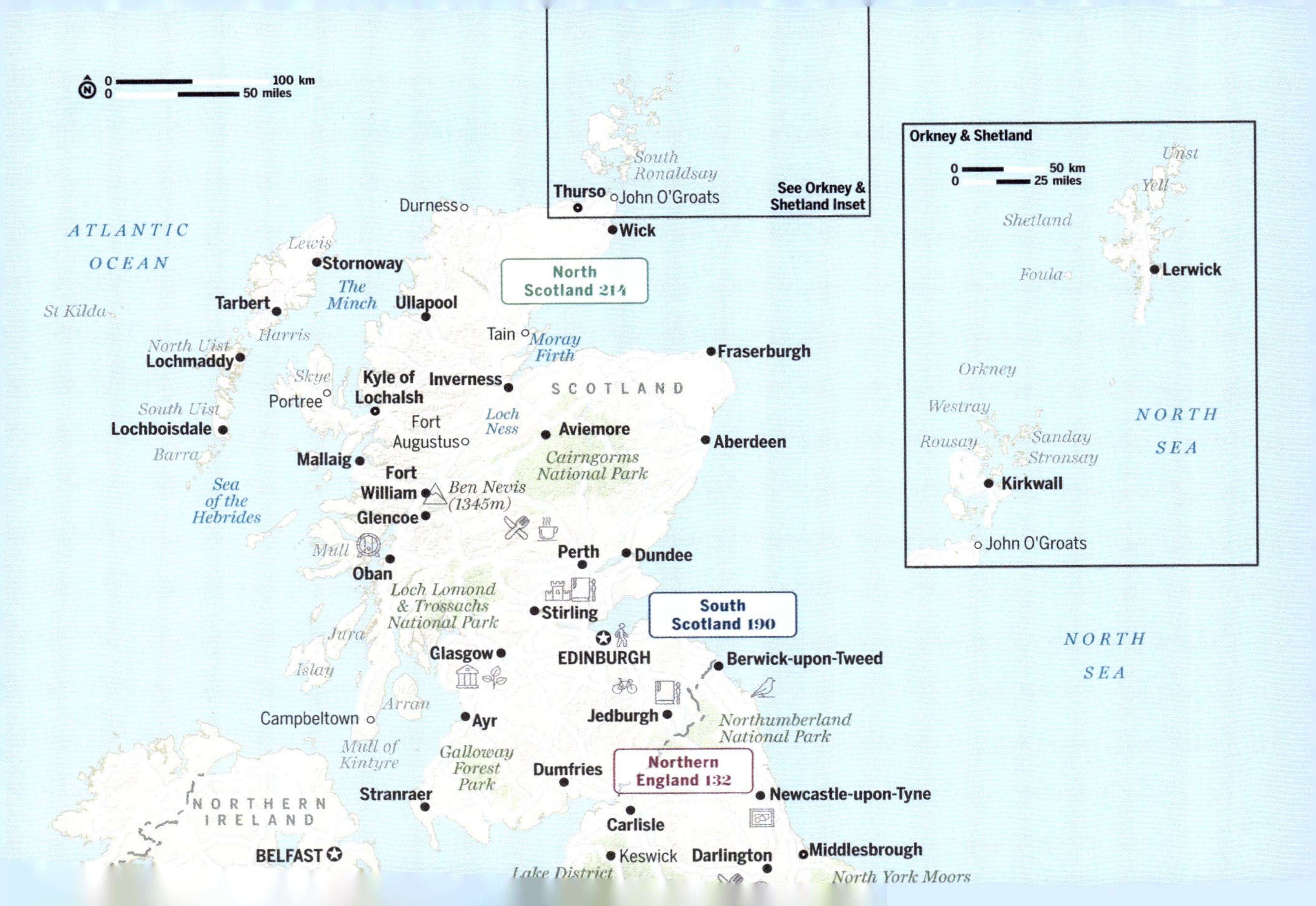

0 100 km
0 50 miles
ATLANTIC OCEAN
St Kilda
Lewis
Stornoway
The Minch
Tarbert
Harris
North Uist
Lochmaddy
South Uist
Lochboisdale
Barra
Skye
Portree
Sea of the Hebrides
Durness
Ullapool
Kyle of Lochalsh
Inverness
Tain
Moray Firth
Fort Augustus
Loch Ness
Mallaig
Fort William
Ben Nevis (1345m)
Glencoe
Mull
Oban
Aviemore
Cairngorms National Park
SCOTLAND
Fraserburgh
Aberdeen
Perth
Dundee
Loch Lomond & Trossachs National Park
Stirling
EDINBURGH
Jura
Islay
Glasgow
Arran
Campbeltown
Mull of Kintyre
Ayr
Galloway Forest Park
Stranraer
Dumfries
Jedburgh
Berwick-upon-Tweed
Northumberland National Park
NORTHERN IRELAND
BELFAST
Carlisle
Keswick
Lake District
Darlington
Newcastle-upon-Tyne
Middlesbrough
North York Moors
North Scotland 214
South Scotland 190
Northern England 132
Thurso
John O'Groats
Wick
South Ronaldsay
See Orkney & Shetland Inset
Orkney & Shetland
0 50 km
0 25 miles
Unst
Yell
Shetland
Foula
Lerwick
Orkney
Westray
Rousay
Sanday
Stronsay
Kirkwall
John O'Groats
NORTH SEA
NORTH SEA

Tharik Hussain
@tharik_hussain @_tharikhussain

Tharik loves bustling, urban Britain; deliciously flavoured by diverse communities from across the globe. Equally, he loves remote, rural Britain where time appears to stand still. For him, somewhere between these juxtapositions is a great Britain.

Emily Luxton
@em_luxton

Emily blames growing up on the Dorset coast for her love of adventure. Her favourite experience is hiking along the Jurassic Coast (p94), or spending as much time in the sea as possible, preferably on her paddleboard.

Mike MacEacheran
@MikeMacEacheran

Mike is a Glasgow-born, Edinburgh-based travel writer who has been exploring Scotland for the best part of four decades. He's commonly found running in the Pentlands south of the Scottish capital, or down the front of a gig in the Barrowlands in Glasgow.

James March
@jmarchtravel

A Birmingham native, James sampled the joie de vivre of France and Canada for three years before returning home to the Second City with the travel bug. Now a travel writer, he's passionate about showcasing everything that's great about Birmingham.

Amy Pay
@YayAmyPay

Amy has always lived in Wales and loves the country's combination of coast, countryside and culture. She loves wandering around Cardiff's Bute Park (p181), kicking back with friends in local coffee shops and exploring wild west Wales (p174).

Kerry Walker
@kerryawalker

Based near London, Kerry is an award-winning travel writer and author, with a passion for good food, mountains and wild places. Whether it's glimpsing puffins and seals, or foraging for edible seaweeds among rockpools, the Pembrokeshire Coast Path (p176) is her happy place.

FIRST SPREAD: WILLIAM TOTI/500PX ©

Contents

Best Experiences 6
Calendar 18
Trip Builders 26
7 Things to Know
About Great Britain..........34
Read, Listen,
Watch & Follow.................36

London 38
Foodie Top & Tail 42
Family Park Life.................44
An Other London..............48
London's Historic
Monuments.......................50
Southern Delights............52
Listings 54

Hidden Muslim Britain 58

Southeast England 64
Best of the
Cotswold Way....................68
A Taste of
English Wine......................70
WWII Spies
& Secrets............................72
An Oxford Education.........76
Boating the
Norfolk Broads..................78
Listings 80

Southwest England 82
Seaside & Steam...............88
Not-So-New Forest 90
Stories in Stone................92
Into the Jurassic...............94
Adventure Dartmoor 96
Protest Culture...............100
Scilly Ferry Hop...............104
Moors & Shores 106
Explore the Shore 108
Listings 110

Birmingham & the Midlands 112
The Workshop
of the World 116
A Gastronomic Haven.....118
Magical Malverns............120
Canal Country 122
Spectacular Ruins...........126
The Tolkien Trail...............128
Listings 130

Northern England 132
Wild Beaches
of the North.....................138
Wild Waters of
the North 140
Outdoor Art 142
Lancashire's Witches......146
The Lake District's
Foodie Icons 148
Cheese Lovers' Tour
of Yorkshire.....................150
Exploring
Hadrian's Wall 152
Listings 158

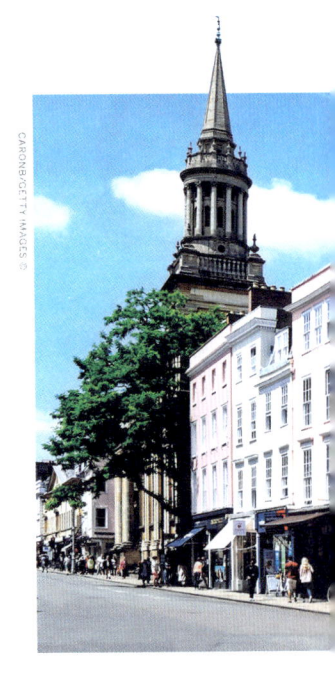

Wales 160
Europe's
Castle Capital..................166
Explore the
Brecon Beacons..............168
Adventure on
the Coast Path.................174
Cardiff's Cultural
Heritage 178
Over the River Taff 180
The Rooftop of Wales......184
Listings 186

Oxford (p76)

South Scotland	**190**
Green Glasgow	196
Witches & Wizards	198
Secret Kintyre	202
South West Coastal 300	204
Biking the 7Stanes	206
Seeking Walter Scott	208
Mackintosh's Glasgow	210
Listings	212

North Scotland	**214**
Remote Tearooms	220
Follow the Jacobite Trail	222
The Sunshine Coast	226
West Highland Wild Swimming	228
Mini Archipelago Adventure	230
Eco-Distillery Hop	232
Wind & Fire	234
Listings	238

Practicalities	**240**
Arriving	242
Getting Around	244
Safe Travel	246
Money	247
Accommodation	248
Responsible Travel	250
Essentials	252

ESSAYS

Anglo Islam	62
The Southeast on Screen	74
Bristol's Black History	102
Diverse Sounds	124
Hadrian's Wall	154
Regional Football Rivalries	156
Cymru Festivities	182
The Festival City	200

VISUAL GUIDES

Awesome Architecture	46
Mid & West Wales Wildlife	172
Up Helly Aa	236

NATURAL FACTS

Nowhere in Britain is more than 75 miles from the sea.

Britain is home to 1800 types of wildflower.

Britain has 11,072 miles of coastline, the third longest in Europe.

ON THE
WILD SIDE

But a whisper away from its cities, Britain is a wild land with an ancient beating heart. Here you can throw on boots to trek through native woodland in search of rare wildlife, be battered by Atlantic waves on ragged stretches of coastline and stand in prehistoric stone circles so old we're still baffled by their true purpose.

Left Wildflower meadow, Cornwall (p108)
Right Scottish bothy (p249)
Below Bottlenose dolphins, Moray Firth (p226), Scotland

→ SLEEP UNDER THE STARS
Whether it's a bothy (p249), a shepherd's hut or a yurt, tune into Britain's wild side by spending a night under the stars.

HOME OF THE NATIONAL PARK
Slip back to nature and be blown away by the drama of Britain's outdoors by visiting any of the country's 15 national parks.

↑ HERE BE WHALES
As well as dolphins, the chilly waters off the coast of Britain are also home to two other rare mammals worth seeking out: the killer whale and the humpback whale.

Best Wild Experiences

▶ Drift gently through the flooded plains of the Norfolk Broads. (p78)

▶ Comb beaches for prehistoric fossils along Britain's Jurassic Coast. (p94)

▶ Spot playful pods of dolphins off the Welsh coast near Cardigan. (p177)

▶ Explore Scotland's wild coastal 'cul-de-sac' at Kintyre. (p202)

PRODUCTION STATS

There are nearly 2000 microbreweries in Britain.

Britain has 387 distilleries.

British wine is booming, with more than 1000 vineyards across the country.

GRAPE & **GRAIN**

Not a lot is more precious to Brits than their right to enjoy a drink. Whether your idea of fun is sipping craft ales in Birmingham's hip microbreweries, crawling through the historic pubs of Victorian London or sniffing out the finest whisky in the distilleries of the Scottish Highlands, this country will leave you in the highest of spirits.

Left Whisky distillery (p232), Scotland
Right Craft beer brewery (p130), Birmingham
Below 'Sausage and mash', a pub-grub classic

→ BRUMMIE CRAFT BEER

With its own craft-beer quarter near Birmingham New Street Station, England's second city is fast becoming Britain's craft-beer capital.

THE LOCAL

For a warm, friendly welcome, classic Sunday roast dinners and cheesy late-night entertainment, it's still difficult to beat grabbing a pint in one of the country's many cosy, local boozers.

↑ PUB GRUB

Once limited to crisps, nuts and pork scratchings, these days pub food is increasingly impressive: from gourmet burgers and chips to cracking Sunday roasts with all the trimmings.

Best Drinking Experiences

▶ Raise a glass to award-winning English fizz in the vineyards of the southeast. (p70)

▶ Go on a gentle pub crawl through the honey-stone inns of the Cotswolds. (p68)

▶ Down a pint in one of London's many old-school pubs and hipster micro-breweries. (p55)

▶ Try a wee dram on a tour of Scotland's much-feted whisky distilleries. (p232)

▶ Forage for ingredients before using them to concoct gin at Goosnargh Gin School. (p159)

BRITAIN'S FOREIGN FOOD

Romans were the first to indulge in eating oysters.

The Vikings introduced smoking and dry-curing fish.

Bangladeshis added spice to British plates with chicken tikka masala.

FOOD, GLORIOUS FOOD

With a raft of ultra-innovative chefs, fresh local produce and influences pinched from every country on earth, Britain has never tasted better. Food is bound to be a big part of your travels: from street-food stalls serving the world on a plate in every city to farmers markets in the countryside, daily fresh seafood on the coast, pubs serving traditional grub and restaurants twinkling with Michelin stars. Dig in.

→ FOODIE MARKETS

Every major city has pop-up food 'trucks' and stalls throughout the week or at weekends such as London's Borough Market. Seek them out for the best street food.

Left Smoked fish (p203), Scotland
Right Borough Market (p43), London
Below Blue Stilton cheese

DISCOUNT EAT OUT

In expensive cities like London, stick to the lunch menus or raid a deli or market for picnic fixings and head to the nearest park.

↑ CHEESY BRITAIN

Often overlooked in favour of its more celebrated Channel counterpart, Britain is actually home to a range of excellent cheeses like a blue Stilton or a crumbly Wensleydale.

Best Foodie Experiences

▶ Embark on a cheese-lover's tour of Yorkshire. (p150)

▶ Treat yourself to a three-starred Michelin meal in the Midlands. (p118)

▶ Try not to break a limb at Gloucestershire's Cheese Rolling Festival. (p81)

▶ Indulge in delicious oysters fished fresh off the coast of Whitstable. (p80)

▶ Grab a tasty dish in the bustling markets of London's Brick Lane. (p43)

MADE FOR WALKING

Come rain or shine, Brits brave the elements by stoically donning coats and boots to hit the trail. Hiking might be slower than driving, but it's the fast track to the country's green and pleasant soul. Criss-crossing this small island are thousands of paths that reveal stirring lakes and mountains, ruins of ancient monuments, bracing coastscapes, mysterious woodlands and crash-bang waterfalls. If you want see Britain, walk it.

Left Brecon Beacons (p168), Wales
Right Scottish breakfast (p220), including haggis
Below Hiking boots

→ **SCOTTISH TEAROOMS**

If you find yourself hiking Scotland's Highlands, stop off at a local tearoom and fill up with a Highlands breakfast complete with black pudding and haggis.

ALTERNATIVE CULTURE

Alternative culture walks in cities like London and Bristol offer a fascinating insight into everything from backstreet history to street art and craft beer.

↑ **BOOTS FOR WALKING**

If you want to make the most of Britain, pack a good pair of walking boots, ideally worn in and waterproof.

Best Hiking Experiences

▶ **Wander through historic market towns and past idyllic churches on the Cotswold Way.** (p68)

▶ **Experience life along the towpaths of Britain's 'Venice' and canal capital, Birmingham.** (p122)

▶ **Hear the ghosts of Roman Britain on a walk around Hadrian's Wall.** (p152)

▶ **Feel the sea breeze as you hike the award-winning Wales Coast Path.** (p174)

▶ **Enter a fairy world in mist-dashed Welsh waterfall country.** (p170)

IMPERIAL PAST

Britain once ruled the waves and some 450 million people across a quarter of the world for almost four centuries. The many people from these former colonies who have since called the country home have enriched its cultural and historical landscape in eye-opening ways.

FROM TOP: RON ELLIS/SHUTTERSTOCK ©, DAN KITWOOD/GETTY IMAGES ©

→ EMPIRE & ENSLAVERY

Britain's involvement in the transatlantic trade of enslaved people has often been ignored. Not anymore. Institutes across Britain, like the Museum of London Docklands, are increasingly highlighting these horrors.

Best Learning Experiences

▶ Learn about the history of enslaved people and protest culture, past and present, in Bristol. (p100)

▶ Understand the story of Britain's Black history at London's Black Cultural Archives. (p49)

▶ Feast on authentic food from the Indian subcontinent in Birmingham. (p118)

▶ Be awestruck by Neasden Temple in northwest London, built by postcolonial migrants. (p46)

★ MUSLIM BRITAIN

Experience three of Britain's finest sites of Muslim heritage in Woking, all established during the period of the British Empire.

This page: Top Neasden Temple (p46), London
Bottom Black Cultural Archives (p49), London
Opposite page: Hever Castle

↘ **OVERNIGHT IN A CASTLE**
Astley Castle, Nuneaton, Warwickshire
Cawood Castle, Cawood, North Yorkshire
Kingswear Castle, Dartmouth, Devon
Clytha Castle, Monmouthshire

MY HOME IS MY CASTLE

Britain is a land of castles, some a thousand years old and a testament to the nation's impressive engineering and love of a good fort. Many have been revamped, revived and restored to their former glory, filled with tales of battling royals, restless ghosts and unimaginable wizardry, making them brilliant picks for a family day out.

Best Castle Experiences

▶ **Meet the beefeaters and ravens at the legendary Tower of London.** (p51)

▶ **Cross the double moats to breach Hever Castle.** (p81)

▶ **Wait for low tide and the magical pathway to St Michael's Mount.** (p110)

▶ **Imagine life as the Red Earl at Caerphilly Castle in Wales.** (p167)

▶ **Visit the home of historic Scottish royalty, Stirling Castle.** (p223)

↘ BRITAIN'S STONE CIRCLES

Maughanby Stone Circle, Cumbria

Castlerigg, Lake District

Ring of Brodgar, Orkney Islands

Druid's Circle, Penmaenmawr

PAGANS & VIKINGS

Up and down this great green island there are signs of Britain's rich cultural past. Two of the most celebrated are the Viking presence, between the 8th and 11th centuries, and the nation's pagan heritage – be that witches, druids or wizards.

Best History Experiences

▸ Go in search of witches and wizards in the city of Edinburgh. (p198)

▸ Feel Britain's pagan heritage at the mysterious stone circles of Stonehenge and Avebury. (p92)

▸ Learn about the former Viking capital of England and York's past at the Jorvik Viking Centre. (p158)

▸ Walk in the footsteps of the condemned Pendle Witches in the wilds of Lancashire. (p146)

▸ Listen to the ghosts of Roman Britain at London's Temple of Mithras, the Mithraeum. (p51)

LEST WE FORGET

The two world wars of the 20th century loom large in Britain's national memory. Cue a raft of gripping museums, monuments and relics that lift the lid on the collective war effort and spotlight the heroes that fought life and limb for their country. These fascinating sites offer a deep dive into history and serve as a reminder for future generations.

→ MUSEUMS OF WAR
In almost every major city in Britain there is a museum dedicated to war, such as the Imperial War Museum London, which contains relics of local and national significance.

Best Memorial Experiences

▶ **Crack the infamous Enigma code at Bletchley house.** (p73)

▶ **Marvel in the ghostly bombed-out beauty of Coventry Cathedral.** (p127)

▶ **Tour the WWII sights of southeast England.** (p72)

▶ **Pay your respects to the soldiers of empire at Woking's Peace Gardens.** (p59)

★ **POPPY SEASON**
On November 11 people wear red poppies to remember the WWI fallen; this is also when creative commemorations are installed across the country.

This page: Top Coventry Cathedral (p127)
Bottom Enigma Machine, Bletchley Park (p73)
Opposite page: Castlerigg

FROM TOP: AVITA ARIKA/SHUTTERSTOCK ©, LENSCAP PHOTOGRAPHY/SHUTTERSTOCK ©

GREAT BRITAIN BEST EXPERIENCES

Demand for hotel rooms goes through the roof in peak summer. Book accommodation, tours and overnight adventures well in advance.

↘ Royal Ascot
Spot the daftest hats and chicest clothes at the highlight of the horse-racing calendar in Berkshire in June.
- Ascot
- ascot.com

↙ Glastonbury Festival
The muddiest and biggest festival of rock kicks off the season in the fields of Somerset in June.
- Glastonbury
- glastonburyfestivals.co.uk

→ Wimbledon
Eat strawberries and cream, and watch the world's best tennis players as they descend on southwest London.
- London

JUNE **JULY**

Average daytime max: 17°C
Days of rainfall: 11

Britain in
SUMMER

→ Cowes Week

The country's biggest yachting spectacle takes place on the waters around the Isle of Wight in late July.
- Isle of Wight
- ▶ cowesweek.co.uk

Womad

This arts, dance and world music fest takes a country park in the south Cotswolds by storm in July.
- Cotswolds
- ▶ womad.org

↓ Edinburgh Festival Fringe

Fizzing with fresh-faced creativity, this mammoth August-long festival brings books, art, theatre, music and comedy to the Scottish capital.
- Edinburgh
- ▶ edfringe.com
- ▶ p200

AUGUST

Average daytime max: 19°C
Days of rainfall: 11

Average daytime max: 19°C
Days of rainfall: 12

Green Man Festival

Probably Wales' best music festival featuring alternative folk, country, world and Americana music in August.
- ▶ greenman.net

Packing Notes

Sun cream for the occasional heatwave; this is officially T-shirt season.

GREAT BRITAIN PLAN BY SEASON

Britain is at its most beautiful as autumn turns woodlands and countryside all shades of gold, crimson and russet.

↗ Braemar Gathering

On the first Saturday in September, Scotland's biggest Highland Games flings you into a traditional feast of dancing, caber tossing and bagpipes.
- Braemar
- braemargathering.org

Abergavenny Food Festival

The mother of all food festivals champions Wales' delicious food scene in mid-September.
- abergavennyfoodfestival.com

↓ Great North Run

The world's biggest half marathon sees 60,000 runners pound the streets of Newcastle in September.
- Newcastle
- greatrun.org

SEPTEMBER

Average daytime max: 16°C
Days of rainfall: 12

OCTOBER

Britain in AUTUMN

↘ Falmouth Oyster Festival

The pretty Cornish harbour town of Falmouth kicks off the traditional oyster-catching season with this foodie fest in October.

▶ falmouthoysterfestival.co.uk

Dylan Thomas Festival

The city of Swansea plays host to this festival celebrating the Welsh laureate's work between October and November.

📍 Swansea
▶ dylanthomas.com

Average daytime max: 13°C
Days of rainfall: 15

↓ Kendal Mountain Festival

Films, talks and a literature festival turn the Lake District's gateway town into a mountain-lover's paradise in November.

▶ kendalmountainfestival.com

NOVEMBER

Average daytime max: 9°C
Days of rainfall: 15

↙ Remembrance Day

Red poppies are worn and wreaths laid across the country on 11 November in commemoration of fallen soldiers.

▶ poppyshop.org.uk

🧳 Packing notes

The rains are back, so pack an umbrella and bring layers with you; the temperature is set to drop.

Avoid long journeys during the weekend before Christmas Day when roads and public transport are chock-a-block.

↗ Stonehaven Fireballs Festival

A riotous celebration of Hogmanay in the Scottish fishing town of Stonehaven wows with a fireball-bearing procession.
▶ stonehavenfireballs.com

New Year Celebrations

New Year's Eve dazzles with firework displays, DJs and street parties up and down the country.

↓ London's New Year's Day Parade

Marching bands, street performers, classic cars, floats and samba dancers bring a carnival-like vibe to London at this flag-waving event.
▶ lnydp.com

DECEMBER

Average daytime max: 7°C
Days of rainfall: 15

JANUARY

Britain in WINTER

Celtic Connections

Britain's premiere celebration of Celtic music sees artists from across the globe descend on Glasgow in late January.
- Glasgow
- celticconnections.com

Jorvik Viking Festival

In the ancient Viking capital of York, this swashbuckling festival celebrates the town's Norse heritage come February.
- York
- jorvikvikingfestival.co.uk

Up Helly Aa

A full-size Viking longship is spectacularly burnt at this January fire festival in the Shetlands.
- Shetland Islands, p234
- uphellyaa.org

FEBRUARY

Average daytime max: 6°C
Days of rainfall: 16

Average daytime max: 7°C
Days of rainfall: 12

Fort William Mountain Festival

Every February the capital of British mountaineering celebrates the sport with workshops, talks and films.
- mountainfestival.co.uk

Packing notes
Bring waterproofs and winter woollies – hats, scarves, gloves and a thick coat.

GREAT BRITAIN PLAN BY SEASON

The weather might not be great, but accommodation rates are, as hotels try to lure visitors after the winter lull.

Stratford Literary Festival

Held in Shakespeare's old stomping ground in early May and fast becoming a must-attend book festival.
- Stratford-upon-Avon
- stratfordliteraryfestival.co.uk

↗ University Boat Race

A tradition since 1829 where the ancient universities of Oxford and Cambridge race each other along the River Thames in April.

→ London Marathon

The country's most famous street run in April where super-fit athletes and dressed-up regulars cover 26.2 miles.
- tcslondonmarathon.com

MARCH

Average daytime max: 9°C
Days of rainfall: 14

APRIL

Britain in SPRING

↓ Spirit of Speyside

Scotland's biggest whisky-producing region hosts the country's largest and only whisky festival between April and May.

▶ spiritofspeyside.com

↓ RHS Chelsea Flower Show

In May the world's most famous flower show is hosted by the Royal Horticultural Society in London's poshest borough.

📍 London

▶ rhs.org.uk

↖ Hay Festival

For 10 days at the end of May the little town of Hay-on-Wye in Wales becomes the centre of the literary world.

▶ hayfestival.com

FROM LEFT: XINHUA NEWS AGENCY/GETTY IMAGES ©, TRAVERS LEWIS/SHUTTERSTOCK ©, ALEXANDRU NIKA/SHUTTERSTOCK ©, DAVID LEVENSON/GETTY IMAGES ©, BACKGROUND: EVGENY KOVALEV SPB/SHUTTERSTOCK ©

GREAT BRITAIN PLAN BY SEASON

Average daytime max: 11°C
Days of rainfall: 12

MAY

Average daytime max: 15°C
Days of rainfall: 11

Glyndebourne

Enjoy world-class opera in the East Sussex countryside from May until the end of summer at this famous festival.

▶ glyndebourne.com

🧳 Packing notes

Lots of layers and a sturdy brolly are the only way to handle erratic British springtime weather.

SCOTLAND
Trip Builder

TAKE YOUR PICK OF MUST-SEES AND HIDDEN GEMS

Energetic cities with proud histories and progressive outlooks dominate the south, while the mountainous north of this myth-steeped country delivers dramatic landscapes, deep, dark, mysterious lochs and remote, storm-battered islands pulsing with wildlife.

Trip Notes

Hub towns Edinburgh, Glasgow, Fort William

How long Allow two weeks

Getting around Hire a car to cover distances at your own leisure. Local trains are reliable and there are good public bus systems in most towns, plus a ferry service to coastal islands.

Tips Driving isn't easy in remote parts of the Highlands. It's important to check forecasts before setting off.

The Small Isles
Grab a bike or step into a kayak and go puffin-spotting and seal sighting around the remote and friendly Inner Hebrides.
1 hr from Oban

West Highland Peninsulas
Find a local guide and head out into the great Scottish wilderness for a swim in a remote, serene loch all to yourself.
1½ hr from Fort William

Glasgow
Be inspired by the genius of architect Charles Rennie Mackintosh in Scotland's Dear Green Place, with its stellar array of vegan cafes, sustainable public transport and green spaces.
1 hr from Edinburgh

Ayrshire Coast
Evoke the spirit of Scottish bard Robert Burns as you wander along Atlantic beaches in search of palatial castles.
1 hr from Glasgow

FROM LEFT: RONTAV/SHUTTERSTOCK © STEVE ALLEN/SHUTTERSTOCK ©

Cullen
Wake up to the sound of gulls and crashing waves in this beautiful fishing village, before walking, swimming or cycling its picturesque coastal trail.

🚌 *3 hr from Aberdeen*

West Highland Line
Ride the scenic train through the wild expanse of Rannoch Moor before stopping for a warm cuppa at the world's most remote tearoom.

🚆 *45 min from Glasgow*

Edinburgh
Eat in Michelin-starred restaurants, go on a witchcraft tour, spend the night in a grand castle, and if you're here during the Fringe Festival, tag on another few days (and book ahead).

🚆 *1 hr from Glasgow*

Roxburghshire
Follow in the footsteps of Sir Walter Scott, through heathery hills, fishing for salmon in the River Tweed and looking for medieval abbeys and baronial mansions.

🚆 *2½ hr from Edinburgh*

NORTHERN ENGLAND
Trip Builder

TAKE YOUR PICK OF MUST-SEES AND HIDDEN GEMS

Ancient monuments that will take your breath away, wind-lashed coastlines, gregarious, music-loving northern towns and wide open moors and mountains where waterfalls plunge into ice-cold lakes all await in the north of England.

🗺 Trip Notes

Hub towns Manchester, Liverpool, Leeds

How long Allow 10 to 14 days

Getting around Cars give you more freedom; buses link the major towns and, if you have the stamina, cycling is a fantastic way to slip under the region's skin.

Tips During summer the Lake District gets ridiculously busy and you'll have no chance of scoring accommodation at the last minute, so book well ahead.

FROM LEFT: HELEN HOTSON/SHUTTERSTOCK ©, MICHAEL CONRAD/SHUTTERSTOCK ©, MATROBINSONPHOTO/SHUTTERSTOCK ©

Lake District
Embrace the growing craze of wild swimming and head for magical spots in Cumbria such as Tongue Pot, an emerald pool beneath a glorious waterfall.
🚆 1½ hr from Manchester

Forest of Bowland
Wander through ancient woodlands, past historic ruins, listening for pagan whispers as you trace the footsteps of the condemned Pendle Witches.
🚆 1½ hr from Manchester

Hadrian's Wall
Look out for the ghosts of ancient Roman soldiers guarding this remote outpost as you explore Britain's Latin past along its most famous historic wall.

🚆 *1½ hr from Carlisle*

Northumberland
Search for the northern lights off the North York coast, before making the pilgrimage to saintly Holy Island (also known as Lindisfarne).

🚆 *1 hr from Newcastle-upon-Tyne*

Whitby
Explore the ruins of the Benedictine monastery high up on a clifftop before visiting the quaint fishing harbour of Whitby, where Bram Stoker's Dracula washed up.

🚆 *2 hr from Middlesbrough*

Yorkshire Dales
Sniff out the region's famous cheese as you take a road trip through the spectacular Yorkshire Dales and North Moors National Parks.

🚆 *30 min from Skipton*

Manchester
Admire world-class street art, taste epic street food and lose yourself in the best of British music in this loud, proud northern town.

🚆 *2½ hr from London*

LONDON
Trip Builder

TAKE YOUR PICK OF MUST-SEES AND HIDDEN GEMS

Divided in two by the snaking Thames, Britain's capital bombards you with never-to-be-forgotten experiences, from phenomenal museums, galleries and theatres to grand royal parks and palaces and a food scene unrivalled across the country. All cultures convene in this vast, intense, enthralling city, which you'll never tire of no matter how often you return. Pick a new neighbourhood and find a different London every time.

Trip Notes

Hub town London

How long Allow five to seven days

Getting around Don't think about driving. Instead use London's network of trains, buses, ferries and even trams, or try the city's cycle and scooter rentals.

Tips Save money by making the most of London's free museums and galleries, and grab yourself a London Pass for the paid sights.

North London
Click into the anything-goes groove of upbeat Camden Market, go for a swim in the ponds at Hampstead, and tuck into authentic Anatolian food as you admire neo-Ottoman mosques.
🚇 *25 min from Liverpool Street Station*

Central London
So much to see for free: an ancient Roman temple, epic museums and galleries, delightful royal parks and historic ruins.
🚇 *20 min from Liverpool Street Station*

FROM LEFT, RICHARD NEWSTEAD/GETTY IMAGES © PAWEL LIBERA/GETTY IMAGES © CHRISPICTURES/SHUTTERSTOCK ©

0 — 2 km
0 — 1 mile

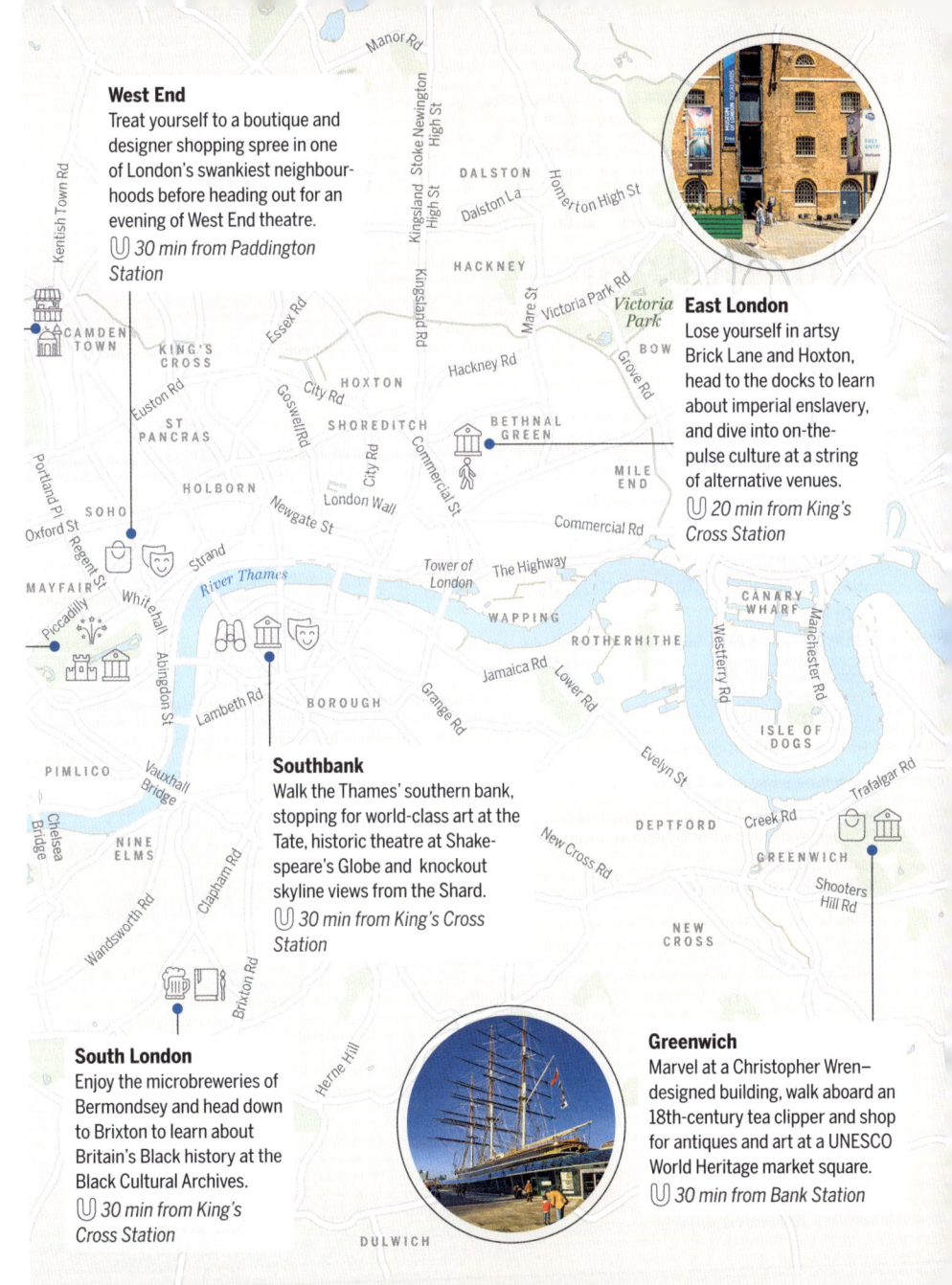

West End
Treat yourself to a boutique and designer shopping spree in one of London's swankiest neighbourhoods before heading out for an evening of West End theatre.
🚇 *30 min from Paddington Station*

East London
Lose yourself in artsy Brick Lane and Hoxton, head to the docks to learn about imperial enslavery, and dive into on-the-pulse culture at a string of alternative venues.
🚇 *20 min from King's Cross Station*

Southbank
Walk the Thames' southern bank, stopping for world-class art at the Tate, historic theatre at Shakespeare's Globe and knockout skyline views from the Shard.
🚇 *30 min from King's Cross Station*

South London
Enjoy the microbreweries of Bermondsey and head down to Brixton to learn about Britain's Black history at the Black Cultural Archives.
🚇 *30 min from King's Cross Station*

Greenwich
Marvel at a Christopher Wren–designed building, walk aboard an 18th-century tea clipper and shop for antiques and art at a UNESCO World Heritage market square.
🚇 *30 min from Bank Station*

SOUTHERN ENGLAND
Trip Builder

TAKE YOUR PICK OF MUST-SEES AND HIDDEN GEMS

The country's warmest region is unsurprisingly home to England's very own award-winning vineyards, and beaches where blue waters on a par with the continent lap the sands. The south of England is also where you will find two of the world's oldest universities, a hidden Islamic gem and the country's most iconic pagan site.

Trip Notes

Hub towns Oxford, Bristol

How long Allow 10 to 14 days

Getting around All the major towns have bus and train links from London, but the extreme southwest only has road links, so a car offers the greatest flexibility.

Tips Devon and Cornwall's warmer weather makes it the most popular region outside of London in the summer, so booking early is extremely important.

Cornwall
Laze around on England's finest beaches, look for pirates in hidden coves, dive for wrecks, visit the world's largest greenhouse and dig into delicious local seafood.
3 hr from Exeter

Isles of Scilly
Hike, kayak, cycle or swim your way around Britain's most southerly island archipelago, set in stunning azure waters.
2¾ hr from Penzance

FROM LEFT: IAN WOOLCOCK/SHUTTERSTOCK ©, CHRISATPPS/SHUTTERSTOCK ©, DENIS CHAPMAN/SHUTTERSTOCK ©

Oxford
Marvel at one of the oldest universities in the world, follow the footsteps of CS Lewis and JRR Tolkien, meander through botanic gardens and read in a historic library.

🚆 1 hr from London

Norfolk
Drift through the Broads at a pace to suit you, looking for rare wildlife, or go beach combing at traditional seaside towns like Cromer.

🚆 3 hr from London

Cotswolds
Wander through chocolate-box villages, photograph traditional stone cottages and take the weight off inside a rustic pub in what is quintessential England.

🚌 1 hr from Oxford

North Sea

- Lincoln
- Leicester
- King's Lynn
- Peterborough
- Birmingham
- Norwich

Norfolk Broads National Park

WALES
- Worcester
- Hereford
- Merthyr Tydfil
- Gloucester
- Northampton
- Cambridge
- Milton Keynes
- Ipswich
- Colchester

- Swansea
- CARDIFF
- Bristol
- Oxford
- High Wycombe
- Chelmsford

- Bath
- Swindon
- LONDON
- Woking

Woking
Discover Britain's forgotten Muslim heritage and marvel at the country's only Grade I-listed mosque, built in 1889.

🚆 30 min from London

- Taunton
- Yeovil
- Salisbury
- Winchester
- Guildford
- Exeter
- Bournemouth
- Southampton
- Brighton
- Exmouth
- Weymouth
- Portsmouth
- Eastbourne
- Torquay
- Isle of Wight

South Downs National Park

Bristol
Immerse yourself in Bristol's proud protest culture, admire the famous suspension bridge and find yourself a Banksy or two to stare at.

🚆 2 hr from London

Wiltshire
Embrace pagan Britain in all its glory at the Stonehenge and then Avebury stone circles, before heading to stunning, Georgian Bath.

🚌 1 hr from Bath

FRANCE

7 Things to Know About
GREAT BRITAIN

INSIDER TIPS TO HIT THE GROUND RUNNING

1 British Beer

To most visitors, British beer is, well, unusual. Traditionally served at room temperature and always flat, it can taste sweet and floral or hoppy and bitter, and look light amber or dark brown. Popular brews include stout, golden ale, lager and brown ale. Needless to say, British beer is an acquired taste but give it a whirl and you might be pleasantly surprised.

2 The Weather

Stereotype though it may be, the Brits really do love to talk (grumble) about the weather, and it's little wonder given you can be thrown the four seasons in a day. A single snowflake can cause rail chaos and when temperatures top 30°C you'll see headlines about the country being 'hotter than the Sahara'. This country doesn't like extremes. If you're looking for an ideal conversation starter, the weather is it.

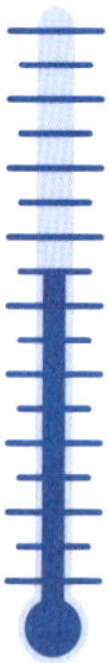

3 Plug It In

The electrical plugs in Britain are unlike those in the rest of Europe, so bring a UK-specific plug adaptor.

▶ For more essential information, see p252

4 Pack a Mac

Speaking of weather, it's true that it's always raining somewhere in Britain, no matter what time of year it is, so always carry a packable rain jacket or umbrella with you.

▶ For more on weather, see p18

01 AKSOL/SHUTTERSTOCK ©, **02** RAMY FATHALLA/SHUTTERSTOCK ©, **03** D-SIGN STUDIO 10/SHUTTERSTOCK ©, **04** NET VECTOR/SHUTTERSTOCK/SHUTTERSTOCK ©, **05** STMOOL/SHUTTERSTOCK ©, **06** GHRZUZUDU/SHUTTERSTOCK ©, **07** MARY LONG/SHUTTERSTOCK ©, **08** SUSSE_N/SHUTTERSTOCK ©

5 Healthcare

Travellers from the EU and all other nations now require private travel insurance to cover medical care. One of the negative impacts of Britain leaving the EU has been the loss of reciprocal healthcare that was available via the old blue EHIC (European Health Insurance Card).

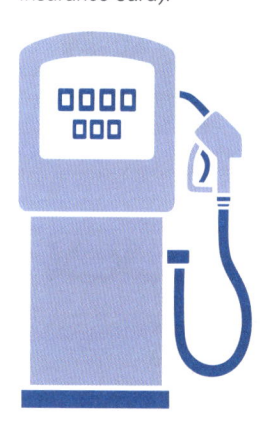

6 Local Lingo

Brits use lots of words that will leave you scratching your head. Here are some organised by country.

With four main dialects and several subdialects, it can be difficult to understand a Scot.

aye yes
bahookie backside or buttocks
bonnie pretty or beautiful
braw excellent or pleasant
dreich dreary, bleak weather
glaikit stupid, foolish or thoughtless
loon boy or son

If it isn't because they're speaking in their own language, you might not understand what the Welsh are saying because they're using these words.

cwtch a cuddle or cubbyhole
lush when something is nice or even awesome

Finally, some English lexical peculiarities.
bants to joke or have a laugh
bloody added for emphasis to mean 'very'
faff waste time or create fuss doing unimportant things
kerfuffle a commotion or a fuss
knackered to be exhausted or very tired
poppycock spoken nonsense or rubbish
the local the nearest pub

7 A Litre or a Pint

Britain confusingly mixes both metric and imperial measurements across the country. For example, the height of a mountain can be in feet or metres but road distance always comes in miles; when you're filling up the car, it's litres but when you're filling up on beer it's pints!

Read, Listen, Watch & Follow

📖 **READ**

Empireland: How Imperialism Has Shaped Modern Britain (Sathnam Sanghera; 2021) Award-winning deep dive into the British Empire's legacy.

The Living Mountain (Nan Shepherd; 1977) Wafer-thin meditation on Scotland's Cairngorms. Masterly nature writing.

Notes From a Small Island (Bill Bryson; 1997) Laugh-out-loud account of the American-British journalist's travels through Blighty.

London: The Biography (Peter Ackroyd; 2000) Definitive delve into the English capital from the Druids to the present day.

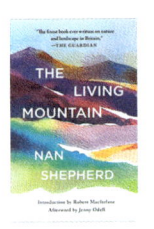

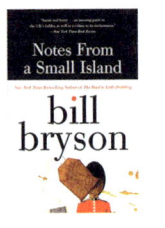

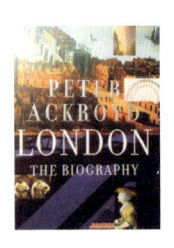

🎧 **LISTEN**

Have You Heard George's Podcast? (BBC Sounds; 2019) George the Poet's (pictured right) fresh take on inner-city life.

Thinking Aloud (BBC Radio 4; 2013) Intriguing introduction to the British class system that includes how it should be measured in the 21st century.

(What's the Story) Morning Glory? (Oasis; 1995) Quite possibly the greatest British indie album ever.

Sgt. Pepper's Lonely Hearts Club Band (The Beatles; 1967) The soundtrack to the Summer of Love remains one of the best British albums of all time.

The English Heritage Podcast (English Heritage; 2017) A walk through English history by the custodians of many of the country's monuments.

WATCH

Wild Isles (BBC One; 2023) National treasure David Attenborough celebrates the beauty of British landscapes and wildlife.

Union with David Olusoga (BBC/OU co-production; 2023) A deep dive into the origins of Great Britain, as seen through the lens of national identity, equality and social class.

Trainspotting (Danny Boyle; 1996) Dark comedy set in Edinburgh that delves into the city's underbelly of drug addiction.

This Is England (Shane Meadows; 2006; pictured above) Dark, gritty urban drama that takes you back to the racism of 1980s Thatcherite England.

Small Axe (Steve McQueen; 2020; pictured below) Fantastic films about British West Indian immigrants from the 1960s to the '80s.

FOLLOW

@VisitBritain
Official X feed for the tourist board of Great Britain.

All Gigs
(allgigs.co.uk) Listings for festivals, music gigs, comedy and clubbing.

Caught Offside
(caughtoffside.com) Leading football gossip blog for a nation obsessed with it.

@BBCNews
News from across the country including regional focus.

Time Out
(timeout.com/uk) From beaches to legal wild camping – it's all in here.

LONDON

CULTURE | DIVERSITY | HISTORY

- **Trip Builder** (p40)
- **Practicalities** (p41)
- **Foodie Top & Tail** (p42)
- **Family Park Life** (p44)
- **Awesome Architecture** (p46)
- **An Other London** (p48)
- **London's Historic Monuments** (p50)
- **Southern Delights** (p52)
- **Listings** (p54)

LONDON
Trip Builder

Relax with a picnic in the beautifully landscaped **Regent's Park** (p45)
🚶 1 min from Regent's Park Station

Take in world-class art for free at the **Tate Modern** (p53) or **Tate Britain** (p54) galleries
🚶 11 min from London Bridge Station

Sample the tasty range of international street food in Brick Lane's **Upmarket** (p43)
🚶 5 min from Shoreditch High St Overground station

Snag a ticket to see the world's longest-running musical at the **Sondheim Theatre** (p55)
🚶 5 min from Piccadilly Circus Underground station

Discover London's other stories on the **Black History Walks** (p49) starting at Trafalgar Sq
🚶 1 min from Charing Cross Underground station

Travel back in time to Roman Britain at the immersive **London Mithraeum** (p51) in the City
🚶 1 min from Bank Underground station

▬▬▬ Experience world-class galleries and museums, listen to globally renowned DJs at iconic clubs, explore other and uncomfortable histories and take in beguiling architecture, spectacular green spaces and vibrant markets before wandering beside the Thames at twilight, looking for that cosy Dickensian watering hole.

PREVIOUS SPREAD: ANDRAS POLONYI/EYEEM/GETTY IMAGES ©
FROM LEFT: YAU MING LOW/SHUTTERSTOCK ©, PETER_FLEMING/SHUTTERSTOCK ©

0 — 1 km
0 — 0.5 miles

Practicalities

ARRIVING
London has numerous transport hubs. The main airport is Heathrow; for trains it's Euston and King's Cross; and for buses, Victoria Coach Station. All are connected to the Underground.

FIND YOUR WAY
The City Information Centre in St Paul's Churchyard is London's main independent, multilingual tourist information centre. It has maps and free wi-fi.

MONEY
Utilise free museums and galleries and purchase the London Pass (londonpass.com) for the paying sites (from £114 per adult).

WHERE TO STAY

Place	Pros/Cons
City of London	Close to major historic sights; pricey accommodation.
City of Westminster	Heart of the shopping district; well connected; expensive.
Southwark	Cheaper accommodation; close to the centre; connections aren't as good.
Tower Hamlets	Hippest hubs; good transport links; cheaper rates.

EATING & DRINKING
Street-food markets and pop-up eateries can be found all over London and offer the tastiest and cheapest eats. Try mouthwatering Caribbean curries in South London and don't miss thick-cut chips with battered fish and mushy peas (pictured top left).

Best local microbrewery beer
Brixton Brewery (p55)

Must-try
Salt beef beigel (pictured left) from Beigel Bake, Brick Lane

GETTING AROUND

Transport for London London's transport system includes the Underground, Overground, TfL Rail, Docklands Light Railway and buses. This is the quickest, cheapest and easiest way to get around.

Alternative transport There are manual and electric cycles to rent on the street, various ferry options and taxis (both the more expensive black ones and those via mobile apps).

DEC–FEB
Christmas lights and cold enough to sometimes snow.

MAR–MAY
Daffodils in the park, outdoor markets start to buzz.

JUN–AUG
Peak season with queues at tourist attractions and lots of music festivals.

SEP–NOV
Scarves and coats as leaves turn orangey-brown.

Foodie Top & TAIL

FINE DINING | HERITAGE | FOOD

Few cities have as much culinary choice or diversity as London, where modern Michelin-starred restaurants sit a stone's throw away from decades-old street-food hot spots. This 'top and tail' foodie experience offers three of the finest dining options and three of the most vibrant street-food spots in the city, each reflecting London's fascinating culinary and cultural heritage.

How to

Getting here All of the places listed here are well served by London buses and the Underground.

When to go The street-food spots are best at the weekends, especially Sunday.

Set menus Michelin-starred restaurants often have affordable set menus – always ask to see one.

Check out The Visit London *(visitlondon.com)* website has great recommendations for other foodie markets and top London restaurants.

Top left Dinner by Heston Blumenthal
Bottom left Camden Market

Michelin-starred dining The only thing modern about double-Michelin-starred **Dinner by Heston Blumenthal** (dinnerbyheston.com) in Knightsbridge is the decor. The food, on the other hand, is a deep dive into English culinary heritage – 16th-century 'meat fruit' (mandarin, chicken liver parfait and grilled bread), and 18th-century hay-smoked salmon with gentleman's relish and sorrel. While there are thousands of 'Indian' restaurants scattered across Britain, few are as sensational as **Tamarind** (tamarindrestaurant.com) in Mayfair. Here chefs riff creatively on the flavours and textures of India to knock up delights like coconut-chilli sea bass with black olives and salmon roe salsa. Finally, the finest of fine dining experiences has to be at London's most highly rated three-Michelin-starred restaurant, **Gordon Ramsay** (gordonramsayrestaurants.com) in Chelsea, where the foul-mouthed celebrity chef's flagship serves up innovative dishes like roast veal sweetbread.

Market street food If street food is more your style, few places offer diverse international cuisine like Brick Lane's **Upmarket** (sundayupmarket.co.uk), where Malaysian curries, Sri Lankan sambal and Mexican burritos are served up under one buzzing roof. For the more gourmet, modern London street-food experience, **Borough Market** (boroughmarket.org.uk) has your stone-baked pizzas cooked in a jiffy and pulled-pork sandwiches, all of which can be washed down with local craft beer. Meanwhile, for sheer atmosphere and fun, you can't go wrong looking for freshly fried churros or kung pao chicken in the nooks and crannies of **Camden Market** (camdenmarket.com) on pretty much any day of the week.

East London's Markets

All three of these markets have their own foodie spots.

Brick Lane Market If you come here looking for street food, be sure to set aside the whole day to wander into the numerous hubs and hidden markets along the lane, filled with flea market bric-a-brac, stylish vintage items, gorgeous antiques and locally produced handicrafts.

Spitalfields Market There have been traders here since the 17th century. These days, the covered market is open every day of the week and home to antiques, vintage and locally produced arts and craft.

Columbia Road Flower Market The country's most famous flower market and an East London institution. Old-school marketeers call out their bargains as visitors descend every Sunday looking for a horticultural bargain or two.

Family
PARK LIFE

PLAY | GREENERY | HISTORY

Few capital cities are as blessed with green spaces as London – and you can thank the Victorians for that. In every quarter, there are vast open spaces with landscaped gardens, welcoming cafes, boating lakes and play parks to be enjoyed. Here are four of the best London green spaces from each quarter offering something for all the family.

How to

Getting here All the parks are served by the Underground, except Greenwich, which is served by the Docklands Light Railway.

When to go Parks are open year-round, but summer is best for picnics and autumn for colourful leaves.

Canal stroll The Regent's Canal runs through Regent's Park and makes for a very pleasant walk. It is also possible to cycle along the towpath or even take a boat cruise.

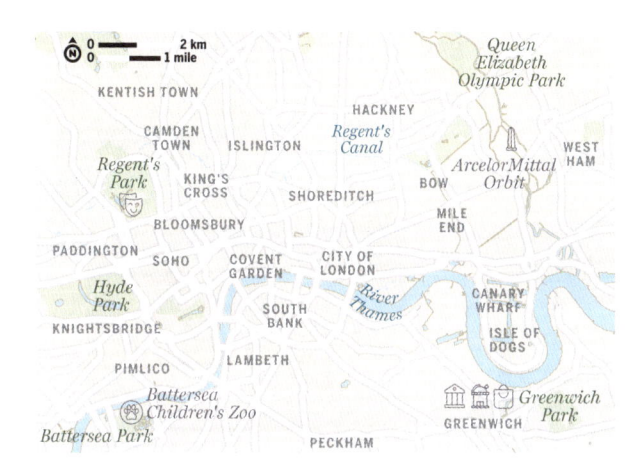

Top left Greenwich Park
Bottom left Regent's Canal

North of the Thames If you find yourself northwest of the City, the world-famous **Regent's Park** (royalparks.org.uk) is a fantastic choice. There's the adjacent London Zoo for the kids, several play parks, a landscaped Japanese garden, boating lake and, of course, the **Regent's Park Open Air Theatre**, which frequently hosts evening performances including a *Midsummer Night's Dream*. In the east, head for the **Queen Elizabeth Olympic Park** (queenelizabetholympicpark.co.uk), which has swathes of landscaped walkways alongside the River Lea, a fantastic adventure play park and the award-winning **ArcelorMittal Orbit** sculpture offering spectacular panoramic views and the world's longest tunnel slide.

South of the Thames Beautiful **Greenwich Park** (royal parks.org.uk), in the east, is home to the Royal Observatory and the Greenwich Meridian line, where families love the intergalactic journey at the Peter Harrison Planetarium. The park offers some of the finest views over London, as well as a small boating lake, a play park and, surprisingly, prehistoric burial mounds. To the west, **Battersea Park** (batterseapark.org) is a cool riverside choice, where young and old can rent bicycles, tandems and pedal karts. The park is also home to a quaint old English garden, a high ropes experience, a boating lake and the iconic peace pagoda, from which four golden Buddhas stare out over the Thames. There's also **Battersea Children's Zoo**, with a large play area complete with sand pits.

⚓ Maritime Magic

Greenwich Park, southeast of the City, has a long regal and maritime history and is a UNESCO World Heritage Site. Anyone visiting the park should take the time to enjoy the other highlights, including a major work designed by master architect Sir Christopher Wren, the spectacular **Old Royal Naval College**, and the Grade I–listed 17th-century former royal residency, the **Queen's House**. Nearby, looking out to the Thames, is the 19th-century tea clipper, the **Cutty Sark**, and finally the old town itself, at the heart of which is the covered **Greenwich Market**, an antique lover's haven.

Get to Greenwich using the Cutty Sark Docklands Light Railway station or the Thames Clipper passenger ferries, which serve the Greenwich Pier.

AWESOME
Architecture

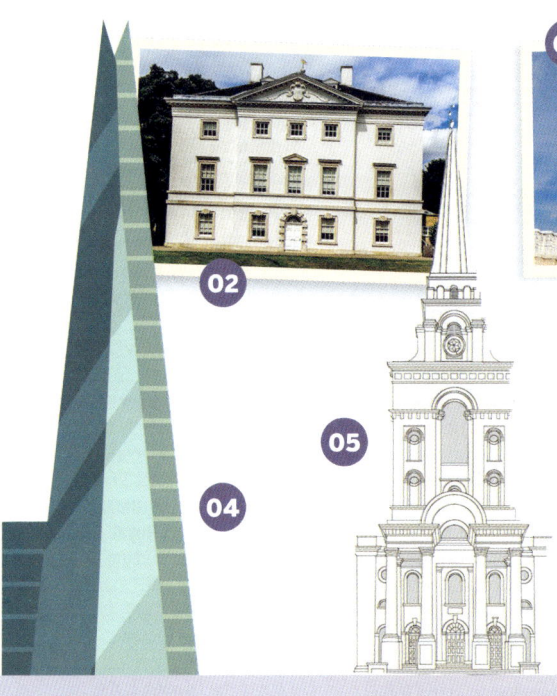

01 National Theatre
Brutalist London at its best: concrete corridors and terraces sprawl in all directions hiding four auditoriums.

02 Marble Hill House
The ideal Georgian town house. Perfectly elegant, intimate and understated, and still accessible by river and road.

03 Neasden Temple
Over 26,000 pieces of stone were sent to 1500 sculptors in Gujarat, India, to construct this Hindu temple.

04 The Shard
Just like a piece of glass, London's tallest building offers something different depending on the light, angle and time of day.

05 Christ Church Spitalfields
An imposingly beautiful, often-overlooked example of English baroque by 18th-century architect Nicholas Hawksmoor.

06 Greater London House
Easily London's finest example of early-20th-century playful art deco, with the added influence of Egyptian revivalism.

07 St Pancras Renaissance Hotel
A spiral frenzy and the primordial luxury hotel; this is London Gothic Revival at its most dramatic.

08 Serpentine Sackler Gallery
The late Queen of Curve, Dame Zaha Hadid, showed how the modern can marry the (neo) classical to birth something beautiful.

09 Lloyd's Building
Like the inner workings of *The Matrix*, this inside-out building by architect Richard Rogers pushed all the boundaries when it was built in 1986.

10 Liberty London
Resembling a giant English pub, this is mock Tudor at its most goading.

11 Aziziye Mosque
Neo-Ottomanism in the shape of a former picture palace beautifully adapted with golden domes and original Iznik tiles.

12 Wilkins Building
Both the design and purpose of London's first university, providing education for all, embody the neoclassicism spirit.

03 An Other LONDON

CULTURE | HERITAGE | ARTS

While most visitors to London are familiar with the city's globally renowned arts and culture venues, few know about the amazing specialist spaces shining a light on the other cultures – Caribbean, African, Arab, South Asian and Turkish, to name just a few – that have helped make London the cosmopolitan and multicultural city that it is today.

How to

Getting here All these institutes are well served by either London's buses, the Underground or Overground.

When to go As these are mostly independent institutes, many do not open daily, so check ahead.

Support and donate Many institutes rely on small private funds, so if you're in a position to do so, support them with a small donation.

Read up Grab a book on London's diverse communities in specialist shops like the Brick Lane Bookshop and the Black Cultural Archives store.

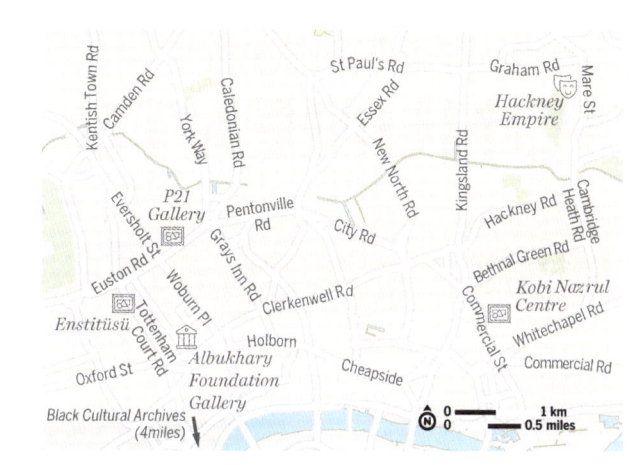

Top left Albukhary Foundation Gallery
Bottom left Hackney Empire

Part of the government-funded British Museum – which was extensively furnished during Britain's colonial period – the **Albukhary Foundation Gallery** is one of the institute's major attempts to 'decolonise' its Islamic collection through a process that saw the new presentation of artefacts led by Muslim curators and advisors. Its diverse display of artefacts include Sir Richard Burton's Hajj zamzam flask through to 19th-century Palestinian bridal headdresses. A short walk northwest is the charming **Yunus Emre Enstitüsü**, which celebrates Turkish culture with regular classes, talks and exhibitions on themes such as the Ottoman Hajj Railway. A little further northeast is the excellent **P21 Gallery** (p21.gallery), dedicated to promoting contemporary Arab art and culture; it has previously hosted work by British-Arab artists like Layla Madanat and Eleanor Nawal.

Heading east, off Brick Lane, is the **Kobi Nazrul Centre**, which hosts arts and theatre inspired by the local Bangladeshi community. Further east is the **Hackney Empire** (hackneyempire.co.uk), a real champion of emerging ethnic artists and comedians, including Guz Khan and Jamali Maddix. Finally, to the south, the **Black Cultural Archives** (blackculturalarchives.org) in Brixton is home to an eye-opening collection of documents and artefacts that tell the stories of Britain's African and Caribbean communities. In 2021 the institute launched the brilliant **Black History Tube Map**, which replaced every station name with that of an amazing former Black resident, such as thinker Stuart Hall and Notting Hill Carnival co-founder Claudia Jones.

🚶 Walking Culture

The growing interest in alternative narratives has seen a mushrooming of tours and walks by guides specialising in the lesser-known stories of the capital.

Muslim History Tours Open-top bus and riverboat experiences that reveal, among other things, the site of London's first mosque and where Arabic was taught in the 1600s (halaltourismbritain.com).

Black History Walks Walking tours uncovering London's 3500 years of Black history to reveal stories about Black freedom fighters of the 1700s and where Bob Marley hung out during his time in London (blackhistorywalks.co.uk).

Open City Fascinating walking tours throughout the year including those that explore colonial legacies like London's forgotten Chinese heritage through to its architectural marvels (open-city.org.uk).

04 London's Historic **MONUMENTS**

RELIGION | HISTORY | MONUMENTS

London has a history that stretches back over 2000 years, starting with its founding as Roman Londinium. A lot has happened since then to make the city the great urban centre it is today. The following are a series of significant historic monuments and buildings that collectively help to map those fascinating two millennia.

How to

Getting here The City is well served by London's buses and the Underground. Better yet, explore as much as possible on foot.

When to go Most of the places are open year-round, though hours do change by season.

Money saver Consider purchasing a saver ticket like the **London Pass** *(londonpass.com)* to visit many of these sights as it will be a lot cheaper.

Cool off In between stops, be sure to down a pint in The Old Bell (95 Fleet St), a pub that was built by Sir Christopher Wren.

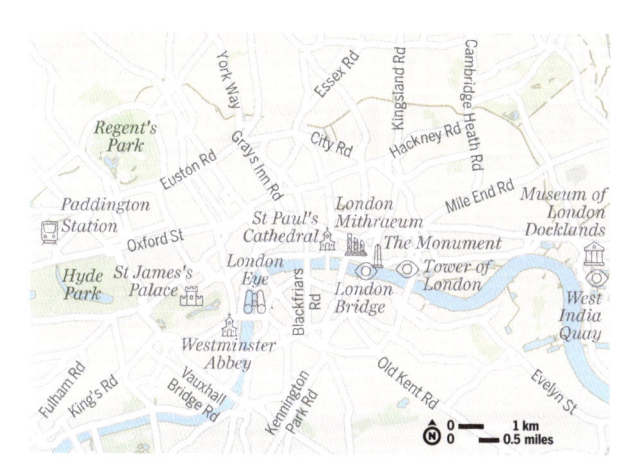

Top left White Tower, Tower of London
Bottom left Westminster Abbey

Roman and Anglo-Saxon The **London Mithraeum** *(london mithraeum.com)*, a temple to Roman god Mithras, features an immersive experience, where carefully curated exhibits and audiovisual highlights evoke Roman Londonium. Another 'relic' of the classical era, albeit in its modern guise, is the **London Bridge**, which has spanned the Thames since 50 CE. Meanwhile, on the other side of the City is **Westminster Abbey** *(westminster-abbey.org)*, where the country's monarchs have been married and buried since the 11th century.

Norman and Middle Ages One of the first monarchs coronated at the abbey was William the Conqueror, who also built the White Tower at the **Tower of London** following his 1066 conquest. Another place where British monarchs have been coronated is **St Paul's Cathedral** *(stpauls.co.uk)*, which burnt down in the Great Fire of 1666, commemorated by **The Monument**, with Sir Christopher Wren starting work on rebuilding it in 1669.

Middle to modern Connect with Tudor London at little-known **St James's Palace**, built by Henry VIII, before exploring a dark part of the capital's history at **West India Quay**, where the 19th-century warehouses were used to store goods sold for or bought with West African enslaved people. Switch to the west of the city to celebrate London's industry and innovation at **Paddington Station**, built by that behemoth of the Industrial Age, English civil engineer Isambard Kingdom Brunel, and where the first underground train journey took place in 1863. Finally, head to the **London Eye** *(londoneye.com)*, built to mark the start of London's third millennium.

London Museum Docklands

Visiting the West India Quay is a wonderful opportunity to explore the free **Museum of London Docklands** *(london museum.org.uk)*, which has permanent interactive exhibitions that provide a rundown of life on the docks and, of course, the trade of the docks. The 'London, Sugar and Slavery' exhibition presents accounts of enslaved people and their enslavers, along with artefacts that bring home the horrors of this lucrative trade in humans. Included is the infamous diagram of the hull of Liverpool ship *Brookes* (p102), which shows the inhuman methods used to transport enslaved people across the Atlantic. The museum runs regular walking tours and talks providing a deeper insight into the docks.

05 Southern **DELIGHTS**

RIVERWALK | ART | DRINKING

Starting at London's most spectacular bridge, stroll along the south bank of the Thames, taking in the city's fantastic river views, stopping off at two cultural heavyweights, and recharging at a riverside watering hole and a restaurant with unparalleled views.

How to

Getting here Use Tower Hill Underground station or bus 15 to start, and Waterloo Station and bus 381 at the end.

When to go If you like the buzz of crowds then the weekends are ideal, but if you don't, go on a weekday mid-morning. A walk at twilight is also magical (although the theatre and galleries won't be open).

Top tip The Tate Modern won't charge you a penny to see world-class art in its permanent collection.

Children's Chill-out

If you have kids in tow, check out **The Scoop** *(london bridgecity.co.uk; pictured)* website, as this delightful sunken amphitheatre near Tower Bridge hosts free films and children's theatre. In summer, pack their swimsuits and let them cool off in the water fountains just behind it.

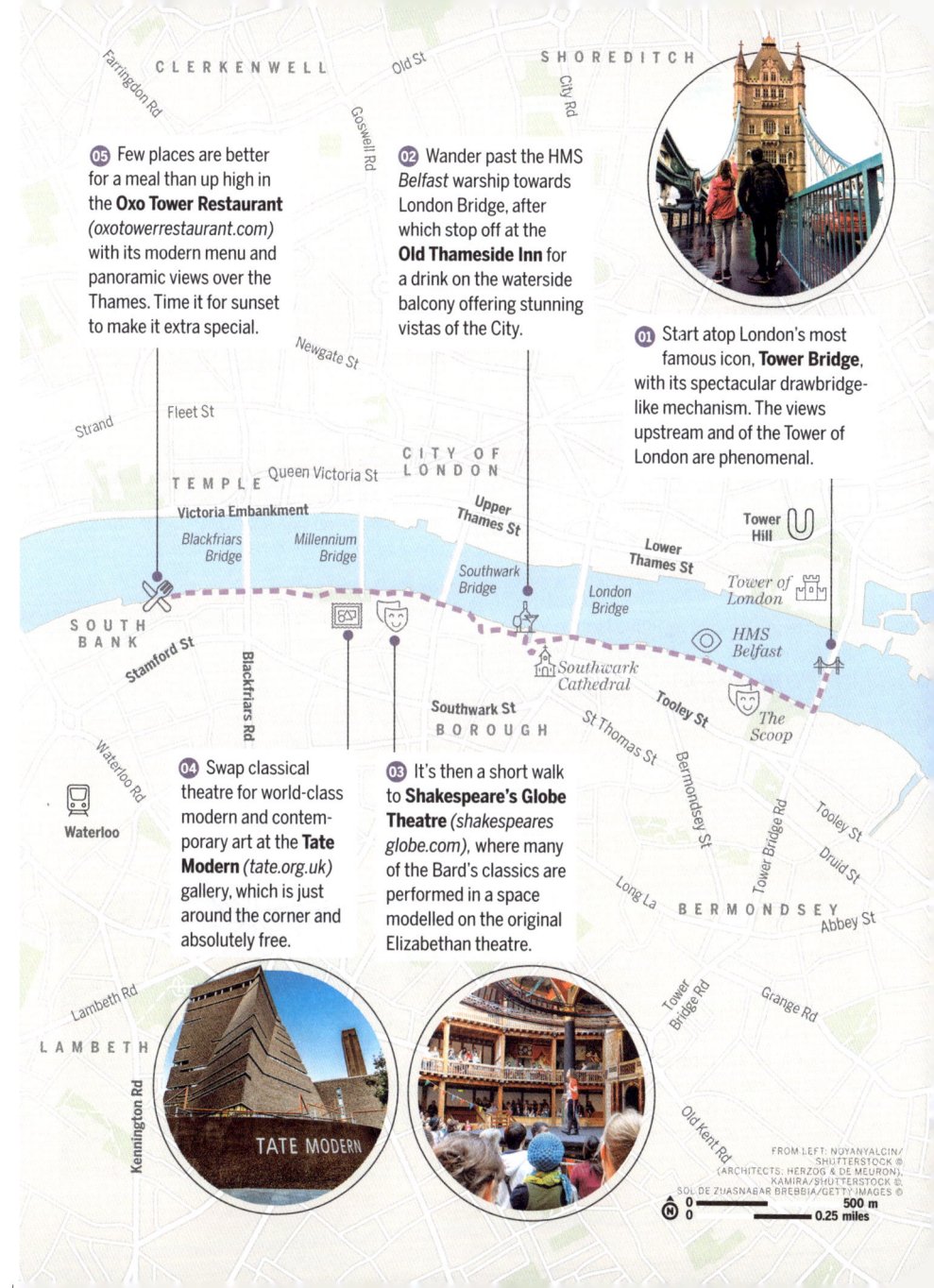

05 Few places are better for a meal than up high in the **Oxo Tower Restaurant** (oxotowerrestaurant.com) with its modern menu and panoramic views over the Thames. Time it for sunset to make it extra special.

02 Wander past the HMS *Belfast* warship towards London Bridge, after which stop off at the **Old Thameside Inn** for a drink on the waterside balcony offering stunning vistas of the City.

01 Start atop London's most famous icon, **Tower Bridge**, with its spectacular drawbridge-like mechanism. The views upstream and of the Tower of London are phenomenal.

04 Swap classical theatre for world-class modern and contemporary art at the **Tate Modern** (tate.org.uk) gallery, which is just around the corner and absolutely free.

03 It's then a short walk to **Shakespeare's Globe Theatre** (shakespeares globe.com), where many of the Bard's classics are performed in a space modelled on the original Elizabethan theatre.

TATE MODERN

FROM LEFT: NOYANYALCIN/SHUTTERSTOCK © (ARCHITECTS: HERZOG & DE MEURON), KAMIRA/SHUTTERSTOCK ©, SOL DE ZUASNABAR BREBBIA/GETTY IMAGES ©

500 m
0.25 miles

Listings

BEST OF THE REST

🏛 Free Culture

British Museum
The country's flagship museum, home to 4.5 million artefacts and fascinating exhibits that have previously covered themes as diverse as the Hajj, Stonehenge and female Japanese artists. *britishmuseum.org*

Tate Britain
The oldest gallery in the Tate family, and famous for its large collection of British artwork by the likes of Hockney, Bacon, Riley and Moore, but in particular the works of JMW Turner. *tate.org.uk*

National Gallery
The artwork on display in the National reads like a who's who of European masters: Rembrandt, Van Gogh, Renoir and Botticelli are among the collection of 2000 pieces. *nationalgallery.org.uk*

Natural History Museum
The evolution of earth is explained through a series of spectacular displays; the dinosaur gallery and the blue whale model are among the standouts. *nhm.ac.uk*

🎭 West End Theatre

Theatre Royal Drury Lane
Every monarch since the restoration has visited this majestic old theatre, which has been open since 1663. In recent years it has been the home of a number of big-name musicals including, *The Tempest, Much Ado About Nothing*, Disney's *Hercules* and *Frozen – The Musical*. *lwtheatres.co.uk*

Her Majesty's Theatre
There has been a theatre on this site since 1705, with the current grand exterior and French Renaissance interior built in 1897. It is in effect the home of one of the world's most famous musicals, *The Phantom of the Opera*. *lwtheatres.co.uk*

Lyric Theatre
Regularly hosting a range of theatre and musicals since 1888, the Lyric has had stellar names like John Malkovich, Glenda Jackson and Ian McKellen perform here, and put on major West End hits such as *Blood Brothers* and *Aladdin*. *thelyrictheatre.co.uk*

Shaftesbury Theatre
With a beautiful Edwardian facade dominating the corner of the avenue it's named after, this theatre was opened in 1911 as the New Prince's Theatre and can hold around 1400 people. Most recently it has had successful runs with musicals like *Mrs Doubtfire*. *shaftesburytheatre.com*

Lyceum Theatre
Resembling a Greco-Roman temple from the front, there has been a theatre on this spot

Lyceum Theatre

since 1765. All 2000 seats get regularly filled up for blockbusters such as *The Merchant of Venice, Wild Rose* and *Coraline – A Musical*. *thelyceumtheatre.com*.

Sondheim Theatre

Renamed in honour of American composer Stephen Sondheim's 90th birthday in 2019, following a major refurb; the former Queen's Theatre on Shaftesbury Ave is the London home of the world's longest-running musical, *Les Misérables*. *sondheimtheatre.co.uk*

Retail Therapy

Oxford Street

Still the most famous of all the shopping streets, Oxford St is home to world-renowned department stores like Selfridges.

Regent Street

Just around the corner from Oxford St, the most famous stores along this elegant parade include the toyshop Hamleys and designer department store Liberty London.

New Bond Street

Adding a few zeros to the retail budget, this is Chanel, Gucci and Louis Vuitton territory, where only very exclusive fashion is to be found.

Knightsbridge

Home to Harrods and Harvey Nichols, along with New Bond St, Knightsbridge is where you are most likely to spot a celeb indulging in their own retail therapy.

Westfield London

There are two of these shopping malls in London, one in Stratford and this one in White City, which just edges it. Great for high-street brands and fast food.

Prospect of Whitby

Pubs & Clubs

Fabric

A central London mainstay for nearly two decades, Fabric is still one of the best nights out in town. Friday is drum and bass with garage and dubstep thrown in; Saturday is all techno, house and hypnotic grooves. *fabriclondon.com*

XOYO

In spite of all the choice in Shoreditch, most clubbers make for XOYO, which has fast developed a reputation for bringing in the best DJs, including Jackmaster and The 2 Bears for weekend gigs. During the week, there are live bands. *xoyo.co.uk*

Prospect of Whitby

In a city renowned for amazing pubs, it's difficult to list a favourite, but the Prospect comes in because there have been Londoners downing pints here, overlooking the waters of the Thames, since the time of Henry VIII.

Brixton Brewery

One of the capital's finest new range of local microbrewers, under a railway arch, with easy-drinking brews inspired by the grit and glitter of Brixton. Try them in the taproom. *brixtonbrewery.com*

🏪 Best for Browsing

Camden Market
Wrapping itself around the famous canal lock, and seeping into every alley and former stable, this popular tourist spot remains one of the most colourful places to pick up something quirky and fun – or just to people-watch. *camdenmarket.com*

Daunt Books
One of the world's most Instagrammable bookshops, Daunt's stunning Edwardian Marylebone store is famous for its wooden balconies, iconic arched windows and claim to being the world's first custom-built bookshop. *dauntbooks.co.uk*

Rough Trade East
Located in East London's famous Old Truman Brewery on Brick Lane, Rough Trade is one of the city's most iconic vinyl stores, and even has its own fair-trade cafe. It also regularly hosts epic free gigs, which have previously featured the likes of indie super band Blur. *roughtrade.com*

Portobello Road Market
Said to be the world's largest antique market, probably because it's actually five markets sprawling through one of London's most iconic neighbourhoods, Notting Hill. The best day to visit is Saturday, when the buzz is great and antiques are aplenty. *portobelloroad.co.uk*

💗 LGBTIQ+ Nights

Heaven
Arguably the most famous LGBTIQ+ nightspot in London, this club on the Embankment has had Kylie Minogue and big names from *RuPaul's Drag Race* up on stage strutting their stuff, which is probably why the queues to get in are so ridiculous. *g-a-yandheaven.co.uk*

The Village
Soho's iconic gay bar was the first of its kind to open in 1991 in London and needs no introduction. Head upstairs to the Soho Bar for the resident GoGo boys and commercial dance music, or the basement for DJ-spun house and tech. *villagesoho.co.uk*

She
A chic exclusively lesbian hang-out in the heart of Soho that often hosts live music mixed in with comedy. It's open daily and noted for its friendly, fun-loving crowd.

The Karaoke Hole
Dalston's standout queer night takes place in a subterranean neon lounge that is all about cabaret and fun-loving karaoke. Great cocktails and drinks are served at a reasonable price. *thekaraokehole.com*

Village 512
Village 512 has a reputation as a neon-lit, cosy, artsy bar perfect for date nights and catch-ups. Among the innovative beverages on offer are CBD-infused lagers. There's karaoke, too.

Sky Garden

London from Above

Sky Garden
This lush, leafy, indoor public 'park' is absolutely free and makes for a truly romantic place to take in the sunset. Floor-to-ceiling glass keeps you from the elements, as you stroll around the landscaped gardens at your leisure. *skygarden.london*

IFS Cloud Cable Car
Sitting way out east, this enjoyable cable-car experience taking you between the Greenwich Peninsula and the Royal Docks is actually part of the Transport for London network. It's very popular for the stunning views upstream towards the City of London.

The View from the Shard
There is no view higher than this in London. The Shard's 360-degree viewing decks – both closed and open-air – are at the top of a building that is twice as tall as any other in the city. It's breathtaking. *theviewfromtheshard.com*

Primrose Hill
Extremely popular, especially during fair weather, this elevated slice of greenery close to Regent's Park is ideal for a picnic rug, some light nibbles and maybe a glass of something gently bubbling, as you take in the wonderful views of London.

Alexandra Palace
Way out north and far less busy than the central green spaces. After exploring the 63 hectares, and admiring the Victorian 'palace' complete with ice rink, plonk yourself down in one of the many spots to admire the chaos that is London, serenely from afar. *alexandrapalace.com*

Hampstead Ponds

Quirky London

Hampstead Ponds
Fancy some wild swimming in the heart of London? Hampstead Heath has three ponds open year-round; one each for men and women, and one open to all. *hampsteadheath.net*

AIM Escape Rooms
Themed escape room experiences that are scarily immersive in Whitechapel. You can choose to save the world, escape a psychopath or do a more lighthearted comedic escape straight out of a *Hangover* movie. *aimescape.com*

Crossbones Garden
This historic graveyard in Southwark contains the remains of paupers, sex workers and children that were considered unfit for a proper burial in holy ground. People tie ribbons of remembrance to the red iron gates to honour 'the outcast dead'. *crossbones.org.uk*

Dans le Noir
This might just be the ultimate sensory food experience. At Dans le Noir you choose a colour-coded menu of either meat, fish, veg or the chef's special, before being led down into the dark basement for your pitch-black dining adventure. *london.danslenoir.com*

06 Hidden Muslim **BRITAIN**

RELIGION | ARCHITECTURE | HERITAGE

Stare in awe at the beauty of a Mughal-style mosque in the Surrey town of Woking. Visit the former royal palace in Brighton where the British Empire's Muslim soldiers were nursed back to health. And try to unravel the mystery of an 8th-century coin featuring the Islamic declaration of faith. Britain's Muslim heritage is a long and storied one.

How to

Getting here and around These sites are located in towns and cities that are well-connected by trains and buses, and have good public transport.

Islamic culture London is home to a host of Islamic cultural institutes worth visiting, including the Arab gallery, P21 (p49) and the Aga Khan Centre.

Muslim food Woking town centre has a host of decent Indian, Bangladeshi and Turkish restaurants. In Liverpool, the finest halal food is around the Liverpool Waterfront. And in Brighton, head to Western Rd for the town's best Middle Eastern.

Woking

Marvel at the stunning pseudo-Mughal beauty of Britain and northwestern Europe's first purpose-built mosque, the **Shah Jahan Mosque**, a Grade I–listed monument built in Woking, Surrey, in 1889. Wander inside and read the 99 names of God, high up on the ceiling, and admire the ornate *mehrab* (prayer niche). The **Sir Salar Jung Memorial House** is home to the mosque's fascinating archives that include rare British-Muslim manuscripts and photos of early British converts and the mosque's illustrious founders.

Walk around the corner to the serene **Peace Gardens** with its beautiful Indian *chattri* (domed cover) above the entrance. Modelled on a classical Islamic garden, complete with central water feature, here you'll

The Oriental Room

Hidden away inside several stately homes are elaborately decorated oriental rooms which mirror the art and architecture of places like Spain's Alhambra and Istanbul's Topkapi Palace. Some of the finest include the Arab Hall at **Leighton House** and the Arab Room at **Cardiff Castle**.

Above left Shah Jahan Mosque, Woking
Above right Arab Room, Cardiff Castle
Left Sir Salar Jung Memorial House, Woking

find the names of some of the Muslims who died fighting for Britain and France during the world wars listed on the back wall. They were once buried here.

Finally, head to Brookwood Cemetery and locate the historic **Muhammadan Cemetery** (now plot 'M1') and read the faded inscriptions on the Marker Stone, planted here in 1884 to identify this as Britain's first Muslim cemetery.

Liverpool

The **Abdullah Quilliam Mosque & National Heritage Centre** (abdullahquilliam.org) in Liverpool was home to England's first public mosque, where local white Muslims prayed in the late Victorian period. Wander through the Georgian House, restored to a functioning mosque in 2014 after more than a century; notice some of the internal arches, rebuilt like the original, and listen to stories about Britain's first Muslim community (p62) told by

Britain's First Muslim Trails

One of the best ways to appreciate the Muslim heritage in Woking is to pick up the maps for **Britain's Muslim Heritage Trails** (everydaymuslim.org), the country's first dedicated to British Muslim history. The maps are available at the **Brookwood Cemetery** and online.

There are two trails: **The Woking Trail**, which takes visitors to the Shah Jahan Mosque, the Peace Gardens and the Muhammadan Cemetery, and **The Muslim Cemetery Walk**, which is a walk through the historic Muslim cemetery locating the final resting place of converted lords, ladies, royals, Ottomans, activists and even the celebrated British-Iraqi architect Dame Zaha Hadid.

■ Sadiya Ahmed, founder of the Everyday Muslim Heritage and Archive Project, the creators of the trails, @Everyday_Muslim

Far left Brookwood Cemetery
Left Queens Hotel, Brighton
Below Brighton Pavilion

members of today's local congregation. Arrange a visit in advance.

Brighton

In this seaside resort town, start at the **Queens Hotel**, which in the 1820s was home to 'Mahomed's Baths' where Sake Dean Mahomet – one of the earliest British-Muslim entrepreneurs – 'shampooed' (an Indian massage using herbal concoctions) Victorian high society. Mahomat also opened Britain's first Indian restaurant in London in 1810.

Nearby is the stunning **Brighton Pavilion**, pleasure palace of King George IV (a client of Mahomat's). Upstairs is the Indian Military Hospital Gallery, which explains how Hindu, Muslim and Sikh soldiers who were injured fighting in WWI were treated here in 'sympathetic' surrounds. Leave the palace via the **India Gate**, a thank you gift from India.

Next, walk up to **Brighton General Hospital**, outside which a huge sign in Urdu and English once read 'The Kitchener Indian Hospital'. This was the 'other' hospital where Indian soldiers were treated – in almost prison-like conditions.

Finally, cross town to the small church of **St Nicholas** and head round the back to visit the neglected graves of pioneering Mahomet and his wife.

Anglo Islam

THIRTEEN CENTURIES OF BRITISH-MUSLIM HERITAGE

Britain's Muslim heritage stretches back to the 8th century. Home to northwestern Europe's first mosques and Muslim cemeteries, this is a nation with a long history of trading with, and ruling over, millions of Muslims, many of whom then came and made their homes in the imperial 'motherland' to help it become one of the most diverse and multicultural countries in the West.

Left William Henry Quilliam
Centre Shah Jahan Mosque
Right Jameel Gallery, Victoria & Albert Museum, London

Early Contact

The most exciting early evidence of Islamic contact with Britain is an 8th-century gold coin minted by the Anglo-Saxon King of Mercia, Offa. Discovered in the pope's coffers in Rome, it has the Muslim declaration of faith and a nod to the Caliph Al-Mansur written in Arabic as well as Offa's name in Latin. Nobody knows why Offa minted the coin, but everyone agrees it was probably minted in England, confirming Britain encountered Islam a century after the Prophet Muhammad's death. The coin is now displayed at the British Museum in London.

Over the next millennium, Britain had a complex relationship with Islam, based largely on trade, diplomacy and empire. Elizabeth I made trade agreements with several Muslim rulers including the Ottomans, for example, and there is evidence that Muslims lived in London throughout this time. In the late 17th century, Britain began colonising Muslim countries, from Africa to Asia; this led to further contact with Muslim cultures and, after the end of the British Empire, large-scale Muslim immigration to Britain from several former colonies in the second half of the 20th century.

The White Muslim Pioneers

The first real community of Muslims in England were a group of white, working-class Liverpudlians. They were led by William Henry Quilliam, who converted to Islam after a visit to Morocco. He founded the country's first mosque in Liverpool in 1887 as well as Britain's first *madrasah* (Islamic school), Islamic library and Islamic journal.

The next community of British Muslims was more mixed and included several influential convert aristocrats and a number of professional Muslims then living in Britain. They gathered around Woking's Shah Jahan Mosque, which was built in 1889 by Hungarian-Jewish orientalist, Wilhelm Gottlieb Leitner. However, activity in Woking really took off following the conversion of Lord Headley in 1913, an influential peer, who along with his friend, Indian lawyer Khwaja Kamal ud-Din, became the driving force of the community.

Settler Muslim Communities

Towards the late Victorian era, there were small pockets of Muslim communities settled in numerous towns and cities across Britain. They were mainly communities of *lascars* (sailors) and traders in towns like Liverpool and Manchester, with the most organised and established being the Yemeni *lascars* in the port towns of Cardiff in Wales and South Shields near Newcastle. The Yemenis are believed to be the founders of Britain's earliest *sufi* (mystical Islam) lodges.

However, the biggest wave of Muslim settlement in Britain came in the postcolonial period, when Muslim men from formerly British-ruled India – modern-day India, Pakistan and Bangladesh – arrived to work in the country from the 1950s onwards. They were later joined by their families and helped to found most of the early mosques in Britain and, in the case of the British Bangladeshis, completely changed the eating habits of British people.

Later waves of Muslims came from North Africa, Somalia, Türkiye and the Middle East as well as from European Muslim countries like Albania, Kosovo and Bosnia and Herzegovina. There is also a sizeable convert community of Brits.

Islamic Art & Artefacts

Having ruled over so many Muslim nations, it will come as no surprise that Britain is home to an astonishing number of Islamic artefacts, and two of the largest collections can be found in London. The **British Museum** (p54) is home to more than 100,000 Islamic objects and some of these have been re-curated for the **Albukhary Foundation Gallery** where treasures from every major Islamic dynasty, including the Ottomans, the Umayyads and the Abbasids, can be seen. Then there is the **Jameel Gallery** in the Victoria & Albert Museum, which is home to almost 15,000 items of Islamic art, including the world's oldest carpet, the Ardabil Carpet, and Qur'anic manuscripts dating back to the 10th century.

SOUTHEAST ENGLAND

HISTORY | COUNTRYSIDE | WINE

- **Trip Builder** (p66)
- **Practicalities** (p67)
- **Best of the Cotswold Way** (p68)
- **A Taste of English Wine** (p70)
- **WWII Spies & Secrets** (p72)
- **The Southeast on Screen** (p74)
- **An Oxford Education** (p76)
- **Boating the Norfolk Broads** (p78)
- **Listings** (p80)

SOUTHEAST ENGLAND
Trip Builder

Easily accessible from London, southeast England mixes historic sights and unspoilt rural landscapes. Explore its array of castles, cathedrals and country houses, escape to the coast's white cliffs and sandy beaches, or head into the countryside for rolling hills, villages and vineyards.

Uncover the lesser-known side of the famous university city of **Oxford** (p76)
🚆 *1 hr from London*

Explore the tranquil **Norfolk Broads** by boat (p78)
🚗 *20 min from Norwich*

Dive into WWII history in the secret tunnels at **Dover Castle** (p73)
🚗 *2 hr from London*

Taste English sparkling wines in the vineyards of **Sussex** (p70)
🚗 *2¼ hr from London*

Enjoy the best bits of the scenic **Cotswold Way** (p68) walking route
🚗 *1 hr from Bristol*

NORTH SEA

Norfolk Broads National Park

South Downs National Park

Strait of Dover

Isle of Wight

English Channel

FRANCE

0 50 km / 30 miles

DONNA GIBBS/SHUTTERSTOCK ©;
PREVIOUS SPREAD: S-F/SHUTTERSTOCK ©

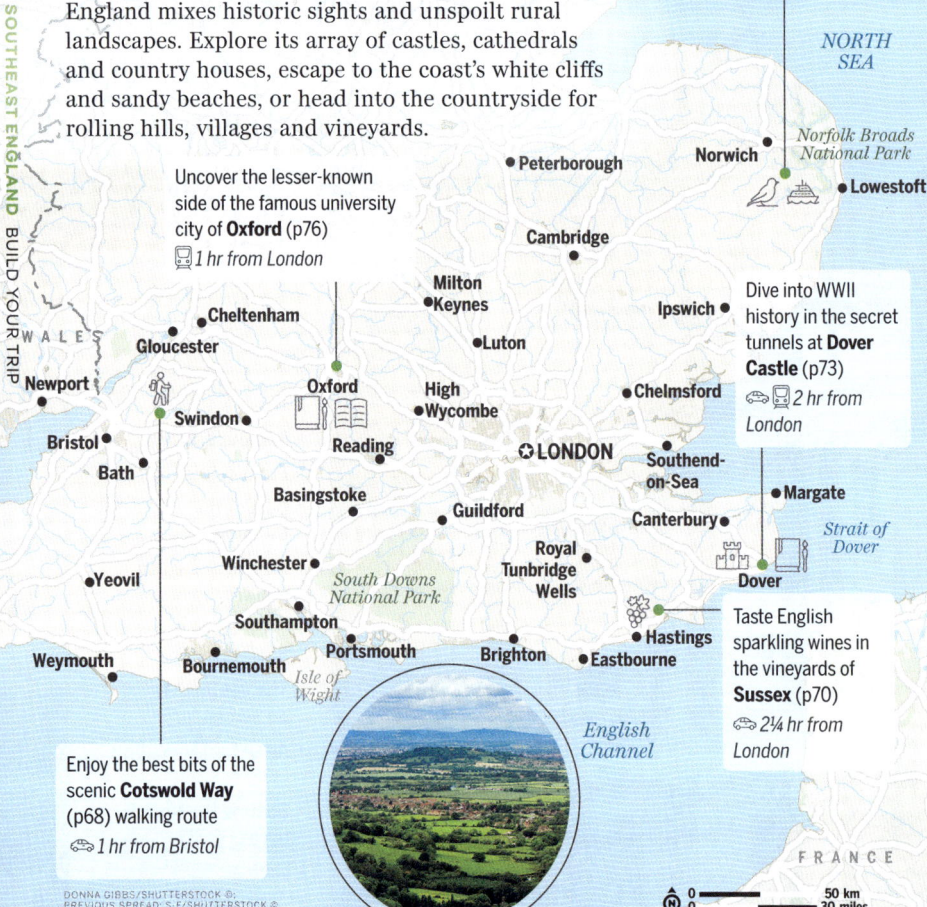

Practicalities

ARRIVING

London's airports provide good access to the southeast. Gatwick is most convenient for Sussex and Kent; Stansted for East Anglia; and Heathrow for Oxford. Bristol airport is also handy for the Cotswolds.

FIND YOUR WAY

Navigation apps and phone signals are generally reliable (except in very rural areas). Ordnance Survey Explorer maps are useful for walkers.

MONEY

If you're using the train, a Network Railcard saves a third on fares in London and the southeast.

WHERE TO STAY

Place	Pros/Cons
Cotswolds	High-end country house hotels and spas, plus cosy cottage rentals; easiest with a car.
Oxford and Cambridge	Stay in historic college buildings outside term time.
Brighton	Wide selection of accommodation. Cool nightlife and arts.
North Norfolk	Camping and glamping. Sandy beaches and nature reserves.

EATING & DRINKING

You'll find world-class dining in the Berkshire town of Bray, which is home to two of the UK's three-Michelin-starred restaurants. While you're here try tasty Cotswold cheeses, from Double Gloucester (pictured top left) to the pungent Stinking Bishop, and meaty Norfolk crabs (pictured bottom left) from Cromer, served with lemon and black pepper.

Best bubbly with a view Rathfinny Estate (p71)

Must-try Whitstable oysters (p80)

GETTING AROUND

Car The best way to reach the region's rural areas.

Train Connects main towns and cities, though you often have to go via London to travel from one area to another.

Local bus Links smaller towns and villages, but can be infrequent.

JAN–MAR Cold and often wet; some sites close for winter.

APR–JUN Sunshine and showers; good-value prices.

JUL–SEP Warmest, driest weather, but can be crowded and expensive.

OCT–DEC Cooling down, fewer crowds and autumn colours.

Best of the
COTSWOLD WAY

VILLAGES | VIEWS | HISTORY

With its chocolate-box villages, rolling hills and historic sites, the 102-mile Cotswold Way is one of Britain's great long-distance walks, connecting Chipping Campden to Bath. But you don't need your walking boots to experience some of the region's most memorable sights, with our guide to highlights of the Cotswold Way also accessible by car.

How to

Getting around While it's easiest to explore the Cotswolds by car, there are train stations in Cheltenham, Stroud and Bath, and infrequent buses connect main towns and villages.

When to go Spring and autumn for the best scenery. Summer weekends get crowded.

How long Allow two to three days to explore the route.

Pub stop The Cotswolds does a great country pub; our picks along the Cotswold Way are the Mount Inn (Stanton), Lion Inn (Winchcombe) and Falcon (Painswick).

Top left Broadway Tower
Bottom left Chipping Campden

Arts and crafts The Cotswold Way starts in the market town of **Chipping Campden**, which has over 250 honey-hued listed buildings. It was a centre for the late-19th-century Arts and Crafts movement, with works by local artists on display at the **Court Barn Museum** (courtbarn.org.uk). Heading south, popular **Broadway** has an array of boutique shops, restaurants and hotels, including the 650-year-old **Lygon Arms** (lygonarms hotel.co.uk). Just outside the village, the **Broadway Tower** is a fairy-tale folly with panoramic views – and a nuclear bunker hidden underneath.

Churches and castles The town of **Winchcombe** is a hub for Cotswold history, from neolithic burial mound **Belas Knap** to 1000-year-old **Sudeley Castle** (sudeleycastle.co.uk), a grand edifice surrounded by beautiful gardens that is the burial place of Henry VIII's last wife, Katherine Parr. At the Cotswold Way's halfway point, **Painswick** is best known for its impressive church surrounded by 99 yew trees. It's also home to England's only surviving **Rococo Garden**, which was painstakingly restored from paintings.

Peace and parkland Heading into the quieter South Cotswolds, the Cotswold Way runs through **Wotton-Under-Edge**, where you can see three sets of ancient almshouses and browse independent shops on the high street. And just before the end of the route in Bath, the peaceful village of **Cold Ashton** is close to the National Trust site **Dyrham Park** (national trust.org.uk), a grand baroque country house in an ancient deer park.

Cotswold Way Walks

Walk a stretch of the Cotswold Way without committing to the full distance with one of these scenic circular walks:

Broadway and the Tower (4 miles) Climb to the hilltop Broadway Tower with views over 13 counties before descending back to the village.

Stanton, Snowshill and the Edge (6 miles) Follow woodland paths to two of the area's prettiest villages, each with a cosy pub.

Cleeve Hill Common Ring (6 miles) Soak up the views from the Cotswolds' highest point in an area of rare limestone grassland.

The Selsey Circuit (5 miles) Mix Cotswold scenery with industrial mill heritage along the Stroudwater canal.

08 A Taste of English **WINE**

WINE | COUNTRYSIDE | FOOD

English wine has gone from a novelty to award-winning industry, with over 140 vineyards in southeast England. The climate and soils of Kent, Surrey and Sussex match those across the Channel, creating sparkling wines that give Champagne a run for its money. New tasting rooms, restaurants and hotels make the UK's wine capital a must-visit for wine lovers.

How to

Getting around The rural locations of the vineyards mean it's easiest if you have a car – and a designated driver. Alternatively, **English Wine Tasting Tours** *(englishwinetastingtours.co.uk)* organises public and private day tours from London.

Opening Prebooking is required for vineyard tours. Cellar door shops are open for drop-in visitors; hours vary.

Events In June, **English Wine Week** *(winegb.co.uk)* sees special events and offers at many wineries.

Top left Grapevine, Rathfinny Estate
Bottom left Sparkling wine, Ridgeview

🍺 Best of the Beers

Prefer the grain to the grape? Try one of these southeast breweries for a tour and tasting.

Shepherd Neame *(shepherdneame.co.uk)* Britain's oldest brewer, at the heart of Kent's hop-growing country, with a wide range of lagers and ales.

Chiltern Brewery *(chilternbrewery.co.uk)* Set among the Chiltern Hills in Buckinghamshire, the amber Beechwood Bitter is its flagship brew and there are several gluten-free beers too.

Hook Norton Brewery *(hooky.co.uk)* Oxfordshire brewers in a quirky Victorian building with original steam engine and beer deliveries by shire horse.

Long Man Brewery *(longmanbrewery.com)* Surrounded by the South Downs National Park, this brewery uses sustainable methods to create award-winning small-batch beers.

Tour and taste The sustainably designed, state-of-the-art winery at **Rathfinny Estate** *(rathfinnyestate.com)* near Beachy Head has vineyard tours, a Michelin-recommended restaurant and B&B accommodation. It's the perfect spot to try the Sussex Sparkling wine, with views of the South Downs. Family-run **Ridgeview** *(ridgeview.co.uk)*, in the South Downs National Park, specialises in sustainably produced sparkling wine. Round out a self-guided tour through the vines with a six-wine tasting.

Dine among the vines At **Chapel Down** *(chapeldown.com)* vineyard in Kent, the award-winning Swan restaurant serves modern British cuisine. Choose from a spot at the chef's table or on the terrace overlooking the High Weald, or pick up local produce from the smart deli to take away. **Balfour Winery** *(balfourwinery.com)* produces Champagne-style wines on its 162-hectare Hush Heath Estate. Head here for a tour and tasting or the weekend Balfour Dining Club dinners, which include four courses paired with matching wines (and music).

Scenic spots Set among the Surrey Hills, **Denbies** *(denbies.co.uk)* is one of England's largest vineyards. As well as award-winning sparkling wines, there are walking and biking routes, a vineyard train, art gallery, farm shop, three restaurants and a luxurious hotel. Alternatively, tranquil **Oxney Organic Estate** *(oxneyestate.com)* in East Sussex is part of an 344-hectare organic farm in the High Weald Area of Outstanding Natural Beauty, with Saturday tours, summer vineyard picnics and quirky accommodation.

09 WWII Spies & SECRETS

HISTORY | MILITARY | MUSEUMS

Head back in time to the 1940s on a tour of WWII sites in southeast England, where underground tunnels, spy stations and mysterious military bases have revealed their wartime secrets. Explore our pick of these former top-secret sites where you can find out about the spies' hidden lives and the important role they played in ending the war.

How to

Getting around There are train stations in Dover and Bletchley, and High Wycombe Station is 2 miles from Hughenden. Orford Ness is only accessible by ferry from Orford Quay.

When to go Orford Ness ferries run April to October. Other sites are open year-round, though opening hours are limited in winter.

Top tip English Heritage (english-heritage.org.uk) and **National Trust** (nationaltrust.org.uk) both offer annual memberships that save you money if you're visiting multiple sites.

Top left Dover Castle
Bottom left Imperial War Museum, Duxford

Secret tunnels Hidden beneath the 11th-century **Dover Castle** *(english-heritage.org.uk)* in Kent lies the wartime HQ of Dover Naval Command. From these tunnels Operation Dynamo was masterminded in 1940 – the evacuation of Dunkirk and rescue of 338,000 men by a flotilla of ships. Today it is run by English Heritage and you can tour the command rooms and underground hospital.

Codebreakers The country house at **Bletchley Park** *(bletchleypark.org.uk)* in Buckinghamshire was the top-secret home of the UK's best codebreakers, who cracked the 'unbreakable' German Enigma code and shortened the war by two years. Bletchley kept its secrets until the mid-1970s when it was declassified; today it's a museum showing how the codebreakers lived and worked.

Mystery base Located on a shingle spit on the Suffolk coast, **Orford Ness** isn't the most obvious military base. But deserted buildings and bunkers scattered across the landscape tell the story of its days as a test site for everything from radar to nuclear weapons – and more that we may never know about. Today it's a peaceful nature reserve accessible only by ferry.

Spy maps Hughenden Manor *(nationaltrust.org.uk)* in Buckinghamshire was the home of former Prime Minister Benjamin Disraeli. It was also the site of a secret wartime map-making operation codenamed Hillside, where skilled cartographers drew maps of Germany from aerial photos to use in bombing missions. Later donated to the National Trust, its wartime role was only discovered in 2004.

WWII Museums

Find out more about WWII in the southeast at the region's military museums.

Imperial War Museum (Duxford) Britain's largest museum of aviation at the historic Duxford aerodrome, with WWII exhibits including Spitfire, Lancaster and Hurricane aircraft *(iwm.org.uk)*.

Chatham Dockyard (Kent) Tour functioning WWII destroyer HMS *Cavalier*, which saw action in the Arctic and Pacific and is preserved as a memorial to those lost *(thedockyard.co.uk)*.

Kent Battle of Britain Museum (Folkestone) Large collection of Battle of Britain artefacts recovered from over 650 crashed British and German aircraft *(kbobm.org)*.

The Southeast on Screen

EXPLORING SOUTHEAST ENGLAND'S FILM AND TV ROLES

From Harry Potter to James Bond, *Bridgerton* to *The Crown,* southeast England has had a starring role in some of the biggest film and TV franchises of recent years. The region's film talent, studios and locations have made it the choice location for everything from period dramas to fashion shoots.

Above left Cliveden House
Above middle Waverley Abbey
Above right Christ Church College, Oxford

The cinematic history of the southeast goes back to the 1920s and '30s, when iconic British film studios like Pinewood, Elstree and Shepperton were founded and which, to this day, are still in production. The recent boom in online streaming services and tax breaks for international productions are also attracting an increasing number of film crews to the UK. Add the southeast's proximity to London and range of locations and it's no surprise that it's become the busiest region outside of London for major film production.

Period Pieces

The castles and country houses of the southeast have provided the backdrop for many period dramas, though they're not always as they seem. Dover Castle became the Tower of London for *The Other Boleyn Girl* (2008) and Chatham Dockyard in Kent the fictional Norwegian port Trollesund for *The Golden Compass* (2007). And the BBC adaptation of Nancy Mitford's *The Pursuit of Love* (2021) used National Trust sites Dyrham Park, Lacock Abbey and Stourhead as locations in Paris, London and Oxford.

But it's not all period pieces. Southeast locations have featured as a WWII RAF base in *Pearl Harbor* (2001; Badminton House), as Prince Charming's palace in *Cinderella* (2015; Cliveden House) and in the final chase scenes of *Hot Fuzz* (2007; Waverley Abbey).

On Location

Emma Clarke-Bolton from the Location Works film location library says it's not just film and TV being shot in the southeast. 'We're asked for locations for music videos and photo shoots, and unmodernised and contemporary buildings are just as in demand.'

With more than 15 years in the locations and film-management industry, Emma has received a few odd requests: 'A lot involve animals – we've had a photographer wanting to bring a lion into an 18th-century country house and a "professional" turkey at Deal Castle. But owners are very accommodating. Fine-art handlers are brought in to make sure art and antiques are safe, especially if there's a party or fight scene in the script.'

> Southeast locations have featured in *Pearl Harbor, Cinderella* and *Hot Fuzz.*

Behind the Scenes

Film tourism has become big business in the UK – and according to Visit Britain 20% of tourists visited a film or TV location on their last trip to the country. Renting out a property as a screen location can lead to a boom in visitors, who get the chance for a behind-the-scenes peek into their favourite shows, from walking up the staircase of Christ Church College Oxford in the footsteps of *Harry Potter* (2001) to seeing the coronation chair from *The King's Speech* (2010) at Ely Cathedral in Cambridgeshire.

For many locations, the ultimate is landing a starring role in a long-running high-profile series, such as Netflix' smash *Bridgerton* (2020–), which counts Badminton House and Stowe Park among its locations. Or *Downton Abbey* – with a second movie released in 2022 – which is filmed in the Oxfordshire village of Bampton. And with over 200 films in production in the UK each year, the next big southeast hit might be on the way.

Southeast Locations to Visit

Blenheim Palace Follow a self-guided tour of locations from films including James Bond's *Spectre* and *The Libertine* at Winston Churchill's birthplace in Oxfordshire *(blenheimpalace.com)*.

Petworth House A baroque-style palace in South Downs National Park, Petworth was in Mike Leigh's 2014 biopic *Mr Turner* as the home of Turner's patron, the third Earl of Egremont *(nationaltrust.org.uk)*.

Basildon Park This 18th-century house in Berkshire hosted a ball in 2005's *Pride and Prejudice* and was in the 2016 comedy-horror spin-off *Pride and Prejudice and Zombies (nationaltrust.org.uk)*.

Woodchester Mansion Half-finished Victorian Gothic Cotswold mansion which appeared as Prince Philip's boarding school Gordonstoun in season two of the TV series *The Crown (woodchestermansion.org.uk)*.

An Oxford **EDUCATION**

ARCHITECTURE | MUSEUMS | LITERATURE

With one of the oldest and most prestigious universities in the world at its heart, the picturesque city of Oxford is a must-visit for its famous golden stone colleges, chapels and cloisters. But as well as exploring the university, why not discover a different side to the city of dreaming spires with some of Oxford's lesser-known sights?

How to

Getting around Oxford is fairly small and easy to explore on foot. Or join the students and rent a bike via the Donkey Republic app.

When to go Spring and autumn when students are in residence. Colleges may be closed during exam periods; many museums don't open on Monday.

Sweet treat Pick up homemade ice cream from Oxford institution G&D's, with three locations across the city.

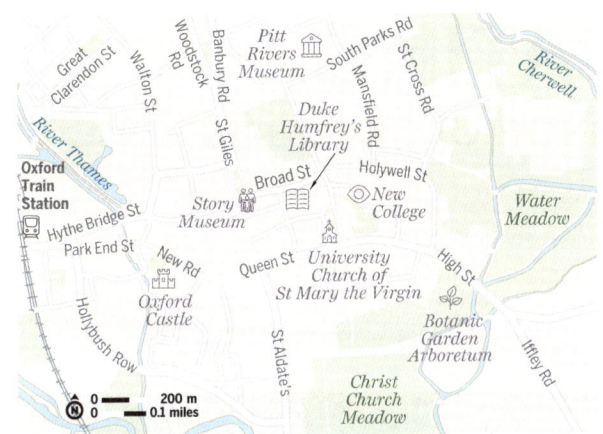

Top left Oxford Castle
Bottom left Pitt Rivers Museum

Quirky collections As an academic heavyweight, Oxford is a great place for museums. One of the most unusual is the atmospheric **Pitt Rivers Museum** (prm.ox.ac.uk). This dimly lit anthropology museum has over 600,000 eccentric artefacts, such as a witch in a bottle. To the south, **Oxford Castle** (oxfordcastleandprison.co.uk) became a prison in 1230 after the English Civil War; theatrical tours of life behind bars are led by costumed guides. You can also sleep in a former cell at the Malmaison Oxford hotel.

Literary links Step inside the pages of a book at the Enchanted Library and Whispering Wood at Oxford's **Story Museum** (storymuseum.org.uk). At this family-friendly interactive museum, stories are brought to life, including those by local authors Lewis Carroll, CS Lewis and JRR Tolkien. Or visit the peaceful **Oxford Botanic Garden & Arboretum** (obga.ox.ac.uk) and make a stop at Lyra and Will's bench, made famous in writer Philip Pullman's *His Dark Materials* trilogy.

Camera ready The domed Radcliffe Camera is one of Oxford's most recognisable buildings. For the best view of it, visit the **University Church of St Mary the Virgin** and climb 127 steps to the top of the tower for views across the city's rooftops. You can also visit medieval **Duke Humfrey's Library**, the Bodleian Library's oldest reading room, with ornately painted ceilings and stacks of ancient books and manuscripts.

Oxford City Walls

Oxford was originally surrounded by medieval stone walls but only a few sections remain – and you have to hunt for them. The best preserved are found in the garden of **New College**; when William of Wykeham founded the college in 1379 he was permitted to buy the land on the condition that the walls were kept in a 'competent manner of reparation'. To check the college is properly maintaining them, the mayor still inspects them every three years. Visit New College to see the wall for yourself. You can also see sections outside the Turf Tavern and on the northern side of Brewer St.

■ **Recommended by Tabby Lucas,** *Oxford Blue Badge Tourist Guide, @cotswold_and_oxford_tours*

11 BOATING
the Norfolk Broads

BOATING | WILDLIFE | WINDMILLS

Set sail through the peaceful Norfolk Broads, where 125 miles of flooded medieval peat workings have formed a network of tranquil waterways, perfect for exploring by boat with their waterside villages, thatched cottages, windmills and nature reserves full of birdlife.

How to

Getting around Hire a boat for a day or longer to explore the Broads' lock-free waterways, which are wide and easy to navigate, or get up close to wildlife on a canoe or paddleboard.

When to go Boat hire is normally available February to November, with spring and autumn quietest and best for wildlife-spotting.

Photo spot Find some of the Broads' most picturesque windmills at Hardley Mill and Thurne Mill.

Wildlife of the Broads

The Norfolk Broads are among the most important landscapes for wetland wildlife in the UK. The Broads are home to otters, winter waterfowl, great crested grebes (pictured) and breeding common terns, and the reedbeds and fens surrounding them support bitterns, cranes, marsh harriers, fen orchids and the Norfolk swallowtail butterfly, which lives nowhere else on earth.

■ Recommended by Norfolk Wildlife Trust, @norfolkwt

NORTH SEA

01 Explore picturesque **Horning**, which dates back to 1020, with its thatched cottages and tearooms. Take a trip on a paddle steamer and stop for drinks at the riverside Swan Inn *(vintageinn.co.uk)*.

02 **Hickling Broad** is the largest of the Broads and a haven for bird species. Tour the nature reserve *(norfolkwildlifetrust.org.uk)* by boat with an expert spotter and climb the 18m tree tower.

03 Visit the atmospheric ruins of medieval monastery **St Benet's Abbey** on the River Bure. Join a free tour or follow the 7-mile circular walk past waterside windmills to How Hill.

05 Unspoiled **Woodbastwick**, linked to Salhouse Broad by a half-mile path, is home to Woodforde's Brewery *(woodfordes.com)* with a visitor centre and brewery tap at the Fur & Feathers *(furfeathernorfolk.com)* pub.

04 On the edge of Malthouse Broad, charming **Ranworth** has panoramic views from St Helen's Church and a boardwalk running through woodland and reed beds to a floating nature reserve.

Norfolk Broads National Park

5 km
2.5 miles

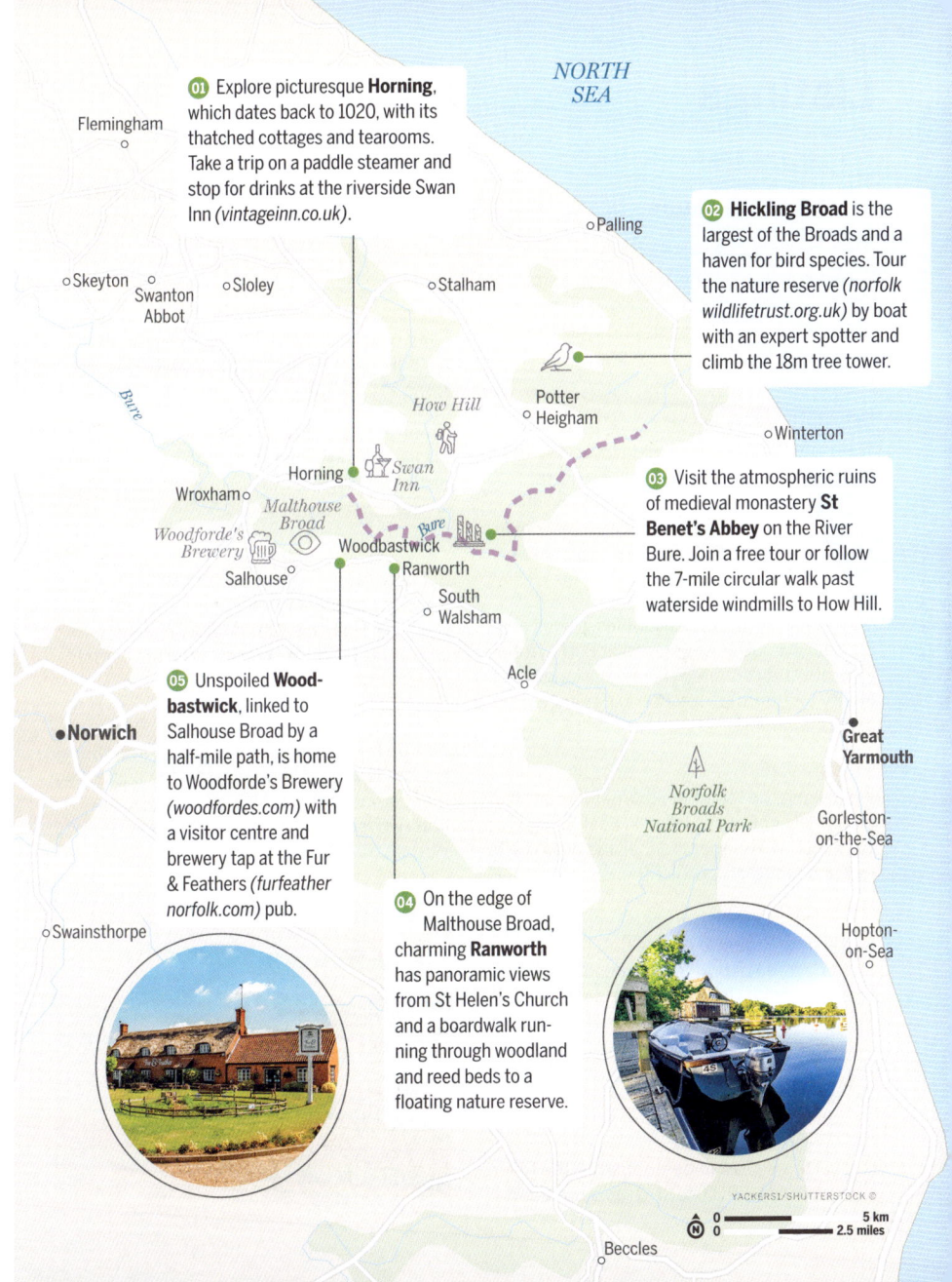

YACKERS1/SHUTTERSTOCK ©

Listings

BEST OF THE REST

🐦 Wildlife & Nature

Seal-watching at Blakeney Point
Take a boat trip to England's largest seal colony at Blakeney Point in Norfolk, home to common and grey seals and where over 3000 pups are born each year. *nationaltrust.org.uk*

Deer Rutting at Minsmere
From late September to mid-November the normally shy red deer stags clash horns during rutting season at the Royal Society for the Protection of Birds (RSPB) reserve in Minsmere on the Suffolk coast. *rspb.org.uk*

Port Lympne
Go on safari with zebras, giraffes, rhinos and big cats in southeast England at Port Lympne in Kent – stay on-site in an animal lodge or luxury tent for the full safari experience. *aspinallfoundation.org*

Beachy Head
Walk along the top of the dramatic 162m-high chalk cliffs of Beachy Head in East Sussex for views out across the Channel and down to its red-and-white-striped lighthouse.

Cotswold Lavender
Fields near Broadway in the Cotswolds become a sea of purple blooms from June to August, with Cotswold Lavender products for sale and plenty of photo opportunities. *cotswoldlavender.co.uk*

🍴 Scenic Dining

Cherwell Boathouse   ££
Converted Victorian boathouse on the River Cherwell in North Oxford. Grab a punt and jug of Pimm's and head upstream before a riverside lunch. *cherwellboathouse.co.uk*

Waterside Inn   £££
Fine dining by the waterside in the foodie hot spot village of Bray in Berkshire. Classic French cuisine, top-notch wine list and three Michelin stars. *waterside-inn.co.uk*

SIX Brasserie & Rooftop Bar   ££
Creative cocktails with views across the Cambridge skyline from the rooftop bar and grilled dishes in the glass-walled brasserie below. *sixcambridge.co.uk*

Victoria Inn   ££
Set between North Norfolk's most beautiful sandy beach and parkland surrounding Holkham Hall, this 19th-century coaching inn serves produce sourced from the estate. *holkham.co.uk*

Whitstable Oyster Company   ££
Pick up half a dozen oysters – best from September to April – and a glass of fizz and enjoy them among Whitstable's colourful beach huts. *whitstableoystercompany.com*

Beachy Head

🏰 Castles & Cathedrals

Canterbury Cathedral
England's largest cathedral, founded in 597 CE. Admire the medieval stained-glass windows, visit the crypt and stand on the spot where Thomas Becket, the Archbishop of Canterbury, was murdered in 1170. *canterbury-cathedral.org*

Hever Castle
Childhood home of Anne Boleyn, the second wife of King Henry VIII, this romantic 13th-century castle in Kent was remodelled in the 20th century by the Astor family. See historic furniture, tapestries and antiques on display. *hevercastle.co.uk*

Bodiam Castle
Medieval Bodiam Castle in East Sussex is straight out of a fairy tale, surrounded by a moat with spiral staircases, battlements and an original wooden portcullis. *nationaltrust.org.uk*

Norwich Cathedral
Norwich's Romanesque cathedral is one of the finest in Europe, with over a thousand roof sculptures, monastic cloisters and even some original medieval graffiti. *cathedral.org.uk*

Weird & Wonderful Events

Jack in the Green
Pagan festival celebrating the coming of spring on the first Monday in May. Dressed in a cloak of leaves, Jack leads a parade of Morris dancers through Hastings before being sacrificed to welcome spring.

Cheese Rolling Festival
Daredevil competitors chase a 3.6kg wheel of Double Gloucester down steep Cooper's Hill in Gloucestershire on Spring Bank Holiday, with the fastest to the bottom in one piece winning the cheese.

Cheese Rolling Festival

Woolsack Races
Started during Tetbury's days as a centre for the wool trade. At this annual event in the Cotswolds in late May, competitors race up a steep hill carrying a 27kg wool sack.

World Pooh Sticks Championships
Inspired by the book *Winnie the Pooh*, in May competitors throw sticks into the River Windrush in Oxfordshire to see which gets under the bridge first.

🗺 Great Journeys

Thames Boat Trip
Cruise up the River Thames along the route of the famous Henley Royal Regatta towards Oxford or Windsor, with self-drive boat hire by the day or week.

Gloucestershire Warwickshire Steam Railway
Head back in time to the Golden Age of steam on the GWSR, a volunteer-run heritage railway through the Cotswold countryside from Cheltenham to Broadway. *gwsr.com*

South Downs Way
This 100-mile stile-free walking route runs from Winchester to Eastbourne along the chalk hills of the South Downs, with shorter sections accessible by bus. *southdownsway.org*

SOUTHWEST ENGLAND

ADVENTURE | BEACHES | CULTURE

- **Trip Builder** (p84)
- **Practicalities** (p86)
- **Seaside & Steam** (p88)
- **Not-So-New Forest** (p90)
- **Stories in Stone** (p92)
- **Into the Jurassic** (p94)
- **Adventure Dartmoor** (p96)
- **Protest Culture** (p100)
- **Bristol's Black History** (p102)
- **Scilly Ferry Hop** (p104)
- **Moors & Shores** (p106)
- **Explore the Shore** (p108)
- **Listings** (p110)

SOUTHWEST ENGLAND
Trip Builder

The experiences are rich in England's wild southwest: ferry-hop between exquisite islands, stargaze beneath ink-black skies, embark on guided swims and discover a culture of powerful protests. Bewitching and surprising, this region demands to be explored.

Catch some waves then feast on surf-inspired street food at **Croyde** (p107)
🚗 2½ hr from Bristol

Feel the heat in the vast greenhouses at the **Eden Project** (p110)
🚗 2½ hr from Bath

Find a favourite castaway beach on the captivating **Isles of Scilly** (p104)
⛴ 3 hr from Penzance

Kayak to secret beaches and hard-to-reach coves near **Falmouth** (p108)
🚆 30 min from Truro

Fall in love with a fairy-tale castle at **St Michael's Mount** (p110)
🚆 30 min from Truro

Carmarthen • Croyde • Bideford • Bude • Padstow • Bodmin • Tavistock • Newquay • Plymouth • St Austell • St Ives • Truro • Penzance • Falmouth • Helston • Land's End • Hugh Town • Isles of Scilly

FROM LEFT: NEIL DUGGAN/SHUTTERSTOCK ©, ASC PHOTOGRAPHY/SHUTTERSTOCK ©, NIGEL JARVIS/SHUTTERSTOCK ©; PREVIOUS SPREAD: SHUANG LI/SHUTTERSTOCK ©

WALES

Merthyr Tydfil

Discover Black history and protest culture in **Bristol** (p100)
🚆 *1½ hr from London*

• Swansea

Look out for wild red deer on wilderness **Exmoor** (p107)
🚗 *1½ hr from Bristol*

Newport
✪ **CARDIFF**
Barry

Severn Estuary

Bristol

Avon

Tour *Bridgerton* backdrops in beautiful **Bath** (p110)
🚆 *15 min from Bristol*

Bath

Bristol Channel

• Minehead

Burnham-on-Sea

• Warminster

Barnstaple

Exmoor National Park

• Taunton

• Salisbury

• Tiverton

• Yeovil

Southampton

• Okehampton

Exe

• Honiton

New Forest National Park

• Exeter

Bridport

• Dorchester

Stour

Bournemouth

Dartmoor National Park

Exmouth

Dine in age-old pubs, hike in the wilderness and camp wild on **Dartmoor** (p96)
🚆 *1 hr from Exeter*

• Weymouth

Isle of Wight

• Torquay

• Dartmouth

English Channel

0 — 50 km
0 — 25 miles

Practicalities

ARRIVING

Air Bristol Airport, Exeter Airport and Cornwall Airport Newquay provide links to UK and European destinations.

Train Direct rail connections to Bristol Temple Meads include those from London Paddington (1½ hours), Birmingham (1½ hours) and Bath (15 minutes). Mainline trains running between London Paddington and Penzance (five hours) call at Exeter (two hours) and Plymouth (three hours) en route.

HOW MUCH FOR A

Local ice cream £3

Pint of cider £4

Cornish pasty £4.50

WHEN TO GO

JAN–MAR
Colder weather and better surf. Seasonal closures in rural areas.

APR–JUN
Boat trips resume, warmer weather, great hiking.

JUL–SEP
Peak season: hotter weather but crowds and higher prices.

OCT–DEC
Good for city breaks, bracing hikes and snug pubs with big fires.

GETTING AROUND

Car Provides the most flexibility, allowing you to explore remote areas at your own pace. Parking can be expensive in cities and is at a premium in resorts and fishing villages in summer. Main routes in and out of the region have traffic jams at peak times.

Bus Services are good in towns and cities. Very rural areas have limited connections but it is possible to explore by bus if you're happy to adjust to their schedules.

Train Frequent mainline services between cities and towns. Branch lines lead to coastal areas including Falmouth and Newquay. See *travelinesw.com* for comprehensive bus and train info.

EATING & DRINKING

The region is awash with chefs specialising in sustainable seafood, especially in ports such as Falmouth. Cafes and village stores stock local, handmade Cornish pasties (pictured top) – beef, swede, potatoes and onions, wrapped in crumbly pastry and crimped on the side (never the top). A proper Devon cream tea (pictured bottom) sees you feasting on just-baked scones, homemade jam and so-thick-you-can-stand-your-spoon-up-in-it clotted cream.

Liquid refreshments include local artisan beers; Bristol in particular has a fine craft-beer scene. Rural pubs specialise in local ciders and ales.

Best castaway pub
Seven Stones Inn (p104)

Must-try surf-inspired street food
Biffen's Kitchen (p107)

CONNECT & FIND YOUR WAY

Wi-fi Most accommodation has wi-fi, though it doesn't always work. Urban areas have plenty of free hot spots, as do cafes and pubs region-wide.

Navigation Apps are reliable but may try to direct you down very rough, narrow lanes. Some rural areas don't have phone signal but dead zones are usually small and signposting is good.

CAR FERRIES

Car ferries shuttle across the region's main rivers. They can shave 30 minutes or so off your journey and they're incredibly scenic too.

WHERE TO STAY

Accommodation spans all price brackets, from campsites and surfer hostels to B&Bs and boutique hotels. Book ahead for weekends and school holidays, when prices also rise.

Place	Pros/Cons
Princetown	Dartmoor village with campsite, bunk houses, inns and B&Bs.
Bristol	Good bases for all budgets include the harbour area and the suburb of Clifton.
Exford	Pretty village with two great inns, B&Bs and a YHA hotel and campsite.
Croyde	Campsites, surf hotels, inns and B&Bs near the beach; reserve well ahead in summer.
Falmouth	Superb range spanning smart hotels, B&Bs and a hostel.
St Mary's	The Isles of Scilly capital has camping, self-catering and hotels.

MONEY

Look out for two- to three-course lunches at top-notch restaurants, which are usually excellent value. In fishing ports, head to the fish and chip shop for super-fresh cheap eats.

Seaside & STEAM

TRAINS | CASTLES | SEASIDE

Journey back in time on the Swanage Railway, a 6-mile trip through the rolling countryside of Dorset's Isle of Purbeck. There are few more dramatic train-window views in England than that of the hilltop ruins of Corfe Castle, glimpsed between puffs of smoke from a lovingly restored steam train as it chugs from Norden to the coast at Swanage.

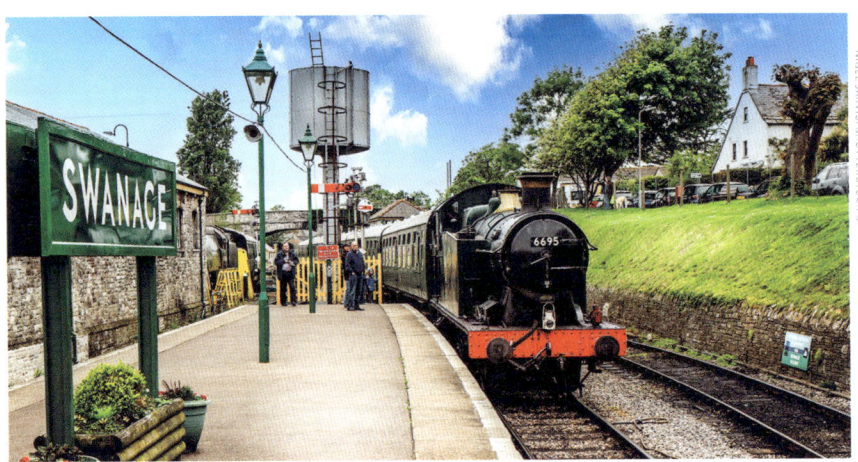

How to

Getting here If you plan to make the return train journey, park at Norden Station. Alternatively, take a train to Wareham then take the Purbeck Breezer 40 bus to Norden Station.

When to go Trains run daily from April to October, and on select dates in winter.

Best views The rear platform at Corfe Castle Station affords the view of the train passing the castle. East Hill also offers great views if you don't mind the climb.

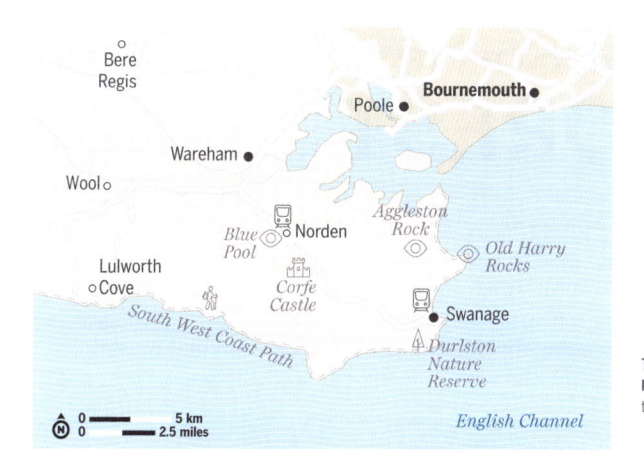

Top left Swanage Railway
Bottom left Corfe Castle Station with the castle behind

All aboard The **Swanage Railway** (swanagerailway.co.uk) has a fleet of vintage steam locomotives and carriages, including two 1940s Southern Railway Bulleid Pacifics. These trains run between a handful of traditionally decorated stations along a historic line, first built in 1885 to bring tourists down to the coast from London and to export Purbeck stone. The line was completely rebuilt by volunteers over a 30-year period after it was demolished in 1972. For the full experience, take the 12-mile return trip from Norden to Swanage, breaking your journey at Corfe Castle Station to explore the picturesque village and castle. Don't miss the free railway museum at the station.

Storied castle Built from grey Purbeck limestone, **Corfe Castle** (corfecastle.co.uk) has been standing tall on its hilltop for over 1000 years. It was partially destroyed in 1646 after being seized by Parliamentarians during the English Civil War, and today is a striking testament to a crucial point in England's story. Even if history's not your thing, the captivating ruin is worth a visit for its superb views and intriguing ghost stories. The neighbouring village, also called Corfe Castle, is home to cosy pubs, a cute model village and a few local art galleries.

The end of the line Swanage is an old-fashioned English seaside town, lying on a sheltered bay with colourful beach huts and golden sands. Beyond the beaches, arcades and quirky vintage shops, the town makes an excellent jumping-off point for exploring the rest of the Isle of Purbeck on foot, by bike or even by boat trip.

Purbeck Pursuits

Explore more of Purbeck on two feet (or two wheels).

From Swanage Hike along the **South West Coast Path** to the chalk stacks known as **Old Harry Rocks**, or cross **Durlston Nature Reserve** to reach the old cliffside quarry at **Dancing Ledge**.

From Norden The **Blue Pool** is another abandoned quarry, now home to a vivid blue lake surrounded by woodland. Explore the wildlife-rich heaths near Studland to find the mysterious **Agglestone Rock** – supposedly thrown there by the devil – or spot sika deer and rare birdlife at **Arne RSPB Nature Reserve**.

13 Not-So-New **FOREST**

GREEN SPACES | OUTDOORS | NATURE

The south of England may be best known for its coastline, but the interior of this region is equally beautiful. Hampshire's New Forest National Park is a popular countryside escape, with ancient woodlands, postcard-perfect villages and a rich foodie scene. Blending forests with heaths, grasslands and coastal landscapes, the park is criss-crossed with walking and biking trails.

How to

Getting around Driving offers more freedom, but roads are often congested during peak seasons. Take a train to Brockenhurst from London and you'll find the park well connected by bus.

When to go In spring and summer for wildflowers, especially the iconic heather; and in autumn, for leaf peeping in the woodlands and stag rutting.

Top tip New Forest is a prime location for foraging, including blackberries, wild garlic and nettle, while samphire is abundant on the coast during August and September.

Top left New Forest Pony
Bottom left Oak Inn, Lyndhurst

Best Lunch Spots

The Pig In Brockenhurst, this is the most iconic dining experience in New Forest, famed for its seasonal 25-mile menu. *thepighotel.com*

Palletts A family-run tea room in Beaulieu serving speciality coffee with tasty cakes and sandwiches. *palletscoffeehouse.co.uk*

Oak Inn This Lyndhurst fave offers a traditional New Forest experience, with low wooden beams and a typical British pub menu – go for the fish and chips! *oakinnlyndhurst.co.uk*

Picnic On a summer's day, a picnic in the shade of Blackwater Woods is hard to beat. Follow Rhinefield Ornamental Dr to get there, going slow to admire the giant redwoods and Douglas firs lining the route.

■ Recommended by Victoria Philpott, *local travel writer and founder of DayOutInEngland.com @vickyflipflop*

Ancient woodland Despite the name, **New Forest National Park** is almost 1000 years old. Founded by William the Conqueror in 1079, the park is known for its ancient pasture woodlands, many of which have remained unchanged for centuries. Explore a diverse range of landscapes, from shingle beaches along the coast to purple heathlands and wide-open grasslands. Keep an eye out for the famous locals: the eponymous wild ponies who roam freely across the park (and its roads!).

Get active Cyclists, ramblers and hikers are spoilt for choice in New Forest, with trails to suit all levels. Plan a route between some of the park's pubs and hotels to discover the excellent local food scene. New Forest's coastal location and numerous rivers mean it's also an ideal place for watersports. Try sailing on the **Solent** or kayaking with **New Forest Activities** (*newforestactivities.co.uk*) along the peaceful Beaulieu River. For something a little different, tackle the floating, inflatable obstacle course at **New Forest Water Park**.

Super reserve Along the coast in Dorset, the Isle of Purbeck is home to the UK's first 'super' national nature reserve (NNR). **Stoborough Heath National Nature Reserve** is a scenic collection of protected heaths, salt marshes and other crucial habitats brimming with rare British wildlife. Keep your eyes peeled for movement in the sand: all six native British reptiles call the lowland heaths at Studland and Godlingston home.

Stories in
STONE

HISTORIC EDIFICES | PREHISTORY | OUTDOORS

One attraction in southwest England stands out above all others. Myth and mystery collide with 5000 years of fascinating history at Stonehenge, but it's far from the only ancient monument of note in the area. Neolithic henges, Iron and Bronze Age hillforts and giant chalk figures pepper the landscapes, adding a touch of intrigue to countryside walks.

How to

Getting here Stonehenge is most easily reached by car. You can also take a taxi or the Stonehenge Tour bus from Salisbury Station.

When to go The beginning and end of the day are generally the quietest times. Entrance is free on the summer and winter solstices.

Learn more Visit Salisbury Museum or Wiltshire Museum for a fascinating insight into Stonehenge, Avebury and the wider area.

Top left Stonehenge
Bottom left Cerne Giant

Stonehenge The neolithic stone circle of **Stonehenge** is perhaps the world's most famous prehistoric sight, thought to have been built around 2500 BCE on the site of an even earlier monument. Scientists have pieced together much of its fascinating story, including how and when it was built, how the larger sarsen stones (weighing 25 tonnes on average) were moved, and the origin of the smaller bluestones – some 150 miles away in southwest Wales. But much still remains shrouded in mystery. Don't skip the excellent **Stonehenge Visitor Centre**, which delves into both history and myth with artefacts, multimedia displays and recreations of neolithic houses.

Get closer The viewing path at Stonehenge is about 8m from the monument. If you want a closer encounter, book the **Stone Circle Experience**, a small group tour held before and after normal visiting hours, which allows visitors to enter the stone circle with an expert guide. During winter, these tours often coincide with sunrise or sunset.

Avebury Just 17 miles north, **Avebury Henge** is less famous than Stonehenge but possibly even more impressive. The henge itself is a vast earthwork enclosing an area of 11.5 hectares, within which is Britain's largest stone circle – originally made up of around 100 stones. From Avebury, you can walk between the paired standing stones of **West Kennet Avenue** towards the **Sanctuary**, another ritual site.

Chalk Mysteries

Dorset and Wiltshire are home to some of England's most famous hill figures – huge chalk drawings made by cutting into the turf on a hillside.

Cerne Giant (Cerne Abbas) A 55m-tall figure of unknown age (possibly late Saxon), depicting a nude giant infamous for his oversized, erect genitalia.

Westbury White Horse (Bratton) The oldest of several white horses in Wiltshire, originally cut in the late 1600s on the side of Bratton Camp Iron Age hillfort.

Osmington White Horse (near Weymouth) Cut in 1808 to represent King George III, a regular visitor to Weymouth.

15 Into the JURASSIC

BEACHES | GEOLOGY | PREHISTORY

A visible echo of 185 million years of history, the Jurassic Coast is England's only natural World Heritage Site, renowned for its extraordinary rock formations and abundance of fossils. Stretching 95 miles from Exmouth in Devon to Dorset's Studland Bay, this diverse coastline is of huge geological significance, also boasting beautiful beaches, quaint seaside towns and quality seafood.

How to

Getting around If not driving, the Jurassic Coaster X53 bus connects most towns and attractions.

When to go Summer is best for seaside outings, but popular spots can be very busy. Spring and autumn are ideal for walking, wildlife and fossil hunting.

Top tip Foodies shouldn't miss the summertime food festivals, particularly Dorset Seafood Festival held on Weymouth's colourful harbourside in early September.

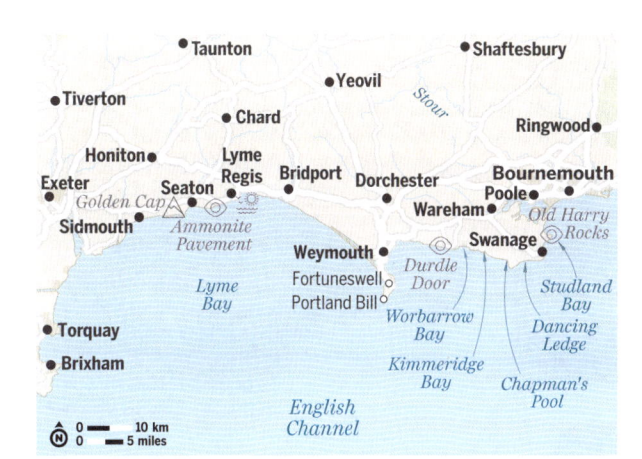

Top left Old Harry Rocks
Bottom left Ammonite Pavement

⭐ Fossil Hunting

According to local geologist Dr Paul Davis, 'The easiest and most productive places to look for fossils are the beaches around Lyme Regis and Charmouth.' Look out for the **Ammonite Pavement** on Monmouth Beach, a rock shelf containing hundreds of fossils visible at low tide.

Frequent rockfalls, changing tides and deep mudflows can make the cliffs and beaches dangerous, so Dr Davis recommends booking a guided fossil hunt. 'The best walks are available from **Lyme Regis Museum** and **Charmouth Heritage Coast Centre** (charmouth.org/chcc).' Be sure to explore the fascinating collections in the museums themselves, too.

■ Dr Paul Davis, Geology Curator (Lyme Regis Museum) and Honorary Scientific Patron (Charmouth Heritage Coast Centre), @pauldavisfossil

Rock icons The Jurassic Coast's wonders are impressive even to those of us without a geology degree. Rock formations carved by millennia of erosion create dramatic backdrops for beach days, such as the chalk rock stacks at **Studland** known as **Old Harry Rocks** – supposedly named after a local pirate – or the towering golden cliffs at **West Bay**, the layers of which reflect falling sea levels 175 million years ago.

Cliff walks The star attraction is **Durdle Door**, a 61m-tall limestone arch over the sea between two pristine bays. For the best views, park in neighbouring **Lulworth Cove** – also worth exploring – and walk the 1-mile cliff path to Durdle Door, then cool off with a dip in the sea. Alternatively, you can take a guided kayaking tour from **Lulworth** to paddle through the arch itself (swimming through, and jumping from, the arch is strongly discouraged). For more cliff walks, try the Isle of Purbeck peninsula (p88), **Portland Bill** or climb to the highest point on the south coast at **Golden Cap**. Head to **Kimmeridge Bay** for rock-pooling, **Studland Bay** for snorkelling, and Weymouth, Lyme Regis or Swanage for a classic English seaside.

Catch the waves The best way to enjoy the Jurassic Coast is to be in, or on, the sea. Take a cruise around **Poole Harbour**, or join a kayaking tour to Old Harry Rocks. Experienced wild swimmers can head to **Chapman's Pool**, **Worbarrow Bay** or the tidal pool at **Dancing Ledge**. For thrill seekers, coasteering at Lulworth Cove or Portland Bill offers an exciting way to get closer to the cliffs and rocks.

Adventure
DARTMOOR

HIKING | CAMPING | MOUNTAIN BIKING

Dartmoor is a massive wilderness in the middle of southwest England, where 368 sq miles of rolling moors are dotted with granite hills, deep wooded valleys and free-roaming ponies, sheep and cows. It's a glorious place to hike, ride mountain bikes, discover stone circles, visit rustic pubs and camp wild under the stars.

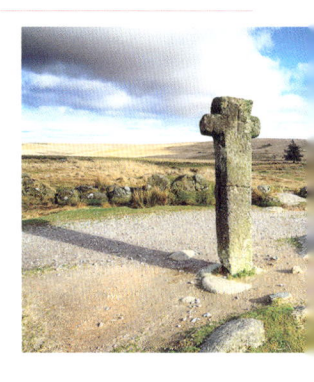

How to

Getting around Bus services can be patchy but the **Dartmoor Explorer** *(firstbus.co.uk)* hop-on, hop-off bus service runs between Exeter and Plymouth across the middle of the southern moor. Stops include Princetown, which makes an ideal base.

When to go Spring through to autumn for warmer days and hopefully better weather.

What to read *War Horse* (1982) by Michael Morpurgo and *The Hound of the Baskervilles* (1902) by Sir Arthur Conan Doyle are set in Dartmoor.

Information
Dartmoor National Park *(dartmoor.gov.uk)*.

Wilderness Walks

Dartmoor is home to more ponies, cows and sheep (50,000) than people (34,000). It's a vast, rugged wilderness with unfenced grazing, some 160 tors (exposed granite hills), ancient woods, steep river valleys and villages.

There are walks for all abilities; some are signed and many traverse open moorland. For a 5-mile blast, head southeast from **Princetown** down the rough track to the ancient granite **Nun's Cross**. A 5.5-mile loop leads from Princetown around **King's Tor** and the disused **Foggintor Quarries**, while a cracking 3-mile hike heads from **Two Bridges** across the open moor to ancient **Wistman's Wood**.

Staff at Princetown's **Dartmoor National Park (DNP) Visitor Centre** can provide maps and information on hiking routes. Alternatively,

Decoding Names & Legends

Dartmoor's mercurial mists, looming rocks and twisted trees have long fed fears and shaped place names. Grim – as in **Grimspound** – meant the Devil. He drove a pack of daemon Wisht Hounds – think **Wistman's Wood** – inspiring Conan Doyle's Sherlock Holmes mystery, *The Hound of the Baskervilles* (1902).

Above left Foggintor Quarries
Above Wistman's Wood
Left Nun's Cross

Moorland Guides (moorlandguides.co.uk) runs regular guided walks and **Two Blondes Walking** (twoblondeswalking.com) runs navigation and wild camping courses.

Megaliths by Moonlight

Finding some of Dartmoor's hundreds of prehistoric remains in the daylight is fun. But it's even better by moonlight or starlight, when the ruined villages and processional stone rows take on a mystical feel. Ancient sites within easy reach of roads include **Grimspound**, near Postbridge, where 24 ruined Bronze Age houses are enclosed by a 150m-diameter boundary wall.

At **Merrivale**, a double stone row, a stone circle and a standing stone sit just half a mile from the road. The double stone rows at **Hurston Ridge** are just a mile north of the excellent **Warren House Inn** pub. Pick a clear night and bring a torch.

Best Dartmoor Cafes & Pubs

Fox Tor Café (Princetown; foxtorcafe.com) Muddy boots and dogs are welcome; hearty menu and bunk beds.

Rugglestone Inn (Widecombe-in-the-Moor; rugglestoneinn.co.uk) Log fires, local ales and Dartmoor's best pies.

Warren House Inn (Postbridge; warrenhouseinn.co.uk) Southern England's highest inn with moorland views and a fire that's burned since 1845.

Home Farm (Bovey Tracey; homefarmcafe.co.uk) Cafe set in National Trust grounds serving delicious local food.

Cafe on the Green (Widecombe-in-the-Moor; thecafeonthegreen.co.uk) Tasty food in one of Dartmoor's prettiest villages – watch ponies grazing on the green.

■ Recommended by Fi Darby, writer and navigation expert with Two Blondes Walking, @fidarby

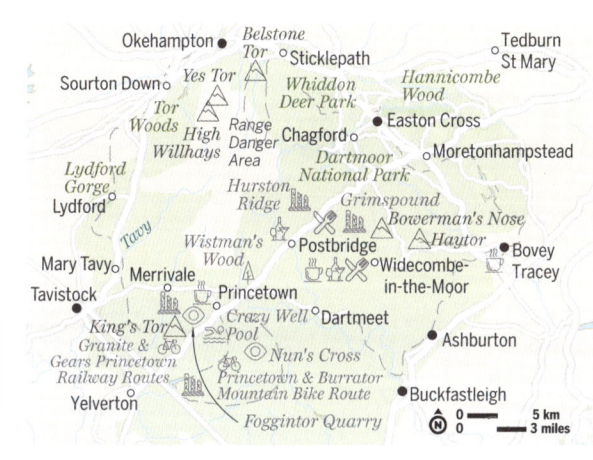

Left Rugglestone Inn, Widecombe-in-the-Moor
Below Mountain biker, Sheeps Tor

Camping Off-Grid

Unlike the rest of England, it's legal to camp outside designated sites on much of Dartmoor. So you can hike off with minimal kit, find your own slice of wilderness, fall asleep gazing up at a glittering Milky Way and wake to the sound of sheep and skylarks. Wild camping is only allowed on some parts of the moor – search for **Dartmoor wild camping map** *(dartmoor.gov.uk)* to find an interactive DNP map and some simple but strict rules.

Moor Mud

Of Dartmoor's off-road mountain-bike trails, two of the best are the 6-mile and 19-mile **Granite and Gears Princetown Railway Routes**. These jolt along tracks on disused railway lines and around rocky outcrops called tors. After taking in **King's Tor**, the longer route then plunges down to forest-framed **Burrator Reservoir**. The 12-mile **Princetown & Burrator Route** crosses open moorland on a loop around **Sheeps Tor** that takes in disused tin mines, medieval granite crosses and the top wild swimming spot: **Crazy Well Pool**. The DNP website has PDFs of the routes.

17 Protest **CULTURE**

BLACK HISTORY | DEMONSTRATIONS | STREET ART

Protest in Bristol is an art form, literally – a local museum featured placards from 2020 Black Lives Matter protests and street art is inspired by anti-capitalist demos. Learning about Bristol's campaigns and causes, past and present, leads you to vibrant counterculture districts spattered with bright murals and also reveals the soul of the city.

How to

Getting around The **Bristol Ferry Boat** *(bristolferry.com)* service from Bristol Temple Meads Station to the M Shed stop runs between April and October. In winter take the m2 bus to Wapping Wharf and walk 1.3 miles northeast to Stokes Croft.

When to go Weekdays are quieter; weekends have a locals-at-leisure feel.

Recharge Head to the Canteen for tasty vegetarian food, free live music and a counterculture vibe, or Caribbean Croft for renowned Caribbean food.

Bridging the past With horned sculptures and hundreds of padlocks, **Pero's Bridge** is an appealing way to head from the Waterfront's bars to the powerful social history displays of the M Shed museum. Alongside, **Bordeaux Quay** is where, in 2020, Black Lives Matter demonstrators dumped a statue of the trader of enslaved people Edward Colston in the water – they toppled it from a plinth 500m away and rolled it here by hand.

Enslavement, abolitionists and a watershed campaign The four towering cranes outside the **M Shed** museum

Top right Edward Colston's statue being thrown into Bordeaux Quay
Bottom right M Shed

📷 Banksy's Bristol Highlights

Bristol's most famous guerrilla muralist is Banksy, whose polemical pieces pop up everywhere from the British Museum to Israel's West Bank barrier wall. In Bristol, seek out the *Girl with the Pierced Eardrum* (Hanover Pl), *Well Hung Lover* (Park St) and *Paint-Pot Angel* (Bristol Museum & Art Gallery).

---

signal Bristol's industrial past. Inside, make a beeline for the **Bristol People** gallery, which explores the city's links to 18th-century enslavers. The gallery's replica model of the **Brookes ship**, which details just how appallingly crowded conditions were, is particularly chilling. A few paces away evocative displays explain how the 1963 **Bristol Bus Boycott** forced a local transport firm to overturn its ban on people of colour working as drivers and conductors.

Riots Also in the M Shed, *Tesco Value Petrol Bomb,* a poster by Bristol street artist Banksy, was created after 2011 anti-supermarket riots in Stokes Croft. A 20-minute walk north past vivid murals leads to the scene. There, outside **Canteen**, another Banksy, *Mild Mild West* (1999), shows a petrol-bomb-wielding teddy bear confronting riot police.

Bristol's Black History

SLAVERS, BOYCOTTS AND BLM PROTESTS

They were among the most striking images of Britain's 2020 Black Lives Matter demos. Crowds toppling enslaver Edward Colston's statue from its plinth, clattering it down the street and pitching it into Bristol's harbour. But what's the history behind those scenes and how does it shape the city today?

Above left Enslavery exhibition, M Shed
Above middle Paul Stephenson
Above right Georgian House Museum

Bristol's Trade in Enslaved People

Edward Colston was one of Bristol's key enslavers. He started trading in the 1650s, initially importing and exporting wine, sherry, cod and silk. But by 1680 Colston had become a member – and eventually deputy governor – of the Royal African Company, which traded in gold, silver and ivory, and also trafficked enslaved people. During his time there, it's estimated that the company trafficked more than 84,000 Africans to the Caribbean and the Americas. When BLM protesters dumped his statue in Bristol's harbour in 2020, they were making a powerful protest against centuries-long racial discrimination and oppression.

The scale of Bristol's involvement in the trade of enslaved people is immense. The city's ships trafficked around 25% of the enslaved Africans carried on British vessels – more than 500,000 people – and in the 1780s the trade of enslaved people made up 80% of Bristol's foreign trade.

Abolitionists, including those from Bristol, circulated diagrams of the *Brookes* ship to highlight the inhumanity of ships laden with human cargo (the M Shed museum displays a copy; p100). Former enslaved people, such as Olaudah Equiano, plus Quakers, Methodists and evangelists were among those who fought to abolish slaving. Guerrilla action by enslaved people and rebellions – one in 1803 succeeding against thousands of troops – helped signal the end. The 'trade' was abolished in 1807 and trading enslaved people was outlawed in British territories in 1834.

Bristol Bus Boycott

After WWII, Britain's labour shortage prompted the country to invite people from the then Caribbean colonies over to work, often even paying their passage. Hundreds of years after enslaved Africans were trafficked to the Caribbean, their descendants made another transatlantic journey. This so-called Windrush generation – named after the former troop ship that carried the passengers – began arriving in 1948.

But when they arrived, these British citizens were subject to racial discrimination. Many faced difficulties finding housing and were limited to working in low-paid jobs. In 1955 a local trade union passed a resolution banning Black and Asian people from working as drivers and conductors for the Bristol Omnibus Company – jobs as maintenance workers, however, were allowed. Led by Bristol's first Black youth officer, Paul Stephenson, local African-Caribbeans campaigned against the policy, calling for a boycott of the city's buses. In 1963, after a four-month boycott, the bus firm overturned the ban. It was a watershed moment – the UK's Race Relations Act, which outlawed racial discrimination, followed in 1965. Despite this, people of colour continue to face racial discrimination and inequalities to this day.

What Next?

The issue of what to do with the physical legacies of the trade of enslaved people and injustice remains contentious. After it was retrieved from the harbour, Colston's statue was temporarily displayed at Bristol's M Shed museum. Dented, battered and spattered with paint, it lay on its side, surrounded by placards from the BLM demonstration. The exhibition, staged with the We Are Bristol History Commission, asked local people – what should we do with it now? In 2024 it went on permanent display in the M Shed's Bristol People gallery.

The Visible Legacy

Georgian House Museum The home of sugar plantation and enslaver John Pinney and his enslaved valet, Pero, who was bought aged 12.

Pero's Bridge Footbridge commemorating all anonymous Africans trafficked by Bristol merchants. Colston's statue was dumped in the harbour alongside.

Bristol Theatre Royal At least 12 enslavers and ship owners helped pay for the original building.

Queen Square Merchants with slaving links lived in the villas surrounding this Georgian park.

Clifton's villas Many fine Georgian buildings in this suburb's Cornwallis and Royal York crescents were owned by merchants with links to enslavery.

18 SCILLY
Ferry Hop

BEACHES | FOOD AND DRINK | WATERSPORTS

Some 30 miles off west Cornwall, the Isles of Scilly are fringed by white-sand beaches and set in azure seas. The 140 islands – only five of which are inhabited – are ripe for hiking, swimming, kayaking, feasting, barefoot beach combing and sunset watching. Fleets of ferries will help you explore.

How to

Getting here and around From March to November, the Scillonian passenger ferry runs between Penzance Harbour on the mainland and St Mary's; there's also a small airport on St Mary's. See *islesofscilly-travel.co.uk* for more info.

When to go Easter to the end of September for hotter days and warmer seas.

Which island? You can stay on any of the inhabited islands. The biggest is St Mary's (pictured above). St Martin's is beach-fringed. Rugged St Agnes feels remote. Chic Tresco has the subtropical Abbey Garden. Bryher has both sheltered and wave-dashed shores.

Best Food & Drink Stops

Troytown Farm (St Agnes) Pure dairy ice cream.

Dibble & Grub (St Mary's) Beachside bistro.

Seven Stones Inn (St Martin's) Shipwreck-chic pub.

Turk's Head (St Agnes) Pint stop beside the ferry quay.

Island Fish (Bryher) Fisher family's seafood hut.

03 Hire kayaks or stand-up paddleboards (SUPs) from Sailing Scilly *(sailingscilly.com)* before touring Tresco Abbey Garden on **Tresco** and having supper at the cool Ruin beach cafe.

01 Wander between Higher Town (try the Island Bakery) and Lower Town (Seven Stones Inn) on **St Martin's**. At high tide walk through dunes, at low tide via sandy St Martin's Flats.

05 Hire SUPs at Hut 62 *(hut62.co.uk)*, then walk the shore to Hell Bay on **Bryher**, before lunch at Island Fish and downing a pint at the Fraggle Rock pub.

04 Book a boat with Scilly Boating *(scillyboating.co.uk)* and head to **Samson**, Scilly's largest uninhabited island, to explore rounded hills, ruined houses and sweeping sandy shores.

02 Low tide on **St Agnes** reveals the causeway to the rocky Gugh headland. Then wander via bird-rich Wingletang Down to the ice-cream hatch at Troytown Farm Campsite.

ATLANTIC OCEAN

0   2 km
0   1 mile

FROM LEFT: KATH WATSON/SHUTTERSTOCK ©, TONY MILLS/SHUTTERSTOCK ©

19 Moors & SHORES

SURFING | STARGAZING | FOOD

The chunk of shore at the top of Devon and Somerset offers an extraordinary range of outdoor adventures in a small space: stargazing on open moors, hiking deer-dotted ridges, plunging into moorland streams and riding cracking surf. Take it all in, and drop into some cosy pubs and surfer street-food stalls along the way.

How to

Getting around It's around 45 miles from moorland Exford to coastal Croyde. The drive is spectacular, especially down plunging Countisbury Hill. Alternatively, hike for three days across the moors and along the South West Coast Path.

When to go Spring brings wildflowers and summer more visitors, but you can always find an uncrowded patch of moor.

Scenic drives Crack across Dunkery Hill then shadow the coast to gaze down onto Porlock Weir, climb out of Lynmouth and see the sweep of Morte Bay.

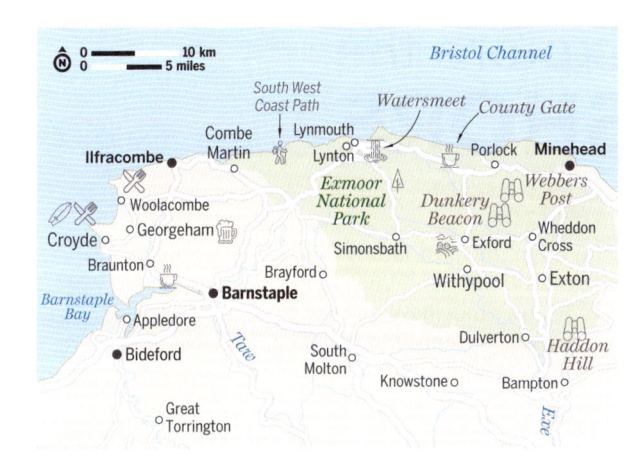

Top left Dunkery Beacon
Bottom left Surfer, Croyde

Ridges and valleys The tiny village of **Exford** huddles in the middle of mighty Exmoor. Superb hikes include a 4-mile walk northeast to **Dunkery Beacon**, Exmoor's highest point, and wrap-around views. Look out for wild Exmoor red deer en route. Visit the **Exmoor Explorer Walks** (exmoorwalks.org/explorers) website for a number of other short routes.

Stargazing Exmoor's plateau of open moorland and minimal light pollution ensure glittering displays. Pick a comfy spot – **County Gate**, **Webbers Post** and **Haddon Hill** are good – then settle back for some of the UK's best celestial sights.

River swims Those open moors and plunging valleys mean miles of tumbling streams. A footpath beside a deep, tree-lined valley stretches east out of **Lynmouth** along the East Lyn River. Locals stop just before the cafe at **Watersmeet** to plunge in pools beside mini waterfalls. Or head half a mile further for quieter trails and the **Long Pool swim spot**; check locally if it's safe to swim.

Exhilarating surf If you're not taking the scenic route, you can drive to **Croyde** from Watersmeet in under an hour. This thatch-studded village backs onto a dune-backed beach with some of the coast's best surf. **Surf South West** (surfsouthwest.com) and **Surfing Croyde Bay** (surfingcroydebay.co.uk) give good tuition; the latter also hires out wetsuits and boards. After catching some waves, head to **Biffen's Kitchen** (biffenskitchen.com) where Biff (a surfer who ditched the day job) dishes up surf-inspired street food at **Ocean Pitch** (oceanpitch.co.uk) campsite within sight of the surf.

Best Foodie Experiences

Cluck Street Food (Croyde; cluckstreetfood.co.uk) Overnight buttermilk fried chicken burgers, vegan seitan fillets and sexy smashed cucumbers in crispy chilli oil.

Kings Arms (Georgeham; kingsarmsgeorgeham.co.uk) The best Sunday roast in North Devon in a friendly pub environment.

New Coast Kitchen (Croyde; newcoastkitchen.co.uk) Modern British dining with seasonally changing menus featuring locally sourced produce.

Gobblebox (Woolacombe; gobbleboxwoolacombe.co.uk) Don't be fooled by the simplicity of the place – staff really know what they're doing when it comes to fast and delicious street food.

Heartbreak Hotel Coffee (Braunton; heartbreakhotelcoffee.com) Delicious coffee and homemade doughnuts en route to the beach.

■ Recommended by George Biffen, *chef and owner of Biffen's Kitchen food van, @biffenskitchen*

Explore the SHORE

KAYAKING | SEA SWIMMING | FORAGING

The edges of places are often the most interesting to explore, especially around Falmouth in south Cornwall. The shoreline here sees rivers carving vast inlets inland, while jagged cliffs and sandy bays line the coast. It's a place for kayaking and paddle boarding, guided swims, foraging and fine local food. Here, by avoiding well-trod trails, you'll encounter a Cornwall many visitors never see.

How to

Getting here and around Falmouth is on a branch line off the London Paddington–Penzance railway line, five hours from the capital. From Falmouth, Fal River *(falriver.co.uk)* runs a wide range of handy ferries and boat trips.

When to go Late spring and early or late summer when hire outlets and ferries are operating, the weather's warmer but it isn't high season.

Where to stay Falmouth. Part busy port, tourist resort and university town, it has several beaches and plenty of cafes, pubs and places to stay.

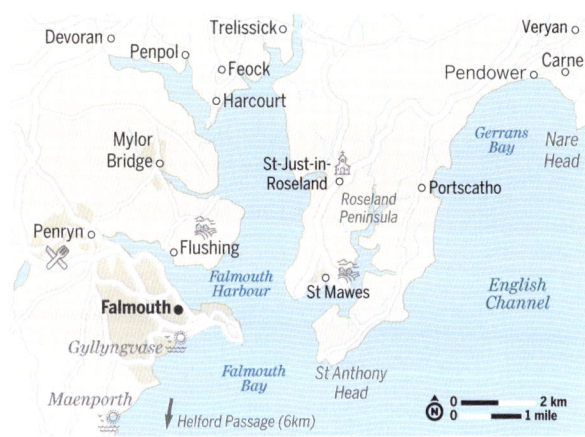

Top left St Mawes Ferry
Bottom left Sea kayaker near Falmouth

Hop on a boat Feel the sheer size of field-framed **Falmouth Harbour** on the **St Mawes Ferry**. The classic wooden boats chug from Falmouth to the pretty fishing village at **St Mawes** on a spray-dashed, 20-minute ride. From St Mawes you can then stroll 3 miles north beside the river to the beautiful 13th-century **St Just-in-Roseland Church**.

Hit the waves Head to **Maenporth**, one of three sandy beaches on Falmouth's southern shore. Here you can hire a kayak or SUP from **Sea Kayaking Cornwall** (seakayaking cornwall.com) then set off to gaze down on the *Ben Asdale* shipwreck and discover otherwise inaccessible gullies and coves. Or don a wetsuit and goggles and plunge into the water for a guided swim trip with Falmouth-based **SureSwim Kernow** (sureswimkernow.co.uk). As you glide along, expect to spot an array of sea life, from pulsing barrel jellyfish to scuttling spider crabs.

Paddle for longer The two- or five-day sea-kayaking trips offered by **Evoke Adventure** (evokeadventure.com) are run by international expeditioner Erin Bastian. These guided explorations see you floating on the serene waters of the nearby **Helford Passage** and powering to the jagged **Manacles**, a shipwreck-strewn stretch of the Lizard Peninsula.

Find your supper Join one of Rachel Lambert's **Wild Walks South West** (wildwalks-southwest.co.uk) seaweed-foraging courses and spot the difference between sea lettuce, sea grass and kelp. Rachel also shares cooking tips and homemade treats, including seaweed hummus, seaweed bread and a spicy seaweed broth.

Best Further Explorations

Gyllyngvase Beach Falmouth's closest beach might get a bit busy, but it's sandy and great for rock-pooling.

Muddy Beach This Scandi-style cafe (muddybeach.com) in Penryn has wholesome food and always interesting estuary views.

Flushing Chug from Falmouth on a tiny boat (falriver.co.uk) to a historic village with a creekside pub.

Place Ferry A 10-minute crossing (falriver.co.uk) from St Mawes to St Anthony on the bewitching Roseland Peninsula.

■ Recommended by **Rachel Lambert**, *author and wild food foraging guide*, @rachel lambertwildfoodforaging

Listings

BEST OF THE REST

🏛 Historic Must-Sees

Roman Baths
Ghostly projections of bathers add to the atmosphere at Bath's superbly preserved Roman spa, where statues fringe pools of steaming 46°C spring water. Online tickets dodge the queues. *romanbaths.co.uk*

Royal Crescent, Bath
Tour 18th-century buildings featured in the Netflix series *Bridgerton,* including the graceful Royal Cres. The Mayor of Bath's Corps of Honorary Guides runs free two-hour tours.

St Michael's Mount
It's a magical sight: a fairy-tale castle near Penzance, clinging to an island in a vast bay. At low tide walk the cobbled causeway; at high tide take the boat. *stmichaelsmount.co.uk*

🌿 Gorgeous Gardens

Eden Project
Feel the heat rise as you enter the immense Rainforest Biome, a greenhouse overflowing with plants and towering trees. Exhibits deliver vital eco-messages with wit and flair. *edenproject.com*

Lost Gardens of Heligan
Wandering Heligan's 81 hectares reveals a secret grotto, whimsical plant sculptures and veg-packed kitchen gardens, all magnificently restored post-WWI. Check out the sunrise sessions in spring and summer. *heligan.com*

Trebah
The gigantic rhododendrons, gunnera and jungle ferns at this garden near Falmouth line the sides of a steep ravine that leads down to a beach. *trebahgarden.co.uk*

🏊 Lidos & Outdoor Pools

Jubilee Pool
Book ahead to luxuriate in the geothermal section of Penzance's 1930s shoreside lido. Or prepare for a bracing plunge in the main pool's unheated seawater. *jubileepool.co.uk*

Thermae Bath Spa
Reserve an evening session at Bath's luxurious contemporary spa then head for the rooftop, geothermal, open-air pool to look down at an illuminated city. *thermaebathspa.com*

Tinside Lido
Spot art deco features as you clatter down the stairs at this gorgeous 1935 lido. The pool's white walls curve out into Plymouth's huge natural harbour. *plymouthactive.co.uk*

Bristol Lido
With water temperatures of 24°C, this Victorian pool is a naturally heated treat. Tickets include use of the spa facilities. Book well ahead. *lidobristol.com*

Roman Baths

🍴 Awesome Eats

Poco £
The chefs at this Bristol bar create imaginative tapas from English fava bean hummus to River Teign mussels with Severn Cider and leeks. *pocotapasbar.com*

Riverford Field Kitchen ££
This organic, plough-to-plate farm near Totnes serves rustic, full-flavour, veg-centric dishes and super desserts. *fieldkitchen.riverford.co.uk*

River Exe Cafe ££
Your table booking at this idyllic floating restaurant in the wide River Exe comes with a seat on a water taxi. Hop aboard for perfectly cooked seafood. *riverexecafe.com*

Woods ££
The pub at Dulverton on Exmoor has season-spun menus packed with full-bodied ingredients: confit leg of free-range duck, asparagus and wild garlic risotto. *woodsdulverton.co.uk*

Tolcarne Inn ££
Tucked in beside Newlyn's harbour wall, this bijou bistro has a chalkboard menu of top-quality seafood and local meats. *tolcarneinn.co.uk*

Star & Garter ££
Once an old Falmouth boozer, now a gourmet gastropub serving nose-to-tail dining and locally sourced foods. *starandgarterfalmouth.co.uk*

🍺 Vineyards & Craft Beer

Bell Inn
Around 500 customers loved this Bath pub so much they bought it. Chat to some of them over table football, bar billiards and fine real ales. *thebellinnbath.co.uk*

Grain Barge
Step aboard this former 1930s cargo vessel moored at Bristol's harbour for local craft ales, wide water views and a top-deck sun terrace. *grainbarge.com*

Polgoon
Guided tours at this edge-of-Penzance vineyard come with five-wine tastings. Best sampled with charcuterie platters at the seasonal restaurant. *polgoon.com*

Trevibban Mill
The balcony and patio at this vineyard near Padstow overlook rolling fields and wildflower meadows. Perfect for sampling its ciders and wines. *trevibbanmill.com*

Pandora Inn
Step into this quintessential smugglers' pub near Falmouth for tucked-away alcoves and beams, or chill out on the creekside pontoon. *pandorainn.com*

🛍 Browsing & Books

Topping & Company
The perfect Bath bookshop: enthusiastic staff, literary events and 50,000 volumes on towering shelves. *toppingbooks.co.uk*

St Nicholas Market
Bristol's Georgian corn exchange is filled with one-off gifts and superb food stalls. There are regular farmers markets outside. *stnicholasmarketbristol.com*

St Michael's Mount

BIRMINGHAM & THE MIDLANDS

HISTORY | FOOD | OUTDOORS

- ▶ **Trip Builder** (p114)
- ▶ **Practicalities** (p115)
- ▶ **The Workshop of the World** (p116)
- ▶ **A Gastronomic Haven** (p118)
- ▶ **Magical Malverns** (p120)
- ▶ **Canal Country** (p122)
- ▶ **Diverse Sounds** (p124)
- ▶ **Spectacular Ruins** (p126)
- ▶ **The Tolkien Trail** (p128)
- ▶ **Listings** (p130)

BIRMINGHAM & THE MIDLANDS
Trip Builder

Forget outdated stereotypes, modern Birmingham is a dynamic metropolis that's proud of its cultural diversity, musical creativity and gastronomic innovation, while the surrounding Midlands region is a beguiling cocktail of ancient hills, literary legend, crumbling castles and pioneering history.

Turn back time at the open-air **Black Country Living Museum** (p117)
🚗 30 min from Birmingham

Explore the historic streets of Birmingham's **Jewellery Quarter** (p117)
🚶 10 min on foot

Sample the seductive and surprising food scene in **Birmingham** (p118)
🚆 no more than 20 min

See the impressive WWII-bombed ruins of **Coventry Cathedral** (p127)
🚆 25 min from Birmingham

Stroll the gentle canal towpaths and rolling rivers of **Stratford-upon-Avon** (p123)
🚆 45 min from Birmingham

Hike above the clouds in the picturesque **Malvern Hills** (p120)
🚆 1 hr from Birmingham

TRINITY MIRROR/MIRRORPIX/ALAMY STOCK PHOTO ©; PREVIOUS SPREAD: JO JONES/SHUTTERSTOCK ©

20 km
10 miles

Practicalities

ARRIVING

Air Several trains per hour run from Birmingham International Airport to New Street Station.
Train New Street Station, Moor Street Station and Snow Hill Station all handle city centre arrivals by train.

FIND YOUR WAY
The tourist office at Library of Birmingham in Centenary Sq offers free city and walking maps to both Birmingham and the Midlands.

MONEY
Most places accept contactless payment. You'll still need some cash in certain situations, such as tipping at restaurants and farmers markets.

WHERE TO STAY

Place	Pros/Cons
Birmingham city centre	Wide variety of accommodation. Walkable and has very good public transport links.
Stratford-upon-Avon	Hotels in town and the countryside. Good base for exploring Warwickshire.
Worcester and Great Malvern	Offers several spa hotels. Best for accessing Malvern Hills hiking trails.

EATING & DRINKING

The city centre is crammed with restaurants, but make sure to explore superb culinary neighbourhoods such as Harborne, Stirchley and Moseley.

Don't miss the signature cocktail The Gambler at neighbourhood cocktail bar Couch or the braised beef shin and cured egg yolk bao from Tiger Bites Pig (pictured top).

Best craft beer
Attic Brew Co (p130)

Must-try balti curry
Shabab's (p119; pictured bottom)

GETTING AROUND

Walking Birmingham city centre is very walkable. Most places can be reached within 15 minutes on foot.

Bus, train and tram A variety of routes depart central Birmingham offering regular connections across the Midlands.

Car The most practical way to explore the hills and countryside.

JAN–MAR
Cold and overcast; ideal for visiting restaurants and galleries.

APR–JUN
Mild temperatures and green foliage return.

JUL–SEP
Peak season for outdoor exploring or enjoying Birmingham's beer gardens.

OCT–DEC
Chilly air returns; autumn colours are perfect for canalside strolls.

21 The Workshop Of
THE WORLD

HISTORY | MUSEUMS | OUTDOORS

The heartbeat of the Industrial Revolution in the 19th century, the Midlands was once a landscape dominated by smoking towers and rumbling factories. While the grass is now greener and the air cleaner, that pioneering period is still preserved in stunning detail across the region. Turn back time and explore what made the Midlands the Workshop of the World.

How to

Getting around Most locations are well served by public transport, although you may want to consider renting a car for Ironbridge Gorge (and perhaps use it to explore the nearby Shropshire Hills).

When to go The shoulder seasons of spring or autumn are best for outdoor attractions to avoid the summer crowds.

Need to know Admission prices can vary as some venues have multiple attractions and museums on-site.

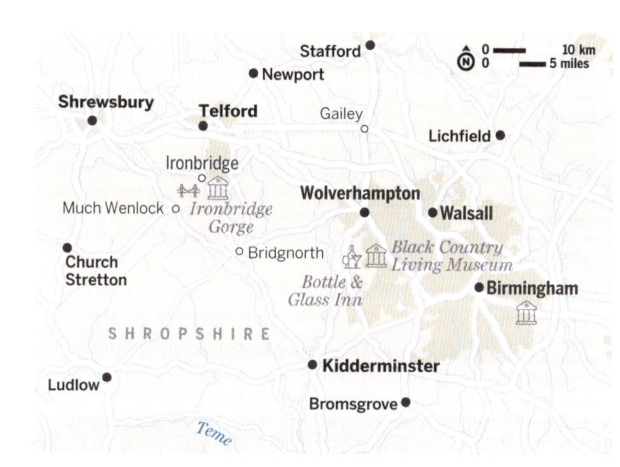

Top left Iron Bridge, Ironbridge Gorge
Bottom left Museum of the Jewellery Quarter

Jewellery Quarter Gems

Pen Museum (*pen museum.org.uk*) Birmingham was once the international centre of pen nib production and, through its cheaper pens, helped to democratise writing. This museum is located in the Argent Centre, a magnificent Renaissance-influenced building.

St Paul's Church What's the relevance for industry? The church was where Industrial Revolution pioneers Matthew Boulton and James Watt both worshipped. Located in Birmingham's only Georgian square (St Paul's Sq).

Coffin Works (*coffin works.org*) A preserved factory where accoutrements to coffins were made – funerals were huge business in the 19th century! There's also a fascinating hidden walk along the canal behind the nearby Shakespeare pub.

A pioneering sight Amid Shropshire's rolling green landscape lies one of the most important structures of the Industrial Revolution. Built in 1779 and now a UNESCO World Heritage Site, the spectacular **Iron Bridge** of **Ironbridge Gorge** was the first bridge to be constructed of cast iron. Meander through the charming riverside village and spend some time in the **Museum of the Gorge** (*ironbridge.org.uk*) and the **Coalbrookdale Museum of Iron**.

History brought to life The **Black Country Living Museum** (*bclm.com*) isn't any old museum. The thick smoke rising from the thousands of ironworking foundries gave the Black Country its name and here the region's 19th-century streets, shops and factories are brought back to life in vivid detail. Speak with curious characters, watch live demonstrations and experience life in an evocative industrial setting spanning 10.5 hectares. Stop for a rustic beer at the **Bottle & Glass Inn**, a working pub as it would have looked in 1910.

An engrossing time capsule Birmingham was known as 'the city of 1000 trades' during the Industrial Revolution, and its Jewellery Quarter was a prominent manufacturing hub. Abandoned in 1981, the workshop at the **Museum of the Jewellery Quarter** (*birminghammuseums.org.uk*) has been immaculately preserved in much the same condition as it had been since the turn of the 20th century. Learn about its fascinating story and explore the gruelling conditions its employees experienced.

■ **Recommended by Carl Chinn,** *a Birmingham-based historian, writer and broadcaster*

22 A Gastronomic HAVEN

FOOD | CULTURE | NEIGHBOURHOODS

A young and diverse generation of chefs have turned tired perceptions of Birmingham's food scene on their head and this wildly creative city now offers a kaleidoscope of flavours, textures and colours. Michelin stars have piled up alongside a flourishing independent scene, while some of Birmingham's finest gastronomy can be found in the city's lively neighbourhood restaurants.

How to

Getting around The city centre is compact and walkable; regular trains and buses offer easy connections to Birmingham's neighbourhoods.

When to go Outdoor and canalside dining make May to September the most attractive time of year to visit.

Need to know Midweek restaurant experiences are quieter and more relaxed; book well ahead if you're visiting at a weekend. Balti restaurants are easier for walk-ins at any time.

Far left Purnell's
Left Chakana
Bottom Meal in the Balti Triangle

Michelin city No British city has more Michelin stars outside of London than Birmingham. With four superb restaurants to choose from, two of the finest are within an easy 10-minute walk of New Street Station. Glynn Purnell's contemporary British fine dining earned him his star at **Purnell's** (purnells restaurant.com) in 2009, while the most recent addition is the sublime **Opheem** (opheem.com). Here chef Aktar Islam's progressive Indian cuisine is a window into Birmingham's gastronomic evolution.

Beyond the bright lights Venture outside the city centre to explore a host of talented independents in a more relaxed setting. Take the 50 bus to **Moseley** where its leafy streets are home to Birmingham's first Peruvian restaurant **Chakana** (chakana-restaurant.co.uk), while over in the craft-beer hub of **Stirchley**, the sizzling kitchen at **Eat Vietnam** (eatvietnam.co.uk) means you're hit by waves of alluring aromas on entering.

Go for a balti Developed by Birmingham's fledgling Pakistani community in the early 1970s, the balti is a fiery one-pot curry that's still popular today and is a symbol of the city's diversity. Just 15 minutes south of the centre, the dish's spiritual home is the colourful and chaotic **Balti Triangle** neighbourhood, where restaurants cook and serve the balti in the same searing hot bowl to retain as much flavour as possible.

Best Balti Houses

Shabab's (163-165 Ladypool Rd) The standard-bearer for the Birmingham balti. A truly iconic restaurant serving amazing, authentic baltis since 1987.

Shahi Nan Kebab House (353 Stratford Rd) Refurbished and refashioned as a Pakistani street food restaurant, Shahi Nan offers friendly service and superb baltis (among other delicious offerings – the lamb chops are a must!).

Royal Watan (602-604 Pershore Rd) Established in 1984, Royal Watan serves authentic baltis alongside freshly prepared Kashmiri and Indian restaurant classics.

■ Recommended by **Andy Munro**, *author of* Going for a Balti *and* Essential Street Balti Guides, X (Twitter)@BaltiBowl

23 Magical MALVERNS

HIKING | OUTDOORS | SPA

Rising starkly from the gentle Worcestershire countryside, the cinematic Malvern Hills are perfect for hiking and cycling, while the spa town of Great Malvern is a quaint mix of quirky shops, Victorian architecture and cosy pubs. Whether taking in views from a wind-whipped hilltop or the front seat of a Morgan sports car, this is the Midlands at its most spectacular.

How to

Getting here and around West Midlands Railway trains run regularly from Birmingham New Street Station to Great Malvern; the journey takes one hour. While a car will make life easier, there are local bus services and plenty of bike-hire options.

When to go The golden sunlight on the hills makes summer (June to August) the most seductive time of year to visit, though the autumnal colours are spectacular too.

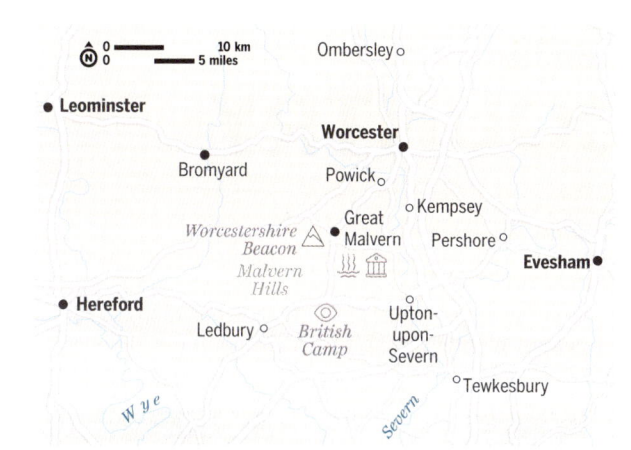

Top left Malvern Hills
Bottom left Morgan Experience Centre

Go above the clouds Looming directly above Great Malvern town, **Worcestershire Beacon** is the highest point (425m) of the Malvern Hills and its summit can be hiked in one hour. Even finer vistas can be enjoyed from the stony windswept trails at the **British Camp** hillfort at the opposite end of the 8.1-mile hills. Cycle trails criss-cross this ancient granite landscape and on a clear day you can enjoy panoramic views of the Severn Valley, the Cotswolds and across Herefordshire into the distant Welsh Hills.

Hire a classic Designed and handcrafted in Malvern Link since 1910, the sleek sports cars produced by the **Morgan Motor Company** *(morgan-motor.com)* are iconic within British motoring. The **Morgan Experience Centre** in Malvern tour gives access to the factory and shows visitors the skill that goes into their production. However, it's the opportunity to hire a Morgan and drive it through the bucolic slopes and meandering country lanes of the Malverns that makes this experience extra special.

And relax While the Malverns' natural spring water had been healing locals for centuries, it was during the 19th century that the 'water cure' craze infatuated Victorian visitors as they poured into the area (including Queen Victoria herself). Get a sense of that spa heritage by passing languid hours at the **Malvern Spa** *(themalvernspa.com)*, with a relaxing indoor-outdoor hydrotherapy pool and soothing steam rooms.

Retro Great Malvern

Carnival Records (83 Church St) Well-curated vinyl record shop that cuts across sub-genres and eras. Offers high-standard new, used and rare vinyl, alongside niche CDs, cassettes, box sets and books.

Hunky Dorey (3 Priory Rd) A quirky high-quality dress agency lying in the shadow of the medieval Great Malvern Priory. Crammed with eclectic antiques, retro furniture and decorative arts.

Malvern Bookshop (7 Abbey Rd) Friendly local bookshop spread across five rooms selling a vast range of antiquarian, rare and quality secondhand books. Head up the creaking stairs to the 1st-floor rooms for a tranquil browse. Handily located next to a cafe.

Canal **COUNTRY**

OUTDOORS | WALKING | HISTORY

'More canals than Venice' is a famous – if rather tongue-in-cheek – local phrase in Birmingham, but the city's extensive canals snake well beyond their watery urban environment and weave into ancient countryside pockmarked by quaint towns and medieval castles. Whether rambling the tranquil towpaths or hiring a boat, there are several ways to explore these historic waterways.

How to

Getting around Accessing the canals is easy as they pass through many of the region's major towns, though hiring a car may be better to visit the more rural stretches.

When to go Summer is best for enjoying the canalside pubs, while the red and golds of autumn are more attractive for walking.

On the water Self-drive narrowboats are widely available; there are also boat tours in Birmingham and Stratford.

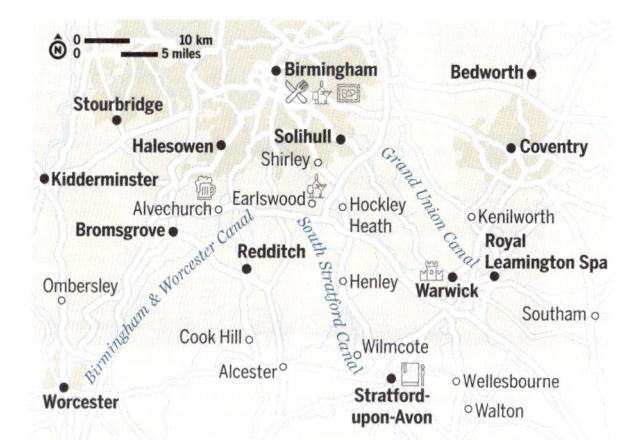

Top left Gas Street Basin
Bottom left Warwick Castle

A city escape With its jaunty waterside pubs, bars and bistros, **Gas Street Basin** is the lively epicentre of Birmingham's canals. Enjoy the atmosphere here before walking the meandering 45-minute stretch of the **Birmingham and Worcester Canal** south to the Birmingham University grounds. This tranquil trail finishes amid some fine Edwardian architecture and it's just a short walk to the **Barber Institute of Fine Arts** (barber.org.uk), a quiet, art deco gallery containing a splendid collection of little-known works from the likes of Monet, Turner and Degas.

Medieval Warwickshire The **Grand Union Canal** passes by many sights on its way south from Birmingham to London, but few are as imposing as the immaculately preserved **Warwick Castle**. Dating back to the 14th century, the castle's rising turrets and formidable walls dominate Warwick's charming landscape and are well worth exploring. Just 3 miles away, the canal towpath connects with the equally historic nearby town of **Leamington Spa**, so consider hiring a bike to explore both on two wheels.

In Shakespeare country With its cobbled streets and quaint Tudor houses, William Shakespeare's home town of **Stratford-upon-Avon** has many attractions but is also surrounded by some magnificent countryside. Hire a colourful narrowboat and explore the picturesque **South Stratford Canal**, before returning to see more of the Bard's most significant sights, such as **Shakespeare's Birthplace** (shakespeare.org.uk) and his final resting place at **Holy Trinity Church**.

Waterside Drinks

The Botanist Gas Street (Birmingham) Perfect for a summer's day. Enjoy the outside beer garden overlooking Gas Street Basin or walk alongside the canal to discover the wide range of bars and restaurants on Brindley Pl.

Bluebell Cider House (Earlswood) Sip from an eclectic range of ciders while admiring the stunning surroundings of Warwickshire. Hit this pub at the right time to watch the sunset over the Avon canal.

The Weighbridge Inn (Alvechurch) A quintessential English canalside pub. This waterside hot spot has a charming character, complemented by a friendly and warm atmosphere.

■ Recommended by Haley Hadley, *Sales and Marketing Director for Midlands-based ABC Boat Hire, @abcboathire*

Diverse Sounds

A MUSICAL CITY THAT REFUSES TO CONFORM

Birmingham's postwar mix of industry and immigration brought people of all races and classes together and inspired some of the most original and influential music these shores have ever produced. Here's how the likes of Black Sabbath and UB40 took their bleak surroundings and turned them into art.

Left Ozzy Osbourne of Black Sabbath
Centre UB40
Right Mike Skinner of The Streets

Heavy Metal Pioneers

Growing up in the grim suburban streets of 1960s Birmingham, the young members of Black Sabbath all felt consigned to a life working amid the crash of machines. Indeed, guitarist Tony Iommi still bears the scars of that alternative life path after getting his fingertips caught in a machine while working at a sheet metal factory in the north Birmingham suburb of Aston aged just 17.

This macabre incident ended up drastically affecting how he played guitar and a dark sound began to emerge. Taking inspiration from Birmingham's smoking chimneys and howling factories, the music pouring out of Sabbath arguably created what we now know as heavy metal. With Ozzy Osbourne's haunting vocals swirling above Iommi's dirty doom-laden riffs, albums like *Black Sabbath* (1970), *Paranoid* (1970) and *Master of Reality* (1971) took rock music into a whole new realm.

Global Sounds, New Romantics & Bhangra

As Birmingham's industry declined, its diversity increased, with immigrants from the Caribbean and the Indian subcontinent invited to Britain to make a new life. That diversity was reflected in Birmingham's music and led to a defining characteristic of the city's music scene: its refusal to conform to any genre or trend.

Could UB40 have come from any other UK city? Maybe. But few parts of the country would have allowed Ali Campbell and his bandmates to have grown up in such a vibrant multicultural environment while hearing reggae beats and Indian rhythms emanating from the city's streets, neighbourhoods and record shops. With this wealth of diversity bringing colour and culture to Birmingham's streets, UB40's multiracial line-up reflected their reality.

Ten years after Black Sabbath introduced the world to metal, Birmingham's musical axis had switched to reggae's punchy drums and thick basslines with seminal albums like Steel Pulse's *Handsworth Revolution* (1978) and UB40's *Signing Off* (1980). From the Handsworth neighbourhood in north Birmingham to Balsall Heath in the south, these albums sounded uniquely local and were full of political bite and stinging social commentary to go along with their catchy tunes.

While this period also saw Birmingham New Romantics Duran Duran conquer the globe's charts, the city – and Handsworth's Soho Rd, in particular – had become the world's epicentre of Bhangra music. While not as mainstream as other forms of music, its fusion of traditional Punjabi dance music and Western popular music has grown into a global cultural phenomenon embraced by members of the Indian diaspora worldwide.

Refusal to Conform

As the 20th century drew to a close and Birmingham's urban landscape had undergone profound change, its status as a cultural melting pot continued to produce unique sounds. From The Streets' garage-infused hip-hop to singer-songwriter Laura Mvula's award-winning neo-soul, Birmingham still refused to conform despite charts consumed by pop and guitars.

Today Birmingham is awash with venues large and small showcasing the city's musical talent. From budding stars on stage at independents like Sunflower Lounge and The Crossing, to more established acts performing at The Mill and the O2 Institute, Birmingham's future feels just as exciting as its boundary-pushing past.

🎧 The Sound of a City

Paranoid, Black Sabbath (1970) Featuring several of the band's signature songs like 'Paranoid' and 'Iron Man', *Paranoid* shot Sabbath to stardom and established them as a force on both sides of the Atlantic.

Signing Off, UB40 (1980) Recorded in the bedroom, garden and basement of producer Bob Lamb's Moseley house, UB40's debut album *Signing Off* was an instant success and introduced the world to their dub-influenced rhythms.

Original Pirate Material, The Streets (2002) With its carefully crafted vignettes of everyday life sung in a distinctly Birmingham accent, The Streets' debut album *Original Pirate Material* was a refreshing landmark in British hip-hop.

25 Spectacular **RUINS**

HISTORY | OUTDOORS | RUINS

From marauding Roman armies to the spectre of Nazi bombers in the night sky, the Midlands has seen conflict spanning centuries. What remains are some of the country's most intriguing ruins. These bizarre and beautiful sights – crumbling castles, bomb-flattened cathedrals – are scattered around the region and can be reached by both train and car.

How to

Getting around Car is the best option, though Coventry is easily reachable from most places by public transport and is just a 30-minute train ride from Birmingham.

When to go The warmer months of May to September lend themselves better to these outdoor sights.

Unusual events Check ahead for concerts or events – the street-food event Coventry Dining Club held at Coventry Cathedral, for example – that might coincide with your visit.

Top left Kenilworth Castle
Bottom left Witley Court

WWII ghosts While its skeletal walls and commanding spire still remain (the third tallest in the UK), the rest of **Coventry Cathedral** (coventrycathedral.org.uk) was devastated by a ferocious German Luftwaffe bombing blitz on the night of 14 November 1940. And yet there's an inspiring beauty about how this 600-year-old structure still stands intact. Don't miss the stunning colours of the stained-glass window in the modernist **new cathedral** next door.

From sieges to celebrations From withstanding a six-month medieval siege to hosting lavish banquets for Queen Elizabeth I, **Kenilworth Castle** (english-heritage.org.uk) is a 900-year-old ruined fortress that's seen plenty of action over its long life. Located on the leafy edges of **Kenilworth** in Warwickshire, the towers give fine views across the county while the landscaped gardens are reminiscent of that decadent Elizabethan period. There's also an on-site tearoom set inside rustic Tudor stables offering cakes and light lunches.

A grand mirage From a distance, **Witley Court** (english-heritage.org.uk) in rural Worcestershire appears the grandest of palaces. A closer look, however, reveals that only the bones of this dramatic Italianate mansion are still standing after a massive fire gutted the building in 1937. What remains is a resplendent example of 17th- and 18th-century architecture flanked by glorious gardens, colourful flowerbeds and ornate fountains. Explore the beautiful surrounding woodlands and lake while you're here.

Roman Midlands

Wroxeter Roman City (Shropshire) Once the fourth-largest city in Roman Britain, the remains of Wroxeter's old bathhouse are fascinating.

Icknield Street (Birmingham) This 1.5-mile section of Roman road, once stretching from Gloucestershire to South Yorkshire, is beautifully preserved in Sutton Park.

Letocetum Roman Baths (Staffordshire) An ancient military staging post near Lichfield with posting station and bathhouse ruins dating back to 130 CE.

Lunt Roman Fort (Coventry) A partially reconstructed example of how the Romans initially made forts using wood rather than stone.

Mancetter (Warwickshire) Heritage centre suggesting Mancetter was the location of warrior-queen Boudica's final battle.

26

The Tolkien
TRAIL

HISTORY | NATURE | LITERATURE

The Lord of the Rings author JRR Tolkien lived in Birmingham during his formative years, where his curiosity was piqued by quirky architecture and mysterious woods. See where Tolkien took inspiration from his childhood neighbourhoods of Hall Green, Moseley and Edgbaston.

How to

Getting around Hall Green/Moseley and Edgbaston, in south Birmingham, are both walkable, but you'll need a car or public transport (bus 1 is ideal) to jump between the two.

When to go May to September is the most pleasant time of year to visit.

How long The trail should only take a couple of hours at most, but allow for transfer time between Moseley and Edgbaston.

Moseley Cafe Stops

Cafephilia (138 Alcester Rd) Watch the world go by at this laid-back independent street-corner cafe.

Damascena (133 Alcester Rd) Sip Turkish coffee amid a wide range of delectable Middle Eastern fare.

Maison Mayci (148 Alcester Rd) Indulgent pastries and handcrafted cakes are on offer at this rustic French cafe.

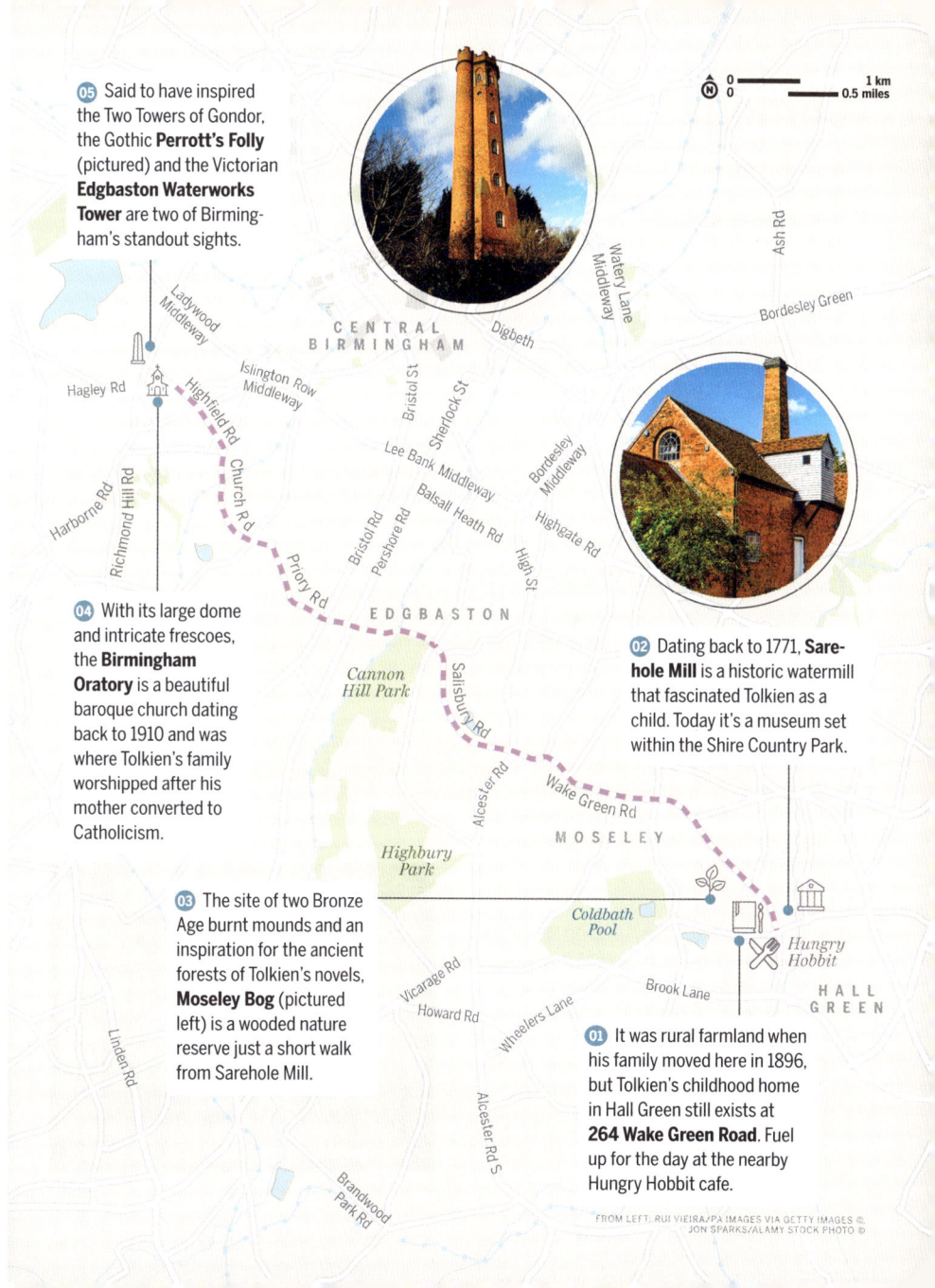

05 Said to have inspired the Two Towers of Gondor, the Gothic **Perrott's Folly** (pictured) and the Victorian **Edgbaston Waterworks Tower** are two of Birmingham's standout sights.

04 With its large dome and intricate frescoes, the **Birmingham Oratory** is a beautiful baroque church dating back to 1910 and was where Tolkien's family worshipped after his mother converted to Catholicism.

03 The site of two Bronze Age burnt mounds and an inspiration for the ancient forests of Tolkien's novels, **Moseley Bog** (pictured left) is a wooded nature reserve just a short walk from Sarehole Mill.

02 Dating back to 1771, **Sarehole Mill** is a historic watermill that fascinated Tolkien as a child. Today it's a museum set within the Shire Country Park.

01 It was rural farmland when his family moved here in 1896, but Tolkien's childhood home in Hall Green still exists at **264 Wake Green Road**. Fuel up for the day at the nearby Hungry Hobbit cafe.

FROM LEFT: RUI VIEIRA/PA IMAGES VIA GETTY IMAGES ©; JON SPARKS/ALAMY STOCK PHOTO ©

Listings

BEST OF THE REST

🛍 Arcades & Food

Great Western Arcade
An ornate Victorian delight located directly across from Birmingham Snow Hill Station's entrance. Packed with independent traders and stylish bistros. *greatwesternarcade.co.uk*

Mailbox
Birmingham's stylish canalside shopping experience, the revamped former Royal Mail sorting office has designer hotels, upmarket restaurants and designer boutiques. *mailboxlife.com*

🍺 Independent Beer, Whisky & Wine

Attic Brew Co
One of the stars of the Stirchley craft-beer scene. Superb beers are brewed on-site and there's plenty of space indoors and outdoors. *atticbrewco.com*

Tilt
Super-central, retro-cool bar in the City Arcade for craft beer, speciality coffee and pinball. You're welcome to bring your own food. *tiltbrum.com*

The Wellington
A gloriously unpretentious pub on Bennetts Hill that's free of pumping music or jaunty decor. The Welly offers eight regular beers and rotating guest ales on tap. *thewellingtonrealale.co.uk*

Grain & Glass
This laid-back bar is the best place in Birmingham for whisky lovers. Sample one of the 300-plus whiskies or come for a tasting event. *grainandglass.co*

Arch 13 at Connolly's
Sit in a comfy booth or at the sleek wooden bar and peruse a menu full of hard-to-find wines and enticing cheese and charcuterie boards.

🏞 Green Spaces & Views

Highbury Park
Highbury Park's winding paths meander through lush forest and quiet lakes despite its location near Kings Heath's bustling High St. Elegant Victorian mansion Highbury Hall is also part of the park.

Edgbaston Reservoir
The walking trail around the reservoir conjures a variety of attractive scenes, but its western shores are the prettiest and offer skyline views of Birmingham city centre.

Beacon Hill
The 248m summit of the Lickey Hills offers stunning views of Birmingham's skyline to the north and the distant Malvern Hills to the south.

Great Western Arcade

Cannock Chase

Elevated heathland 20 miles north of Birmingham. Cannock Chase was a former royal forest and is populated by dense woodland and small lakes with extensive walking and cycling trails.

Art Galleries

BMAG

Birmingham Museum & Art Gallery houses fine art, archaeology and ceramics. Most impressive is the Round Room, where exhibitions zoom in on underrepresented people and historically overlooked stories. *birminghammuseums.org.uk*

Ikon

A free contemporary-art gallery located in a wonderful neogothic school building at Brindley Pl. Features a regular programme of multimedia exhibitions, events, workshops and seminars. *ikon-gallery.org*

Exquisite Eating

The Wilderness £££

Eating here is unlike most fine-dining experiences largely thanks to its charcoal-black interior and pounding rock soundtrack. The 10-course tasting menu features Birmingham's most creative dessert course. *wearethewilderness.co.uk*

Upstairs by Tom Shepherd £££

Lichfield restaurant serving exceptionally well-prepared food in a beautiful former crafts workshop. Multicourse tasting menus are designed by award-winning chef and owner Tom Shepherd. *upstairs.restaurant*

Oyster Club ££

The Oyster Club's creamy battered halibut and Jenga-stacked triple-cooked chips are the best fish and chips in the city. *the-oyster-club.co.uk*

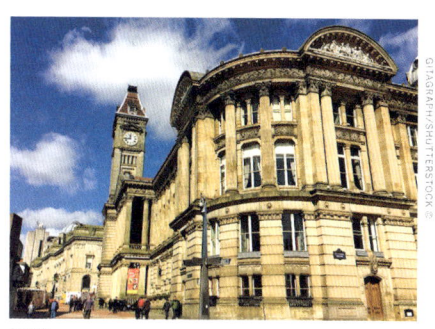

BMAG

Tiger Bites Pig £

Intimate East Asian street food joint specialising in delicately cooked bao packed with rich flavours. *tigerbitespig.co.uk*

Lunch, Pizza & Sunday Roast

Ju Ju's £

Canalside cafe serving the heartiest of Sunday roasts using locally sourced ingredients inside a cosy space. Breakfasts are excellent too.

Grace + James ££

Part of a vibrant scene on Kings Heath's York Rd, Grace + James' handcrafted sandwich menu rotates every other week. Also great for wine and cheese.

Otto ££

Wood-fired pizzas served in a laid-back atmosphere in the Jewellery Quarter. Pick from a handful of regular signature combinations made from fresh ingredients and a revolving cast of specials. *ottopizza.uk*

Peacer ££

Relaxed restaurant in Moseley serving New York–style vegetarian pizzas by the slice. Take out or dine in with a cold craft beer. *peacer.co.uk*

NORTHERN ENGLAND

CULTURE | OUTDOORS | FOOD

- **Trip Builder** (p134)
- **Practicalities** (p136)
- **Wild Beaches of the North** (p138)
- **Wild Waters of the North** (p140)
- **Outdoor Art** (p142)
- **Lancashire's Witches** (p146)
- **The Lake District's Foodie Icons** (p148)
- **Cheese Lovers' Tour of Yorkshire** (p150)
- **Exploring Hadrian's Wall** (p152)
- **Hadrian's Wall** (p154)
- **Regional Football Rivalries** (p156)
- **Listings** (p158)

NORTHERN ENGLAND
Trip Builder

Northern England is best known for its world-class cities, but its great outdoors also shines bright: think surfing and canoeing, spotting dinosaur footprints, following the trail of some ill-fated 'witches' and even spotting the northern lights from an iconic pilgrimage island.

Make a foodie pilgrimage to **L'Enclume** (p149), part of Simon Rogan's gastro-empire
🚗 *30 min from Windermere*

Go wild swimming at **Tongue Pot waterfall** (p141) amid classic Lakes scenery near Holmrook
🚗 *around 1 hr from Windermere*

See where the Pendle Witches spent the night before execution in the **Trough of Bowland** (p147)
🚗 *25 min from Lancaster*

Spot endangered red squirrels and natterjack toads among the dunes of **Formby Beach** (p138)
🚆 *40 min from Liverpool*

Watch the tide claim the statues of **Another Place** (p144) at Crosby Beach
🚗 *25 min from Liverpool*

Hike over the sands to see the UK's rarest flower on **Holy Island** (p139)

🚗 around 1 hr from Newcastle

- Berwick-upon-Tweed
- Alnwick

Make traditional Yorkshire cheeses at Laceys in the heart of the **Dales** (p151)

🚗 around 1 hr from Harrogate

- Newcastle-upon-Tyne
- Sunderland
- Durham
- Middlesbrough
- Darlington
- Richmond

The Pennines

NORTH SEA

North York Moors National Park

- Scarborough

Take to the waves in the increasingly popular surf spot of **Scarborough** (p141)

🚗 around 1 hr from York

Yorkshire Dales National Park

Forest of Bowland

- Harrogate
- York
- Preston
- Bradford
- Leeds
- Blackburn
- Hull
- Huddersfield
- Wigan
- Bolton
- Grimsby
- Manchester
- Doncaster
- Warrington
- Sheffield
- Chesterfield
- Lincoln

Take in remarkable street art in Manchester's old **cotton mills** (p145)

🚶 half a day on foot

Paddle past the Mersey's nature reserves or Britain's first canal in **Manchester** (p141)

🛶 half a day to 1 day

- Derby
- Nottingham

FROM LEFT: PHIL KIERAN/SHUTTERSTOCK © JON DUNN/ALAMY STOCK PHOTO © SIMON ANNABLE/SHUTTERSTOCK © PREVIOUS SPREAD: WIG WORLAND/GETTY IMAGES ©

Practicalities

ARRIVING

Air There are international airports in Manchester (pictured), Liverpool, Leeds-Bradford and Newcastle.

Train Manchester, Liverpool, Leeds and Newcastle are the main rail stations in the region.

Car The main motorways are the M62 (Liverpool–Manchester–Leeds), M1/A1(M) (Leeds to Newcastle) and M6 (Manchester and Liverpool to the Lake District).

HOW MUCH FOR A

Pint of Yorkshire ale £4.50

Sunday roast £15

Canoe rental £20

GETTING AROUND

Car The best option to explore the landscapes of the north, with the freedom of stopping off for wonderful walks.

Bus Buses link some of the main cities and towns; see *gonorthwest.co.uk* and *gonortheast.co.uk* for routes and timetables.

Bicycle A great way to get around within different regions or on longer routes linking destinations.

WHEN TO GO

JAN–MAR
The coldest months; evenings are noticeably brighter after March.

APR–JUN
Longer, warmer days towards June but risk of showers.

JUL–SEP
Warmest months, with long summer nights; always expect rain.

OCT–DEC
Stronger wind and waves; much colder, especially in December.

EATING & DRINKING

Shrimps (pictured top) are fished from Morecambe Bay, cooked in seawater and spices, then potted and sealed with butter. Fish and chips, one of Britain's national dishes, is best sampled at Whitby's Magpie Café, with harbour and abbey views. Craster kippers (pictured bottom), the famed smoked fish popular with the Royal Family, is best tried in the fishing village itself.

Kendal Mint Cake is a sweet bar made with peppermint oil; it's popular as hikers' fuel in its native Lake District.

Best for tea and cakes
Betty's cafe and tearooms, Yorkshire (various locations)

Must-try cheese
Wensleydale in Hawes (p151)

CONNECT & FIND YOUR WAY

Wi-fi Available at most accommodation and likely to be high speed except in very remote locations. Remote locations may also have patchy phone signal and 4G/5G coverage.

Navigation If you are using your phone to navigate while hiking or exploring remote areas, have back-up maps and communication just in case.

TRANS PENNINE TRAIL

This 215-mile route for walkers, cyclists and horse riders takes you coast to coast between the North and Irish Seas, alongside rivers and canals and through some of northern England's most historic towns and cities.

WHERE TO STAY

Cities and towns can get busy in high summer and on holiday weekends, so book well in advance, especially for the Lake District.

Place	Pros/Cons
Manchester	A great base for culture, nightlife and food, with plenty of accommodation options ranging from hostels to five-star hotels; can get busy during festivals and events.
York	The walled city founded by the ancient Romans is an atmospheric place to stay as well as a jumping-off point to the Dales and Moors; but can be busy during events.
Windermere	Hot spot for lovely hotels and restaurants in the Lakes; suffers from over-popularity in high summer.
Northumberland Coast Area of Outstanding Natural Beauty (AONB)	A glorious windswept stretch with everything from boutique hotels to cosy cottages; but does bear the brunt of storms.

MONEY

Credit and debit cards are accepted almost everywhere, and there are ATMs in the main towns.

27 Wild Beaches of THE NORTH

WILDLIFE | GEOLOGY | WALKING

Lashed by the North Sea on one side and the surprisingly rough Irish Sea on the other, the north of England is no classic beach destination. Yet its many vast stretches of sand include some of Britain's most spectacular beaches – many of them with treasures all of their own, from ammonites in Yorkshire to endemic orchids on Northumberland's Holy Island.

How to

Getting around Coastal England is best discovered by car, but on a local level, walking and cycling paths are great ways to explore.

When to go Summer sees the fairest weather, but in winter these windswept beaches offer some gorgeous sights, from Arctic geese to the aurora borealis (northern lights).

Top tip Part of the National Cycle Network, the Coast and Castles South cycle route is a great way to see Northumberland, including Holy Island (also known as Lindisfarne).

Red squirrels and natterjack toads Between the bright lights of Liverpool and the quintessentially English seaside resort of Southport, **Formby Beach** in Merseyside is a surprising spot for a nature haven. Visit its National Trust reserve of sand dunes and pine woods and you're likely to spot endangered red squirrels (seen all year round but most active in spring and autumn) and natterjack toads (most likely spotted in the March to June breeding season), and even dino footprints bearing witness to the prehistoric life that lived here.

Top right Robin Hood's Bay
Bottom right Natterjack toad, Formby

Across the Sands to Holy Island

Holy Island is accessed by road causeway or on foot across the sand and mud, with the safe route marked by wooden poles. Study tide times before you set out, or go with local guide, scientist and teacher Mary Gunn of **Holy Island Hikes** (holyislandhikes.co.uk).

Ammonites and northern lights On the North York Moors coast, the old fishing and smuggling village of **Robin Hood's Bay** and its estuary **Boggle ('hobgoblin's') Hole** is one of the best fossil-hunting sites in the UK, as well as one of the country's most likely spots for observing the aurora borealis. For likely appearances, sign up for alerts at *aurorawatch.lancs.ac.uk/alerts*.

Arctic geese and orchids Come to mystery-swathed tidal **Holy Island** off the coast of Northumberland not only for the history but for the dunes, salt marshes and mudflats of the **Lindisfarne National Nature Reserve**, where 11 species of orchid include one of the rarest plants in the UK, the endemic Lindisfarne helleborine. Other sightings might include migrating seabirds, grey and harbour seals, and 'St Cuthbert's Beads' (marine animal fossils).

28 Wild Waters of THE NORTH

SWIMMING | SURFING | CANOEING

Raw and elemental, northern England's landscapes are perfect for those wanting to do some watersports. Wild swimming has become almost a national obsession in recent years, and the seas, rivers and lakes of the north are perfect for it. But this region is also increasingly popular for canoeing, kayaking and even surfing.

How to

Getting around Most of the north's best spots for watersports are in fairly remote locations that are most easily accessed by car.

When to go Summer is the most pleasant time for wild swimming and canoeing, while the ideal conditions for surfing come in winter and spring.

How much Canoe hire from £18; surf lessons from £40. For canoe hire and guided trips contact **Venture Out** *(venture-out.co.uk)*.

Top left Kayakers, Bridgewater Canal
Bottom left Surfer, Scarborough

River Mersey Canoe Trail More typically known for its industrial heritage, it may come as a surprise to learn you can paddle along this iconic river. Running 17 miles from **Stockport**, Britain's first-ever National Canoe Trail takes you through a long green corridor of nature parks and reserves before joining the Manchester Ship Canal. You can also tackle the historic **Bridgewater Canal** (Britain's first, built in 1761) to either central Manchester's **Castlefield Urban Heritage Park** with its Roman relics or to **Dunham Massey** stately home.

Tongue Pot, Lake District When choosing among Cumbria's many waterfalls, tarns and larger lakes, you go can't go wrong with a dip in Tongue Pot. Beside a pebble beach and a pack-horse bridge, this legendary emerald pool beneath a roaring cascade has 5m-high sheer rock walls perfect for jumping from. You'll find it at the confluence of the River Esk and Lingcove Beck, far west of the madding crowds of the main Lakes. Get here via a 4-mile round-trip hike from **Holmrook** through stunning scenery.

Scarborough This former spa town that became one of Britain's first seaside resorts (it pioneered rolling bathing machines in 1735) is becoming a hip alternative to the often overcrowded surf beaches of southeast England. Come here as a beginner or a pro or something in-between: there are locations and conditions for all levels, from slow learner waves in **South Bay** to the left-hand point break of **Cayton Bay**.

The Mermaid of the Lakes

Suzanna Cruickshank moved to Cumbria on a whim in 2008. Having never swam in wild water before, she was coaxed into Derwentwater by her landlady and never looked back – she now writes books on outdoor swimming as well as leading guided swims and swim-hikes in the Lakes. 'A day spent wandering the valleys in search of an exciting waterfall to swim in is a day well spent,' says Suzanna. 'We have lakes, rivers, tarns and waterfalls to swim in. As long as you can access the water without trespassing, it's usually OK to swim there.'

■ **Suzanna Cruickshank**, author of Swimming Wild in the Lake District (2020), Cumbria, @suzannaswims

29 Outdoor ART

ART | WALKING | CYCLING

You don't need to venture indoors to see great art – from Grizedale Forest in the Lake District to the walls of Manchester's former cotton mills, northern England abounds in open-air artworks combining culture with a fresh-air-filled day out.

Above *Angel of the North*
Above far right Yorkshire Sculpture Park (p144)
Right *Another Place*

How to

Getting around You'll need a car to access most of the outdoor art in the north of England, but the sites themselves are mainly discoverable on foot.

When to go All year, but the least rainy months – May, June, September and October – are especially good.

How much Most of these art experiences are completely free to enjoy; the only exception is the **Yorkshire Sculpture Garden** (adult/child £11/free).

The Angel of the North

Visible from the A1 as you approach Gateshead, the **Angel of the North**, the largest sculpture in Britain, has been greeting visitors to the northeast since 1998 – its wings angled to create, in sculptor Sir Antony Gormley's words, a 'sense of embrace'. Although most visitors drive past it, it's worth more than a glance through a car window to grasp not only its size (24m in height with a 54m wingspan) but also its resonance. It's sited on a spot where miners laboured for centuries and was conceived to symbolise the region's transition from the industrial to the information age. The hilltop setting is a great spot for a picnic with views.

Another Place

If you like the *Angel of the North*, head over to Merseyside's **Crosby Beach** (just south

Icons of MCR Street Art

Vietnamese-French Akse came to Manchester in the early '90s and hooked into a graffiti scene active since the '80s, including the **Outhouse MCR** public art project in the Northern Quarter. He also recommends a trip out of the centre to **Withington Walls**, which includes his portrait of footballer Marcus Rashford.

■ Recommended by Akse, @akse_p19

of Formby with its red squirrels; p138). Here Gormley created not one but 100 life-size cast-iron figures (modelled from his own naked body) dotted along 2 miles of the foreshore and out to sea – meaning at certain times they are part-submerged by the tide. Come to **Another Place** to meditate on how we fit into the bigger picture: the statues face the sea as if contemplating, as Gormley expresses it, 'Human life […] tested against planetary time'.

Yorkshire Sculpture Park

Human figures are also among the 100 or so open-air sculptures and installations by British and international artists that dot the splendid 202 hectares of the **Yorkshire Sculpture Park** (ysp.org.uk) at the 18th-century Bretton Hall estate in West Yorkshire. But also note the number of works linked to the landscapes of the north: Castleford-born Henry Moore's **Large Spindle Piece** is inspired by a rock formation he remembered seeing as a very young

Unmissable Art Collections

Whitworth Art Gallery (Manchester; whitworth.manchester.ac.uk) Focused on modern artists, the UK's first art gallery built in a park includes an art garden, sculpture terrace and orchard garden.

Walker Art Gallery (Liverpool; liverpoolmuseums.org.uk) The national gallery of the north houses one of the largest art collections – of European art from 1300 to the 20th century – in England outside London.

Hepworth Wakefield (hepworthwakefield.org) This museum was named for local artist and sculptor Barbara Hepworth but embraces other major artists, many from Yorkshire, including Henry Moore and David Hockney.

BALTIC Centre for Contemporary Art (Newcastle; baltic.art) Situated in a landmark converted mill on the banks of the Tyne, this is a major international venue for contemporary art.

Left Hepworth Wakefield
Below Sculpture, Grizedale Forest

child in Leeds, while **Squares with Two Circles** by English sculptor Barbara Hepworth was designed to react to its setting by changing appearance according to the time of day and season.

Grizedale Sculpture Trail

Stone, wood and other materials predominate in the nature-inspired artworks in **Grizedale Forest** in the Lake District – discover them along its extensive network of walking and cycling trails, accompanied by glorious Fells views. As well as fixed artworks, look out for changing installations inviting you to immerse yourself in nature through the likes of woodland-inserted virtual reality that allows you to see the forest through various animals' eyes.

Manchester's Northern Quarter

Switch from remote trails to the heartland of the Industrial Revolution (Manchester's first **cotton mill** was built in the now-hip **Northern Quarter** in 1783) to dive into the UK's most compelling street-art scene. Here colourful, often political works by the likes of Akse (p143), Qubek and Nomad Clan continue the transformation of this ever-evolving city while keeping the past firmly present – these artists paint over other works adorning the walls of former warehouses and factories in an ongoing temporal layering.

30 Lancashire's **WITCHES**

WALKING | ROAD TRIP | HISTORY

Lancashire's wild landscapes are often overlooked as people flock to the Lake District. But they're among the UK's most compelling – especially the Trough of Bowland within the Forest of Bowland Area of Outstanding Natural Beauty (AONB) – and they harbour a fascinating past. Walk in the footsteps of the Pendle Witches, marched to trial at Lancaster Castle in 1612 and executed in the moors above it.

How to

Getting around Covering 45 miles from Barrowford to Lancaster, the trail is best experienced by car, but factor in time to stop off for fantastic walks.

When to go Any time of year; winter rewards hardier travellers with cosy pubs for warming up en route.

Top tip Visit *visitlancaster.org.uk* for more info on the route and *forestofbowland.com* for info on Forest of Bowland walks, camping and glamping (including wild camping).

Top left Trough of Bowland
Bottom left Pendle Heritage Centre

Those accused The nine women and two men accused of murder by witchcraft were marched through the gorgeous countryside of the Forest of Bowland from the picturesque village of **Barrowford**. Begin your own journey here to learn about their tragic history at the **Pendle Heritage Centre** (pendleheritage.co.uk) with its museum, walled garden, bluebell wood and tearoom.

A scenic walk Armed with their story, head over Pendle Hill and into the **Forest of Bowland**, stopping off at **Clitheroe** for its castle and museum along the way. From here proceed through the heart of the AONB. A Site of Special Scientific Interest, the **Trough of Bowland** is home to just a couple of farms. The rest of it is pure, empty, unspoilt countryside, the rolling fells, moors and crystal-clear streams of which have led to it being described as the Switzerland of England. You might have the valley and high pass of the Trough of Bowland all to yourself (although it's popular with cyclists for its steep climbs and sweeping panoramas – this is where Sir Bradley Wiggins prepared for his Olympic and Tour de France wins).

A sombre end Memories, hearsay and superstition combined to form the basis for the 'evidence' given at the Lancaster witchcraft trials of August 1612 – nothing that would hold water in a modern courtroom. **Lancaster** itself is worth at least a day or two for exploring its castle with 19th-century prison cells, **Maritime Museum** and **Williamson Park** with woodland walks, a butterfly house and sea views.

Forest of Bowland Walks

You won't be able to resist stopping off for a walk or two when driving this historic route. Perhaps the best is the **Haredon and Langden circular route** (around 6 miles), taking in some of the most beautiful valleys in northwest England.

The Pendle Witches are said to have spent a night at Langden Castle – actually a humble shelter that was used by the land keepers and which still stands today.

You'll have to cross the brook by the shelter, so make sure you wear waterproof walking boots or be prepared to take them off!

31 The Lake District's FOODIE ICONS

ROAD TRIP | FOOD | HOTELS

Even outside its cities, northern England has some truly spectacular dining. These five iconic northern restaurants can be linked to form the gastronomic road trip of which foodie dreams are made.

A Chef's Tips

Considered by many the UK's best restaurant, three-Michelin-starred L'Enclume (dish pictured) is the baby of chef Simon Rogan, for whom stunning local produce is behind the growing migration of talented chefs to the Lakes. His hot tips on where to go include the **Drunken Duck** (Ambleside), **Chesters by the River** (Ambleside), **Punch Bowl Inn** (Crosthwaite) and **Old Stamp House** (Ambleside).

■ Simon Rogan, *Michelin-starred chef in the Lake District*, @rogan_simon

How to

Getting around A car is the best way to reach these fairly remote locations – all have guest rooms so you can make a night of it.

When to go Booking ahead is essential for each venue as they are popular with visitors and locals.

How much You'll pay between £75 and £250 for a tasting menu. Lunches often feature the same dishes at half the price.

05 In the heart of the Lake District, north of Windermere, **Holbeck Ghyll** (holbeckghyll.com) is a grand country house hotel with a seasonal British fine-dining menu and a chef's table among its options. The views are astonishing.

01 Start at Michelin-starred **Angel at Hetton** (angelhetton.co.uk) set in a 15th-century inn in the Yorkshire Dales. The UK's original gastropub, today it combines boundary-pushing food by chef Michael Wignall with sleek accommodation.

03 Head due north for the 17th-century **Sun Inn** (sun-inn.info) in Kirkby Lonsdale, where dishes feature hearty seasonal produce with a foraged touch, inspired by the three counties it sits between: Lancashire, Yorkshire and Cumbria.

04 Carry on to the southern Lake District, to the village of Cartmel, where Michelin-starred chef Simon Rogan has his iconic **L'Enclume** (lenclume.co.uk), wowing with ingenious season-spun flavours, Aulis chef's table, neighbourhood joint **Rogan & Co** (roganandco.co.uk), farm and guest rooms.

02 Slip over the border into Lancashire, where the glorious 17th-century **Inn at Whitewell** (innatwhitewell.com) sits lost in time in the heart of the Forest of Bowland. Expect classic British food with a local, seasonal twist.

FROM LEFT: DEBRA O CONNOR/ALAMY STOCK PHOTO ©, ROB COUSINS/ALAMY STOCK PHOTO ©

32 Cheese Lovers' Tour of YORKSHIRE

ROAD TRIP | FOOD | NATURE

Crumbly, honey-scented Wensleydale was first made by Cistercian monks from France's Roquefort region who had settled in the valley of that name. Today it is among several iconic Yorkshire cheeses best discovered on a road trip through the Yorkshire Dales and North York Moors National Parks.

Cheeses on Tour

Look out for the **Yorkshire Cheese Grill** (yorkshirecheesegrill.co.uk) street-food van as it pops up around the county, at markets, beer festivals and the **Yorkshire Dales Cheese Festival** each October. Try the Fill Thi Booits grilled cheese sandwich with Wensleydale Fountains Gold Cheddar, English mustard and local red onion chutney.

Jamie Wilson, *founder of Yorkshire Cheese Grill, @yorkshirecheesegrill*

How to

Getting around You'll need a car to really explore the Yorkshire Dales and Moors with all their cheese-related stop-offs. There are also many lovely walks.

Origins Wensleydale is a valley also famed for its ales from Theakston Brewery and Black Sheep Brewery in Masham.

How much From £100 per person to spend a day learning to make French cheese at Laceys.

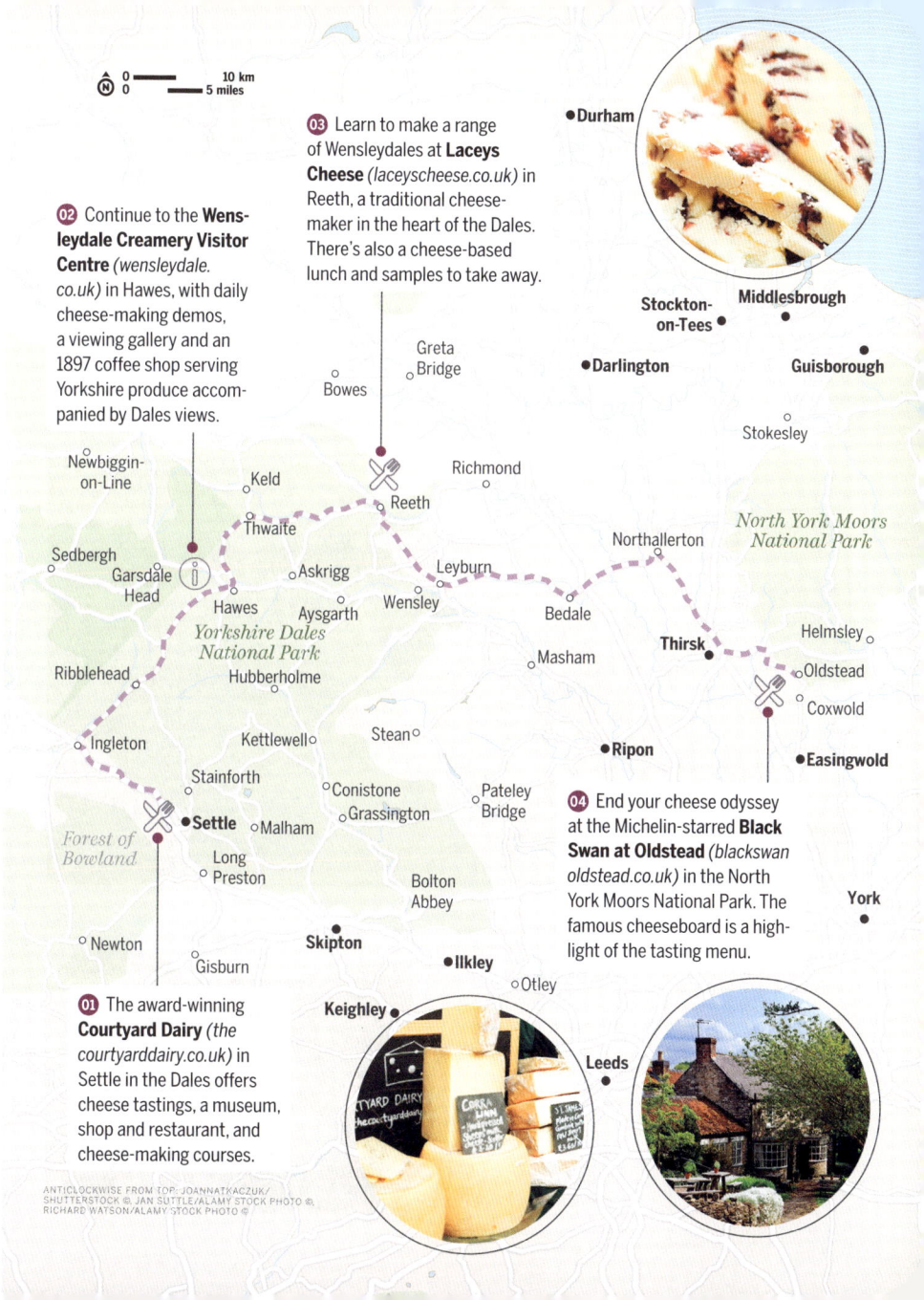

02 Continue to the **Wensleydale Creamery Visitor Centre** (wensleydale.co.uk) in Hawes, with daily cheese-making demos, a viewing gallery and an 1897 coffee shop serving Yorkshire produce accompanied by Dales views.

03 Learn to make a range of Wensleydales at **Laceys Cheese** (laceyscheese.co.uk) in Reeth, a traditional cheese-maker in the heart of the Dales. There's also a cheese-based lunch and samples to take away.

04 End your cheese odyssey at the Michelin-starred **Black Swan at Oldstead** (blackswanoldstead.co.uk) in the North York Moors National Park. The famous cheeseboard is a highlight of the tasting menu.

01 The award-winning **Courtyard Dairy** (thecourtyarddairy.co.uk) in Settle in the Dales offers cheese tastings, a museum, shop and restaurant, and cheese-making courses.

ANTICLOCKWISE FROM TOP: JOANNATKACZUK/SHUTTERSTOCK ©; JAN SUTTLE/ALAMY STOCK PHOTO ©; RICHARD WATSON/ALAMY STOCK PHOTO ©

33 EXPLORING Hadrian's Wall

OUTDOORS | WALKING | HISTORY

Exploring the most spectacular surviving stretches of Hadrian's Wall involves time spent outdoors in open countryside. The 84-mile Hadrian's Wall Footpath follows the ancient monument's undulating route from coast to coast and can be walked in sections on day trips or completed over several days. With England's oldest purpose-built prison and a medieval abbey, Hexham offers a perfect base west of Newcastle.

How to

Getting here Arrive early for a spot in popular car parks such as Steel Rigg and Housesteads. The AD122 bus stops at points of interest between train stations in Haltwhistle and Hexham.

When to go Avoid summer weekends and bank holidays when the footpath alongside Hadrian's Wall draws a legion of visitors. Springtime brings opportunities to view lambs gambolling in surrounding fields. Be prepared for changeable weather and wear good footwear.

Far left Hadrian's Wall
Left Sycamore Gap
Bottom Housesteads Roman Fort

Hadrian's Wall in Newcastle

The well-curated Hadrian's Wall Gallery at the **Great North Museum: Hancock** (greatnorth museum.org.uk) provides an overview of the structure. It also showcases Roman artefacts excavated in the region, ranging from coins to inscribed altar stones. They include altars dedicated to the god Antenocitus found at **Benwell Roman Temple**. Bus 38 runs close to the Benwell site, 2.5 miles west of the city centre, as well as the nearby Vallum crossing.

A turret and knee-high stretch of wall stands 1.5 miles further west at **Denton Hall**. A low section is also visible by the side of the A69 in West Denton.

Twelve miles east of Newcastle, **Arbeia South Shields Roman Fort** (arbeiaromanfort.org.uk) provides insights into life and army service on the wall. Open from March to September, the site has a reconstructed gate, barrack block and commanding officer's house plus a compact museum.

A circular walk Hadrian's Wall remains shoulder high as it snakes over Highshield Crags in **Northumberland National Park** (northumberlandnationalpark.org.uk). Spend a day exploring one of the best maintained sections of the ancient monument during an 8-mile **circular walk** starting from Steel Rigg car park. Partially following the **Pennine Way** and **Hadrian's Wall Footpath**, which converge here, the route also sweeps through nearby fields. In places the footpath is steep and challenging, such as the descent to **Milecastle 39**, where up to 30 Roman soldiers would have been stationed.

Picnic stop Once famous for its much-photographed tree (felled by vandals in October 2023), the U-shaped dip of **Sycamore Gap** is still a striking spot, with the ancient wall clambering across the rugged terrain. The hills here provide decent shelter from wind, making it a good spot to pause for a picnic or drink.

Family fun The footpath provides views of the Crag Lough glacial lake, before dropping towards **Housesteads Roman Fort** (english-heritage.org.uk). The family-friendly on-site museum holds original artefacts, introduces the fort's story and gives kids the opportunity to dress up as soldiers. Known to the Romans as Vercovicium, 800 soldiers were garrisoned at the site, whose exterior wall and interior layout can be seen.

Views of the wall Near Milecastle 36 the trail turns at King's Wicket and skirts north of the wall. Here you can see fine alternative views of Sycamore Gap on the way back to Steel Rigg.

Hadrian's Wall

A ROMAN RELIC ON THE ENGLISH LANDSCAPE

Running across northern England, Hadrian's Wall today forms part of UNESCO's transnational Frontiers of the Roman Empire World Heritage Site. It bears the name of the emperor who ordered the construction of the 73-mile structure in 122 CE as part of wider efforts to consolidate his territory.

Left and centre Sections of Hadrian's Wall
Right Benwell Vallum Crossing

Standing between Wallsend on the River Tyne and Bowness-on-Solway by the Solway Firth, the purpose of the wall is much debated. Importantly, it helped discourage barbarian raids into the upper reaches of the province of Britannia. Other than for a 20-year stint from 142 – when the Antonine Wall was garrisoned – troops stationed in forts, milecastles and turrets along the length of Hadrian's Wall guarded the empire's northern frontier for nearly 300 years.

An Imposing Structure

The purpose of the wall was not just defensive. Archaeological evidence excavated in the vicinity of the wall suggests it was rendered and whitewashed. In an era of few stone structures, any such barrier that rose to a height of 3.6m and spanned the horizon would undoubtedly have sent a profound psychological message about the power and resources of the Roman Empire.

Gates in the wall facilitated control of the flow of goods and taxation. They also enabled Roman troops to patrol north of the wall, with cavalry units strategically stationed in forts at Vindolanda and Stanwix. Notably, military campaigning took place in 210 and 305–06 to suppress serious uprisings involving tribes living outside the empire.

Building the Wall

Estimates suggest that the wall's initial construction phase took place from 122 to 128. The II Augusta, VI Victrix and XX Valeria Victrix legions, each with approximately 5000 soldiers, were involved in quarrying and transporting stone as well as building the wall. Despite that dedicated labour force, initial plans to build the wall about 4m high and 3m thick were downscaled to a width of 'just' 2.3m. In the Cumbrian countryside near Gilsland a section of the so-called 'narrow wall' rises from a base built to the broader dimensions.

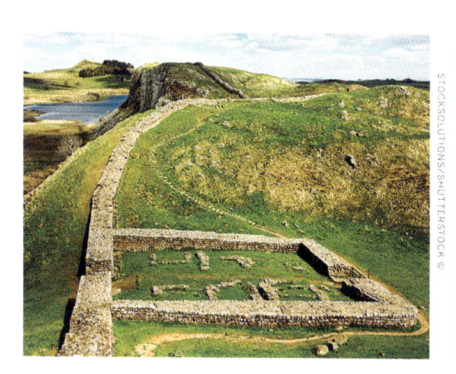

West of the River Irthing the scarcity of easily accessible building stone resulted in the wall being constructed from cut turf.

> Any such barrier that spanned the horizon would undoubtedly have sent a profound psychological message about the power of the Roman Empire.

Despite the inevitable dearth of employment records from 1900 years ago, we know that a Flavinus Carantinus was in the quarry at Fallowfield Fell at some point. He inscribed his name and carved a phallus into the sandstone. The graffiti is now displayed in the museum operated by English Heritage at Chesters Roman Fort.

The Wall's Legacy

After the collapse of Roman power in Britain early in the 5th century, the stone wall provided a ready source of masonry for later building projects. This explains why the ancient structure is most impressive away from human settlements. Stone from the wall was used in buildings including Hexham Abbey, Lanercost Priory and Langley Castle. Nonetheless, much remains to be seen as Hadrian's Wall crosses the centre of the country.

The Vallum

The Vallum is a huge earthwork constructed southward of Hadrian's Wall. Measuring approximately 36m across from north to south, the Vallum encompasses a deep ditch, about 6m wide, flanked by mounds of earth roughly 2m high. It may have demarcated the frontier zone. A gateway excavated in Newcastle's Benwell district also indicates that movement through the Vallum was controlled.

Centuries of erosion have softened the shape of what would once have been a formidable barrier. That may explain why many visitors to the ancient frontier fail to notice the Vallum.

Regional Football Rivalries

LOCAL RIVALRY LIVED THROUGH SPORT

Many people living in northeast England support their local football club, and average attendances of both Newcastle United and Sunderland rank among the top 100 in Europe. No fixture excites passions like the local derby, where intercity rivalry comes charging to the fore on the pitch.

Left 1904 illustration of a match between Newcastle and Sunderland at St James' Park, Newcastle
Centre Entrance to the Stadium of Light, Sunderland
Right Newcastle United flag

When Newcastle and Sunderland clash on the football field during derby matches, they give vent to a longstanding Tyneside–Wearside rivalry that was simmering even before the English Civil War of the 1640s.

The cities stand 10 miles apart. Newcastle overlooks the River Tyne while the River Wear flows through Sunderland. During the 17th century, tensions were growing between merchants in the northeast, as crown monopoly rights granted to glass producers on Tyneside prevented the industry from developing on Wearside. The story is summarised succinctly in a display at the National Glass Centre, an attraction by the Wear's north bank in Sunderland.

Coals from Newcastle

The region had plentiful access to coal, used to heat glass furnaces, but only the Company of Hostmen, based in Newcastle, was permitted to transport the fuel to London. That trade was lucrative and eyed enviously.

In 1637, needing money to finance military campaigns, King Charles I raised taxes on coal. As a concession, he permitted the Company of Hostmen to set the commodity's price. With tensions rising and the nation polarising, boycotts of coal from Newcastle ensued and in 1640 a Scottish army cut supplies.

Commercial self-interest prompted the decision makers in Newcastle to stay loyal to the crown as civil war loomed. Wearside, meanwhile, sided with the Parliamentarian cause. While the Tyne was blockaded, shipments of coal from Sunderland grew.

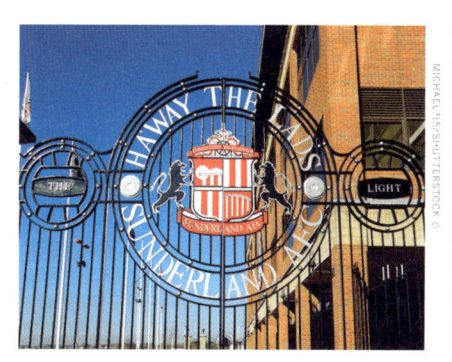

Identities in the Industrial Age

In the 19th century proximity to fuel, raw materials and ports facilitated the boom of heavy industries in northeast England. The Saturday half-day holiday provided time for the workforce to participate in and watch sports, and sporting clubs became focal points of local identities.

Founded in 1879, Sunderland Association Football Club soon enticed talented players from Scotland and won the first of their six league championships in 1892. That year teams from the east and west ends of Newcastle merged, explaining the name of the club that has won the FA Cup six times and four league championships.

> Today most fans exchange good-natured banter but occasionally tensions still escalate into physical confrontations.

A Fixture with History

By the early 20th century Newcastle's home ground could hold 30,000 spectators. Yet more than double that crammed into St James' Park for the clubs' fixture on the Good Friday of 1901. Fans spilled onto the pitch and the match was abandoned and fighting escalated into a riot. Today most fans exchange good-natured banter but occasionally tensions still escalate into physical confrontations.

Head-to-head results between the two clubs are stacked evenly. Derby matches tend to be keenly contested but on the way to winning the league championship in 1908–09, Newcastle suffered a 9–1 mauling at home to Sunderland. That remains Newcastle's record defeat at St James' Park and Sunderland's biggest away win.

Winners in Striped Shirts

Sunderland wear red and white home jerseys. Remarkably, they are the most recent club to play in striped shirts and win England's top football division. That was back in the 1935–36 season. The club played the 2024–25 season in English football's Championship second tier.

Competing in the top tier Premier League, Newcastle United play in black and white and regularly attract crowds of more than 50,000 to home games. A takeover by a wealthy consortium in 2021 gave the club's fans hope that Newcastle will be the next league winner wearing stripes. That, however, is by no means a universal dream across the region.

Listings

BEST OF THE REST

🌿 Nature Immersion

Northumberland & Kielder Water & Forest International Dark Sky Park
Head to the second-largest area of protected night sky in Europe for heavens so dark that the Milky Way and even Jupiter can cast shadows. The observatory has a packed calendar of events.

Gordale Scar
Climbing this gorge deep in the Yorkshire Dales, carved by torrents of glacial meltwater over successive Ice Ages, is easier than it looks. It's part of a circular walk from Malham, including the rock amphitheatre of Malham Cove.

24 Peaks Challenge
With stamina and two days to spare, you'll find this 31-mile route a great way to see the Lake District. Best done with a guide, it takes in some of the best ascents in the national park, including Scafell Pike.

WWT Martin Mere
If you're looking for a gentler day out, perhaps with kids in tow, venture to this wetlands nature reserve and wildfowl collection in Lancashire, with canoe safaris and boat tours.

The Pinnacle
Rock climbers delight in this dramatic stack of three gritstone pillars at Raven Stones Brow near Greenfield Reservoir in the Yorkshire section of the Peak District.

🏛 History & Tradition

Beamish Living Museum of North
Learn about life in northeast England during the 1820s, 1900s, 1940s and 1950s at this world-famous open-air museum complete with vintage trams and costumed actors bringing history to life. *beamish.org.uk*

Whitby Abbey
Be spooked by the Benedictine monastery that inspired Bram Stoker's *Dracula* in its wind-lashed setting high on a clifftop overlooking the quaint fishing harbour of Whitby on the North York Moors Coast. *english-heritage.org.uk*

Jorvik Viking Centre
Find out all about York's ancient past – including just how bad it smelt in those days! – at this time-capsule museum that takes visitors past life-size dioramas in small carriages. *jorvikvikingcentre.co.uk*

Castlefield Urban Heritage Park
Deep-dive into Manchester's history in this area of waterside walks on the site of Britain's first modern canal (1764), the world's first railway station (1830) and the Roman fort of Mamucium.

International Slavery Museum
Discover the history of enslaved people, including those linked with Liverpool's maritime

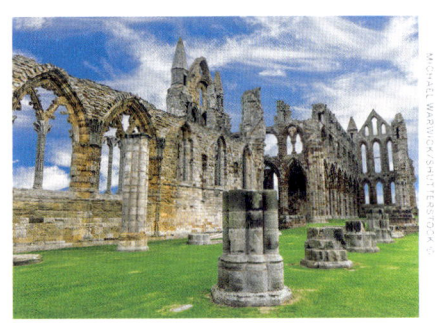

Whitby Abbey

heritage, as well as learning about contemporary slavery. *liverpoolmuseums.org.uk*

Adventures & Tours

Northern Experiences Wildlife Tours
Set sail off the Northumberland coast for fantastic marine sightings, from pelagics (white-beaked dolphins, harbour porpoises, minke whales and more) to otters. Night photography and astronomy sailings are also available. *northernexperiencewildlifetours.co.uk*

North Yorkshire Moors Railway
When you're not walking and hiking in the area, this atmospheric heritage steam train journey takes you through the region in historic style – with lunch or dinner aboard if you wish. *nymr.co.uk*

Cross-Bay Walks, Morecambe
Experience the ever-changing flats and channels of Morecambe Bay stretching from southwest Cumbria to Fleetwood in Lancashire with a guide to keep you safe. *exploremorecambebay.org.uk*

River Explorer Cruises, Liverpool
Drink in views of the city's world-famous waterfront from the deck of the iconic Mersey Ferry on this 50-minute jaunt, including a food and drink stop. *merseyferries.co.uk*

Dave Gray's Puffin Cruises, Amble
Board an ex–Royal Navy lifeboat for a one-hour cruise around Coquet Island to spot bird species including Eider ducks, kittiwakes and rare Roseate terns, the island's grey seal colony and puffins galore. *puffincruisesamble.com*

Flavours of the North

Lakes Distillery
Immerse yourself in whisky making at this renovated Victorian farmstead on the shore

Mersey Ferry, Liverpool

of Bassenthwaite Lake, with tastings, tours (including whisky and chocolate pairings), a bistro and even alpaca to meet. *lakesdistillery.com*

Goosnargh Gin School & Atelier Experiences
Find out how to make gin and even forage for local botanicals for your ingredients, or sign up for sessions with the master potter who makes the firm's stone bottles. *goosnarghgin.co.uk*

Scranchester Tours
Learn about Manchester's cultural history on these half-day foodie outings which include eight tastings in Chinatown and Ancoats' Little Italy with its ice-cream vendors. *scranchestertours.com*

York's Chocolate Story
Go beyond York's Viking and Roman history to learn about its famous chocolate makers, then watch a chocolate-making demo or even team up with the chocolatier to make your own bar. *yorkschocolatestory.com*

Northumbrian Coastline Food Tour
Sample some of the North Sea's freshest seafood including Lindisfarne oysters on this day-long itinerary that also takes in quaint little fishing villages.

WALES

WILD | ADVENTURE | CULTURE

- **Trip Builder** (p162)
- **Practicalities** (p164)
- **Europe's Castle Capital** (p166)
- **Explore the Brecon Beacons** (p168)
- **Mid & West Wales Wildlife** (p172)
- **Adventure on the Coast Path** (p174)
- **Cardiff's Cultural Heritage** (p178)
- **Over the River Taff** (p180)
- **Cymru Festivities** (p182)
- **The Rooftop of Wales** (p184)
- **Listings** (p186)

WALES
Trip Builder

A land of majestic castles, undulating hills, vast mountain ranges and 830 miles of impeccable coastline, Wales is a petite country that proves size doesn't matter. It's a friendly, natural playground underpinned by its unique culture and heritage.

Go wild swimming in the mountainside lakes of **Snowdonia National Park** (p184)
🚗 *30 min from Bangor*

Spot dolphins, otters and rare birds in the wonderful hideaway of **Cardigan** (p177) in Ceredigion
🚗 *2 hr from Cardiff*

Try paddleboarding, or jump off a cliff and swim in caves coasteering in **Pembrokeshire Coast National Park** with TYF (p175)
🚗 *2 hr from Cardiff*

IRELAND
- Dungarvan
- Waterford
- Wexford
- Rosslare

Fishguard
Solva
Haverfordwest
Pembroke

ATLANTIC OCEAN

0 — 50 km
0 — 25 miles

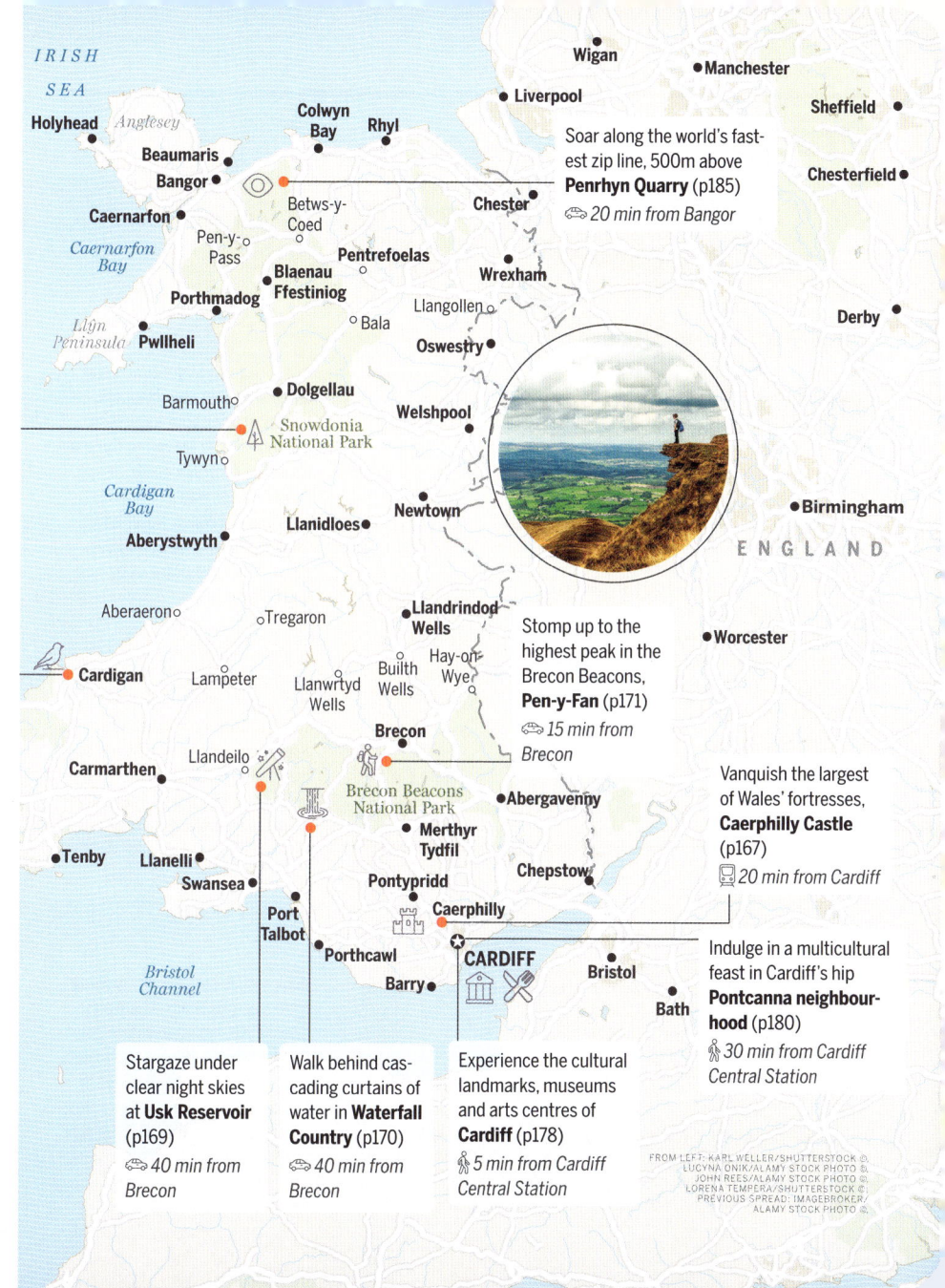

Soar along the world's fastest zip line, 500m above **Penrhyn Quarry** (p185)
🚗 *20 min from Bangor*

Stomp up to the highest peak in the Brecon Beacons, **Pen-y-Fan** (p171)
🚗 *15 min from Brecon*

Vanquish the largest of Wales' fortresses, **Caerphilly Castle** (p167)
🚆 *20 min from Cardiff*

Indulge in a multicultural feast in Cardiff's hip **Pontcanna neighbourhood** (p180)
🚶 *30 min from Cardiff Central Station*

Stargaze under clear night skies at **Usk Reservoir** (p169)
🚗 *40 min from Brecon*

Walk behind cascading curtains of water in **Waterfall Country** (p170)
🚗 *40 min from Brecon*

Experience the cultural landmarks, museums and arts centres of **Cardiff** (p178)
🚶 *5 min from Cardiff Central Station*

FROM LEFT: KARL WELLER/SHUTTERSTOCK ©,
LUCYNA ONIK/ALAMY STOCK PHOTO ©,
JOHN REES/ALAMY STOCK PHOTO ©,
LORENA TEMPERA/SHUTTERSTOCK ©.
PREVIOUS SPREAD: IMAGEBROKER/
ALAMY STOCK PHOTO ©.

Practicalities

ARRIVING

Cardiff Airport The main airport in Wales is 12 miles from Cardiff city centre. To get to Cardiff, take the 905 shuttle bus to Rhoose Train Station, then the train to Cardiff Central Station. In total, this journey costs £5.40 and takes an hour. Taxis take 30 minutes but will cost around £35.

Cardiff Central Station This central transport hub provides rail connections across Wales and to points further afield.

HOW MUCH FOR A

Welsh cake 50p

Local craft beer £4.50

Castle entry fee £11

WHEN TO GO

MAR–MAY
Sunny, mostly dry and fairly quiet. The countryside comes alive with colour.

JUN–AUG
The hottest and busiest period. Great for exploring the coast.

SEP–OCT
Milder, autumnal days and smaller crowds. Perfect walking weather.

NOV–FEB
Cold and rainy, especially around mountains. Outdoor activities are limited.

GETTING AROUND

Bus and train Major towns and cities are connected by public transport. Plan your journey in advance on the **Traveline Cymru** (traveline.cymru) website or app. Transport For Wales (tfw.wales) sells Explore Wales, Rover and Ranger passes that permit one day or four days of travel by train and bus.

Car and taxi A car is necessary to reach some remote areas not accessible by public transport. Hire costs from £30 a day. Alternatively, check for taxi operators.

Walking There are many walking routes across Wales. The Wales Coast Path (walescoastpath.gov.uk) is signposted from end to end. Waypoints are commonplace in the countryside and along routes. Some taxi operators offer luggage transfer.

EATING & DRINKING

Welsh cakes (pictured top) are subtly sweet, lightly spiced, bready raisin cakes that are dusted with sugar.

Cawl (pictured bottom) is a hearty, flavourful broth loaded with chunky root vegetables and soft lamb pieces. Glamorgan sausages are meat-free croquettes made from Caerphilly cheese, leeks and breadcrumbs.

Welsh rarebit is the ultimate cheese on toast: grilled bread topped with a molten cheese, ale and mustard roux.

Best coffee and beer social
Hard Lines, Cardiff (p181)

Must-try Welsh cakes
MamGu Welshcakes, St Davids (p188)

CONNECT & FIND YOUR WAY

Wi-fi Often freely available in cafes, pubs, restaurants, shopping centres and transport hubs. Mobile phone reception and 4G coverage are good but get patchier in remote locations.

Navigation Easy in populated areas; people are willing to give directions and the main navigation apps are accurate. Use Ordnance Survey maps in remote areas.

LANGUAGE

Welsh is an official language of Wales, but English is the first language for the majority of people living here.

WHERE TO STAY

Wales is a small country, but getting from one end to the other takes a long time. Stay in or near to the regions you wish to explore.

Place	Pros/Cons
Cardiff	Accommodation to suit most budgets and lifestyles; the capital city boasts entertainment, sports and nightlife.
Llanberis	Simple B&Bs, guesthouses and dorms within walking distance of the base of Snowdon; quiet village dwarfed by mountains.
St Davids	Independent hotels, campsites and self-catering; Britain's smallest city, loved by surfers, pilgrims and outdoors enthusiasts.
Abergavenny	Traditional Welsh market town with luxury hotels, independent shops and easy access to the Brecon Beacons.
Cardigan	Off-grid accommodation and self-catering studios; a haven for wildlife lovers, craftspeople and young explorers.

MONEY

Most places accept card and contactless payment, but carry cash for markets, remote locations and car parks. Public beaches, forests, mountains and parks are usually free to visit, well maintained and picturesque.

34 Europe's Castle **CAPITAL**

CASTLES | DAY TRIP | CULTURE

Wales has more castles per square mile than any other European country. Since its formation, the country has had around 600 castles, and over 100 still remain, showcasing styles from the 11th to the 19th century and in varying levels of disrepair. Thick stone walls, pierced with arrow holes and slitted windows, tell tales of battles past. Visit them individually, or combine a few fortresses into an historic day trip.

How to

When to visit Many castles open year-round (hours are shorter in winter). Most have picnic areas, ruins or surrounding countryside to explore. Springtime brings daffodils and autumn ochre trees.

Combining castles Most castles are remote but reachable by car. Road trip from Caerphilly Castle to Beaumaris Castle, overnighting at Powis Castle en route.

Check for tickets Some castles, including **Cadw** *(cadw.gov.wales)* and **National Trust** *(nationaltrust.org.uk)* ones, require entry tickets. Budget £5 to £15 per person.

Big and bold The largest castle in Wales and second largest in Britain, the 13th-century **Caerphilly Castle** is monumental yet accessible. It sprawls over the Valleys town, with hilly mounds and waters buffering it from the public. Its best feature is arguably the southeast tower; it leans more than the Leaning Tower of Pisa, but with far fewer tourists posing for photos by it.

Florals and fancy Sitting on an enormous rock, medieval **Powis Castle**, outside Welshpool, is lavishly decorated inside, with an abundance of wall and ceiling murals, furnishings and Indian artefacts in the **Clive Museum**. The garden, however, is breathtaking. The Europe-inspired arched terraces, 14m yew hedges, rare plants, statues and herbaceous borders are lovely to stroll around.

World-renowned architecture Created by Edward I and his architect, **Beaumaris Castle** was the last of their four builds in northwest Wales. Along with their other Gwynedd castles (Caernarfon, Conwy and Harlech), Beaumaris is recognised as a UNESCO World Heritage Site. Incomplete but nevertheless impressive, the castle is a beast beside the Menai Strait. Two concentric double-walled rings encircle the inner ward, while six towers, two hefty gatehouses and a moat keep trouble out. The towers aren't as tall as planned, and the gates aren't complete, but Beaumaris is still spectacular.

Top left Caerphilly Castle
Bottom left Powis Castle

Other Notable Castles

Cardiff Castle (*cardiffcastle.com*) The capital's central stronghold combines Roman, medieval and Victorian Gothic styles. Tour the lavish interiors then climb the clock tower for views across the city.

Caernarfon Castle (*cadw.gov.wales*) Brother of Beaumaris Castle and equally ambitious, Caernarfon Castle is a fortress fanatic's dream. With multifaceted towers, thick walls of coloured stone and a vast moat, it is delightfully domineering.

Pembroke Castle (*pembrokecastle.co.uk*) This oval-shaped castle, with a knot of passageways, staircases and tunnels to unravel, is best known for being the birthplace of Henry Tudor. It's perched on the Pembroke River, with views stretching to Milford Haven.

35 Explore the Brecon **BEACONS**

HIKING | WATERFALLS | MOUNTAINS

The Brecon Beacons National Park showcases geographical highs and lows, from deep gorges and dark caves to sky-grazing peaks, waterfalls and stargazing spots. Its four mountain ranges emerge between market towns, where local produce is celebrated.

Above Milky Way over the Brecon Beacons
Above far right Felin Fach Griffin, Brecon
Right Sgwd yr Eira (p170)

How to

Getting around A car is a must here, as are sturdy walking boots. Bring change for car parks.

When to go Start activities early in the day to beat busy periods. For stargazing, aim to go when there are clear skies.

Bring a picnic Stock up on locally made goodies (cheese, smoked fish, fresh bread and the like) in Abergavenny, Brecon or Crickhowell beforehand.

Starry Nights

As the great sails and glacier-carved valleys of the Brecon Beacons fall into darkness, it can get cold up on these moors, alone with the hoot of a tawny owl, the night-time chorus of bleating sheep – and the universe beyond. On clear, moonless nights, the heavens sparkle with an eternity of stars and distant planets feel close enough to reach out and touch in the Brecon Beacons, which put Wales on the celestial map when it became the world's fifth **International Dark Sky Reserve** in 2013.

Your first port of call should be **Bannau Brycheiniog National Park Visitor Centre** in Libanus, just south of the A40. The **Usk** and **Crai Reservoirs** in the western Brecon Beacons are ideal for stargazing, with road access, little light pollution and flat areas for telescope twitching. But medieval **Carreg Cennen** castle,

Where to Eat Well

Felin Fach Griffin ££ Menus feature ingredients from the garden. *eatdrinksleep.ltd.uk*

Walnut Tree £££ Shaun Hill shakes the pans at this Michelin-starred wonder in Llanddewi Skirrid. *thewalnuttreeinn.com*

International Welsh Rarebit Centre £ One-of-a-kind rarebits are served in a converted schoolhouse in Defynnog.

The Hours £ Charismatic bookshop-cafe rustling up delicious lunches and Sunday roasts. *thehoursbrecon.co.uk*

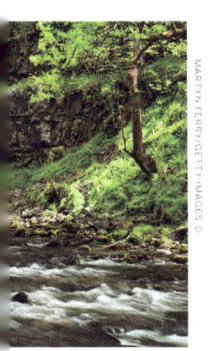

high atop a limestone crag, is more atmospheric. Further east, ramp up the dark sky romance at **Llanthony Priory** in the secluded Vale of Ewyas, at **Sugar Loaf** in the heart of the Black Mountains, or at 677m **Hay Bluff** on the road over the Gospel Pass to Hay-on-Wye. The national park website *(breconbeacons.org)* has the lowdown on stargazing accommodation.

Chasing Waterfalls

According to Welsh mythology, the southwestern Brecon Beacons are riddled with subterranean passages that are the entrance to the fairy underworld. And indeed the ivy-draped, fern-brushed woodlands and steep, rocky gorges at **Ystradfellte** look the part. This southwestern chunk of the Brecon Beacons is nicknamed Waterfall Country, with wispy falls created by five rivers as they tumble through gorges and over rock formations towards the River Neath.

The finest torrent is the wispy **Sgwd yr Eira** (Snow Waterfall), floating over a cliff, which you can walk behind; or, go for a wild swim at the base. At one point the River Mellte disappears into **Porth-yr-Ogof** (Door to the Cave), the biggest cave entrance in Britain (17m wide and 5m tall), reappearing 100m south. The **Four**

The Lady of the Lake

Llyn-y-Fan Fach appears in Welsh epic, the *Mabinogion*. Legend tells that a young farmer peered into the lake and saw a beautiful maiden. He coaxed her ashore and begged for her hand in marriage. The couple lived happily and raised three sons. But when the farmer struck his wife three times, she returned to the fairy world forever.

Here myth merges with fact, as the sons were the first in a long line of royal healers. The village of Myddfai was a medieval centre for herbalist activity. Today Pant-y-Meddygon (Physicians' Valley) on Mynydd Myddfai is still rich in the plants used to make the remedies described in the late-14th-century *Red Book of Hergest*.

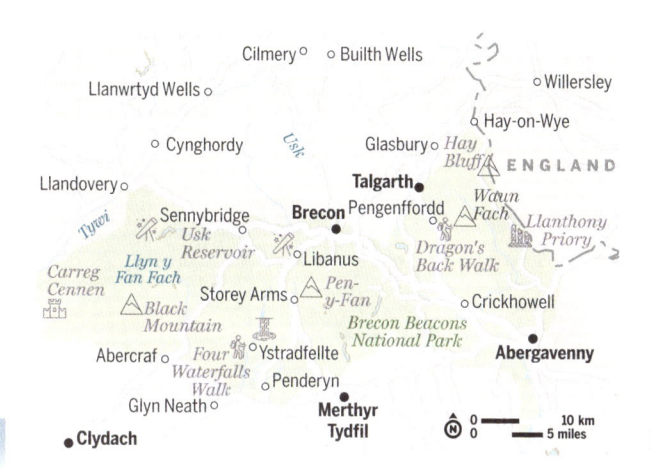

Left Llyn-y-Fan Fach
Below Dragon's Back Walk

Falls Walk takes in the lot. It's a challenging 5.5-mile hike (allow three hours). The trailhead is **Cwm Porth** car park, 3 miles north of **Penderyn** (of gin and whisky distillery fame) on the A4059.

Peaks & Ridges

Rain, bog and fog be damned: puffing up to the highest peak in the Brecon Beacons, 886m **Pen-y-Fan**, is irresistible. On cloud-free days, views stretch over bald, glacier-scoured peaks and deep valleys to the Black Mountains, Bristol Channel and Eryri (Snowdonia) beyond. The quickest route to the top begins at **Pont ar Daf** car park. It's a steep but straightforward ascent (4.5 miles return; allow three hours). Or to tick off a quartet of peaks – **Corn Du**, **Pen-y-Fan**, **Cribyn** and **Fan-y-Big** – hook onto the 10-mile horseshoe walk (allow five hours), which begins at the Lower **Neuadd Reservoir**.

For views without crowds, trek up lesser-known peaks. The **Dragon's Back Walk**, a 7-mile circular route from Pengenffordd to **Waun Fach** mountain, has soul-stirring views of the Black Mountains. Or head to the glacial cirque lake of **Llyn-y-Fan Fach** near Llanddeusant. A 4-mile trail shadows a stream to this myth-steeped lake, before cresting the knife-edge ridge to open moors. Pick a clear day and bring a copy of *OS Explorer OL12: Brecon Beacons National Park*.

MID & WEST WALES
Wildlife

01 Red kite
See over 100 of them up close during daily feeding sessions at Bwlch Nant yr Arian, Aberystwyth.

02 Starling
Every night at dusk during autumn and winter, thousands of starlings swarm in murmurations to roost under Aberystwyth pier.

03 Osprey
Dyfi Osprey Project, housed at Dyfi Wildlife Centre in Machynlleth, usually has nesting ospreys from mid-March to September.

04 Puffin
Over 22,000 puffins nest on Skomer Island and Skokholm Island in Pembrokeshire. Boat trips are run by Pembrokeshire Islands.

05 Grey seal
At low tide, grey seals rest on coastal rocks and beaches in Pembrokeshire. Fluffy seal pups arrive from August.

06 Manx shearwater
Almost 320,000 breeding pairs of Manx shearwater call Skomer and Skokholm home. It's the world's largest

known concentration of them.

07 Bottlenose dolphin
Between May and September, these beautiful dolphins are regularly spotted in Cardigan Bay. In winter they move further offshore in pods.

08 Harbour porpoise
Smaller than dolphins but still visible from land, porpoises gather along Cardigan Bay, particularly around the headlands.

09 Otter
Head to Cardigan's Welsh Wildlife Centre or Teifi Marshes at dawn or dusk to see otters fishing in the River Teifi.

10 Lapwing
These endangered tufted birds have found safety on the estuary salt marsh and lowland wet grasslands at Ynys-hir RSPB Reserve, Machynlleth.

01 ERNI/SHUTTERSTOCK ©. 02 ERIC ISSELEE/SHUTTERSTOCK ©. 03 DENNIS JACOBSEN/SHUTTERSTOCK ©. 04 ALFMALER/SHUTTERSTOCK ©. 05 LUCA NICHETTI/SHUTTERSTOCK ©. 06 KEITH PRITCHARD/SHUTTERSTOCK ©. 07 NEIRFY/SHUTTERSTOCK ©. 08 ANNA L. E MARINA DURANTE/SHUTTERSTOCK ©. 09 ERIC ISSELEE/SHUTTERSTOCK ©. 10 NICOLAS PRIMOLA/SHUTTERSTOCK ©

36 Adventure on the
COAST PATH

COAST | BEACHES | ACTIVITIES

Wales was the first country in the world to have a footpath skim its entire coastline. Dust off your walking boots, don a wetsuit or grab binoculars to discover hundreds of outstanding beaches, caves, bays and cliffs along this 870-mile playground.

Above Tenby Harbour
Right South Beach, Tenby

How to

Getting around Walk, drive or use Traveline Cymru buses to get between coastal locations.

When to go Beaches are busiest in summer. Check rules for specific beaches and tide times before visiting.

Activity providers Hook up with a watersports expert – including coasteering, cliff-diving and stand-up paddle boarding – as they know of hidden dangers in the water. TYF in St Davids hires equipment.

Top tip The Wales Coast Path waymarker is a blue and yellow circle, inside which is a white shell with a dragon's tail. Red versions indicate alternative routes.

West is Best

No point in **Pembrokeshire Coast National Park** in west Wales is more than 10 miles from sea, and all of its seaside perimeter is on the **Wales Coast Path** *(walescoastpath.gov.uk)*. The area is largely unspoiled and thrums with rare wildlife in volcanic outcrops, limestone cliffs, tangled hedgerows and golden shores. Indented with scores of beaches – from dune-backed shores to castaway coves – the backbeat here is the booming Atlantic and the trill of seabirds.

For a quadruple hit of beaches, kick off in **Tenby**. **North Beach**, below a hill of pastel-coloured houses, is sheltered and scenic. It connects to **Harbour Beach**, with bobbing boats and crabbing opportunities aplenty. Recharge at the Stowaway cafe inside a harbour arch, or sample locally caught fish and chips. **South Beach** and the adjoining **Castle Beach** form nearly 2 miles of gently sloping sand and azure sea, backed by Pembrokeshire hills and dunes.

Saints & Shores

St Davids is the UK's smallest city, with a population of just 1600, and a major site of pilgrimage for Christians and coastal fans alike. The spectacularly ornate valley-based cathedral was built high and mighty in the 1100s on the site of a 6th-century monastery founded by St David, patron saint of Wales. Right on the **Pembrokeshire Coast Path** (nationaltrail.co.uk), St Davids is a characterful base for exploring. Indie shops and a raft of enticing restaurants and hotels ramp up its appeal, as does adventure specialist TYF. Near St Davids Head, **Whitesands** is one of the finest surfing beaches in the UK – a broad arc of sand with a steady flow of impeccable waves.

The nearby harbour town of **Solva** is quite the coastal dream, with a rewarding walk up a gorse-laden cliff to panoramic views. Behind **Abereiddi Beach**, in the opposite direction from St Davids, is the **Blue Lagoon**. It's a 25m-deep former slate quarry filled with seawater, popular with coasteerers, climbers and divers. The water has an emerald hue from the minerals below.

The Birthplace of Coasteering

Coasteering takes people closer to the wonders of nature than any other activity. There's nothing like it for stoking a love of the ocean's wild places. Wales' TYF introduced the world's first guided coasteering trips in 1986, drawing on the skills and resources needed for surfing and climbing to create coasteering's blend of excitement, discovery and learning.

If you want to try coasteering, always use an activity provider. We recommend **Cardigan Bay Active** (Cardigan), **TYF Adventure** (North Pembrokeshire) and **Outer Reef** (South Pembrokeshire).

■ Bonnie Middleton, *Community Co-ordinator at TYF,* @tyfadventure

🥾 Want a Challenge?

It's possible to do a circular walk of Wales' entire perimeter (1047 miles) by combining national trails. At the southerly end of the Wales Coast Path, near Chepstow, join the ancient **Offa's Dyke Path** (nationaltrail.co.uk) to go north, up to the official start of the Wales Coast Path near Chester.

Back to Nature

Where Pembrokeshire spills over into Ceredigion, castle-topped **Cardigan** is a chilled hideaway. There's a welcoming community of artists, creatives and wildlife watchers. This is epitomised at **Fforest Farm** (coldatnight.co.uk), an Instagram-perfect site run by art school graduates that embraces small pleasures. Sleeping options include a thoughtfully converted Georgian farmhouse and a geodesic dome, with access to a cedar barrel sauna and rustic, fire-warmed pub. The **Welsh Wildlife Centre** and Teifi Marshes next door are hot spots for otter and rare bird sightings.

Beyond the West

While west Wales has the densest stretch of unbeatable coast, the rest of the Wales Coast Path delivers too. The island of **Anglesey**, far north, is a peaceful escape with whales, porpoises and dolphins visible from land. Slinging its hook into the Irish Sea, the **Llŷn Peninsula** is full-on drama, with memorable beaches like surf-smashed **Porth Neigwl** and entrancing **Porthor**, famous for its 'whistling sands'. The **Gower Peninsula** captivates with its coves and colour-charged sunsets. **Worms Head**, which resembles a sea snake, looks sensational from 3-mile **Rhossili Bay**. If you're lucky, you might spot seals on the rocks.

Left Blue Lagoon, Abereiddi Beach
Top Cardigan
Above Worms Head and Rhossili Bay

37 Cardiff's Cultural HERITAGE

ARTS | ENTERTAINMENT | CITY SCOURING

When it comes to culture, variety is encouraged and embraced in Cardiff. Art galleries, performance spaces and music venues entertain fans of the mainstream and the niche, while the city's independent shops showcase and encourage creativity.

How to

Getting around Cardiff is a walkable city. If needed, there are frequent bus services *(cardiffbus.com)*, trains (Cardiff Central, Queen St and Cardiff Bay) and taxi ranks throughout the city.

Book ahead Most galleries have free admission, but some exhibitions require tickets. Gigs and shows vary in price and can sell out.

What's on Visit Minty's Gig Guide on Facebook or see *Buzz Magazine* (printed and online at *buzzmag.co.uk*) for listings.

Arcade Pit Stops

Spillers (Morgan Arcade; pictured) The world's oldest record store where vinyl reigns supreme.

Wally's Delicatessen (Royal Arcade) Trove of Welsh produce, craft beer and spirits.

Rules of Play (Castle Arcade) Board-game shop with hundreds of titles.

The Pen & Paper (Royal Arcade) Stationery shop for amateur and professional artists.

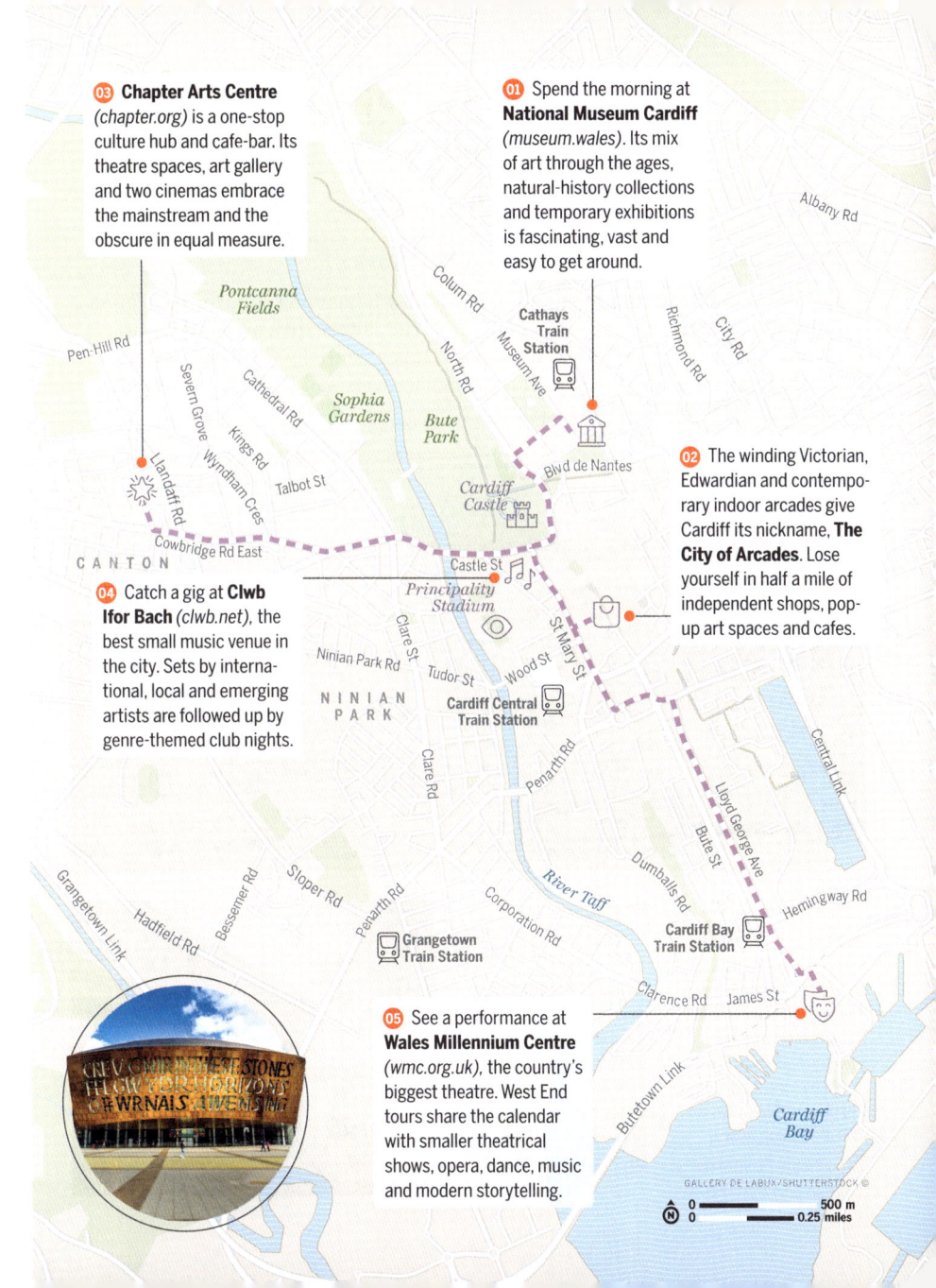

01 Spend the morning at **National Museum Cardiff** (museum.wales). Its mix of art through the ages, natural-history collections and temporary exhibitions is fascinating, vast and easy to get around.

02 The winding Victorian, Edwardian and contemporary indoor arcades give Cardiff its nickname, **The City of Arcades**. Lose yourself in half a mile of independent shops, pop-up art spaces and cafes.

03 Chapter Arts Centre (chapter.org) is a one-stop culture hub and cafe-bar. Its theatre spaces, art gallery and two cinemas embrace the mainstream and the obscure in equal measure.

04 Catch a gig at **Clwb Ifor Bach** (clwb.net), the best small music venue in the city. Sets by international, local and emerging artists are followed up by genre-themed club nights.

05 See a performance at **Wales Millennium Centre** (wmc.org.uk), the country's biggest theatre. West End tours share the calendar with smaller theatrical shows, opera, dance, music and modern storytelling.

GALLERY DE LABUX/SHUTTERSTOCK ©

0 — 500 m
0 — 0.25 miles

38

Over the River
TAFF

MULTICULTURAL FOOD | PARKS | INDEPENDENT SHOPS

Cross the River Taff to enter Cardiff's most happening suburb: Pontcanna. A breeding ground for star chefs, small breweries, alternative arts and nature, it's a hub of creativity and multiculturalism. It is essentially the upmarket part of an area known as Canton, which is grungy in parts and a treasure trove of small businesses and eateries.

How to

Getting around Pontcanna is close to the city centre. You can reach it on foot via Castle St then Cathedral Rd, but the walk through Bute Park is much more scenic. Check *cardiffbus.com* for information on buses.

Two wheels Explore on a rented bike from **Pedal Power** *(cardiffpedal power.org)* in Pontcanna Fields and Cardiff Bay.

Dress code During the day, things are casual in the eateries. By night, some restaurants and their customers smarten up for the occasion. Somewhere in the middle, smart casual, is safest.

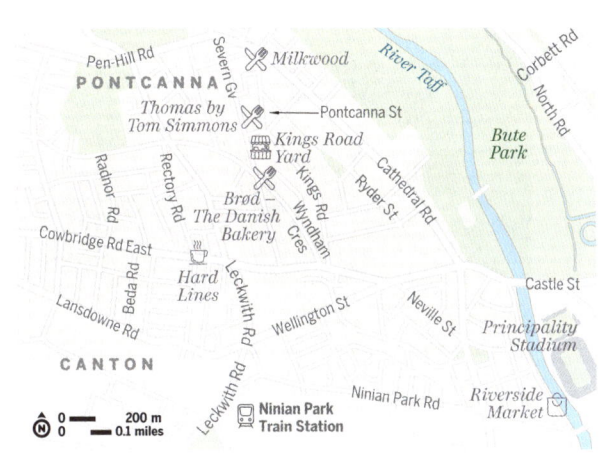

Top left Bute Park
Bottom left Riverside Market

Lungs of the city The suburban edge of Cardiff city centre is softened by **Bute Park**. With 57 hectares of green expanses, woodland, wildflowers and river life, it's a peaceful haven that hushes the capital's buzz. Take the **Champion Tree Trail** – a route that showcases the highest number of 'champion trees' (the tallest or broadest of their type) in any UK public park – then cross the red bridge by the Summerhouse Cafe kiosk towards Canton.

Capital cuisines Cardiff has had a multicultural population since welcoming workers from over 50 countries in the 1900s to work on the docks. The championing of other cultures is what makes **Pontcanna** the best place to eat in the city, where cafe owners and restaurateurs give inherited recipes a Welsh twist using local produce. **Milkwood** (milkwoodcardiff.com) bistro puts imaginative global riffs on contemporary Welsh flavours, while **Thomas by Tom Simmons** (thomas-pontcanna.co.uk) flaunts French-inspired cuisine and local beers on tap, including its own (there's a speakeasy-style cocktail bar on the top floor, too).

Coffee and cake For lazy Sunday cosiness, choose **Brød – The Danish Bakery** (thedanishbakery.co.uk). It's owned by a Danish dough master who dreamt of having a hygge heaven in which to share her country's delights. It'd be wrong not to mention **Hard Lines** (hard-lines.co.uk), the diner run by a Cardiff-born coffee roastery. Baristas sling impeccable espressos from Hard Lines beans, best paired with the irresistible counter treats.

To Market, to Market

Community spirit runs high in Cardiff. People turn out in droves for goods at the weekly markets, perusing the wares of local makers, street-food stalls and allotment keepers.

Riverside Market This large street market is held on Fitzhamon Embankment (opposite the Principality Stadium) every Sunday (10am to 2pm), except on match days. Typical fare includes artisanal cheese, bottles of microbrewery ale and authentic curries. Walk here from Pontcanna via Bute Park. *riversidemarket.org.uk*

Kings Road Yard In Pontcanna itself, Kings Road Yard houses noteworthy permanent food stops and a Saturday morning farmers market, plus other themed markets throughout the year. *kingsroadyard.co.uk*

■ Written with **Helia Phoenix**, writer, DJ, photographer and film-maker who works for Visit Wales. Follow her on Instagram or X @heliaphoenix

Cymru Festivities

A CHRONOLOGICAL SHOWCASE OF WALES' ANNUAL FESTIVITIES

As a patriotic country with a history of myths, legends, community gatherings and merriment, Wales has a suitably packed calendar of events that are celebrated each year. Everyone is welcome to join in or look on – regardless of where they're from.

Left Wooden lovespoons
Centre Wales flags and rugby fans, Cardiff
Right Mari Lwyd

Santes Dwynwen

St Dwynwen, patron saint of lovers, is celebrated on the Welsh alternative to Valentine's Day on 25 January. She has a tragic backstory involving star-crossed lovers, an arranged marriage to the wrong man and transformation into ice, but we spread love by exchanging cards and romantic gifts (like carved wooden lovespoons) and spending time with our loved ones. Some make the pilgrimage to St Dwynwen's Church on Ynys Llanddwyn, Anglesey, an island where Dwynwen set up a convent and lived as a nun.

Dydd Miwsig Cymru

A celebration of Welsh-language music on 5 February, which has a lively scene across the country. On this day, gigs take place in unusual places covering many genres, with lyrics in Welsh.

Six Nations Rugby Championship

Rugby brings everyone together in February to indulge in national pastimes: drinking, making merry, wearing sheep hats and traditional costumes, singing our hearts out and cheering on the boys. The entire nation glues itself to coverage of the matches.

St David's Day

On the national day of Wales (1 March), expect street parades and nods to tradition. Children wear Welsh lady costumes or rugby shirts, Welsh cakes and cawl are consumed en masse, and leeks and daffodils, national emblems of Wales, adorn shirt collars and shop windows. The Welsh flag – Y Ddraig Goch (the Welsh Dragon) – is flown with pride.

International Dylan Thomas Day

This is a celebration day of the life and work of Welsh poet Dylan Thomas, marking the anniversary (14 May) of when *Under Milk Wood* was first read on stage in 1953. Arts organisations, libraries and cultural venues put on events, readings and online activities to acknowledge Thomas' contributions to the world. The Dylan Thomas Centre and the town of Laugharne, where he lived for much of his life, celebrate him all year.

National Eisteddfod

An eisteddfod is a festival that celebrates Welsh literature, music and performance. Held the first week of August, the peripatetic National Eisteddfod, the biggest, is a chance to celebrate and promote the past, present and future of the Welsh language across multiple art forms. There's music, singing, dancing, drama and workshops, with events for all the family. Thousands of young people from around Wales participate in poetry and dance competitions, while others aim for arts and crafts prizes.

Mari Lwyd

Probably the most bizarre Welsh tradition is that of Mari Lwyd (late December and early January), meaning 'grey mare' or 'grey Mary'. A horse's skull is put on a pole that's decorated with Celtic runic symbols, bells and ribbons. The skull is carried by a crowd who go from door to door around the village or town. At each house, the Mari and its entourage chant and sing, then the homeowners chant back. Eventually Mari is allowed inside, where she brings good luck for the new year. This ancient pagan tradition is still going strong in parts of Wales, and even in other parts of the world, where Mari Lwyd pub crawls are enjoying an explosion in popularity.

National Symbols

Daffodil A yellow flower that blooms in early spring, coinciding with St David's Day. It is a symbol of hope and growth for the season.

Leek A root vegetable that looks like an enormous spring onion but tastes sweeter. As far back as the 7th century, rulers ordered their soldiers to wear them for identification purposes.

Lovespoon A handcrafted wooden spoon, traditionally given by a man to the woman they love. Symbols of love are carved into the wood as messages.

Triple harp A harp with three rows of strings, typically played by traditional Welsh folk musicians.

39 The Rooftop OF WALES

MOUNTAINS | LAKES | ADVENTURE

Standing above the rest of Wales, Snowdonia National Park's peaks include the country's highest, Snowdon. Rugged mountains surrounded by dramatic coast, dense forests and tranquil lakes are ready for adventuring, from trampolining in a disused mine to ziplining over slate caverns.

How to

Getting around Driving is easiest: Snowdonia National Park is well connected to motorways and A roads, which become minor further in. Alternatively, Conwy Valley Line railway connects Snowdonia National Park to Betws-y-Coed and Blaenau Ffestiniog. Use local taxi services to go further afield.

When to go Routes are busiest in summer, less crowded but rainy in spring and autumn, and often treacherous in winter.

Safety Before walking Snowdonia's peaks, check the **Llanberis Mountain Rescue** (*llmrt.org*) website for safety advice.

Wild Lake Swimming

Llyn Padarn (Llanberis; pictured) Large shallow lake with panoramic views, suiting most abilities.

Llyn Dinas (Beddgelert) Tranquil glass-clear lake, backed by ancient trees and mountains.

Llyn y Foel (Moel Siabod) Glorious sub-summit lake off the trail towards the craggy peak of Moel Siabod.

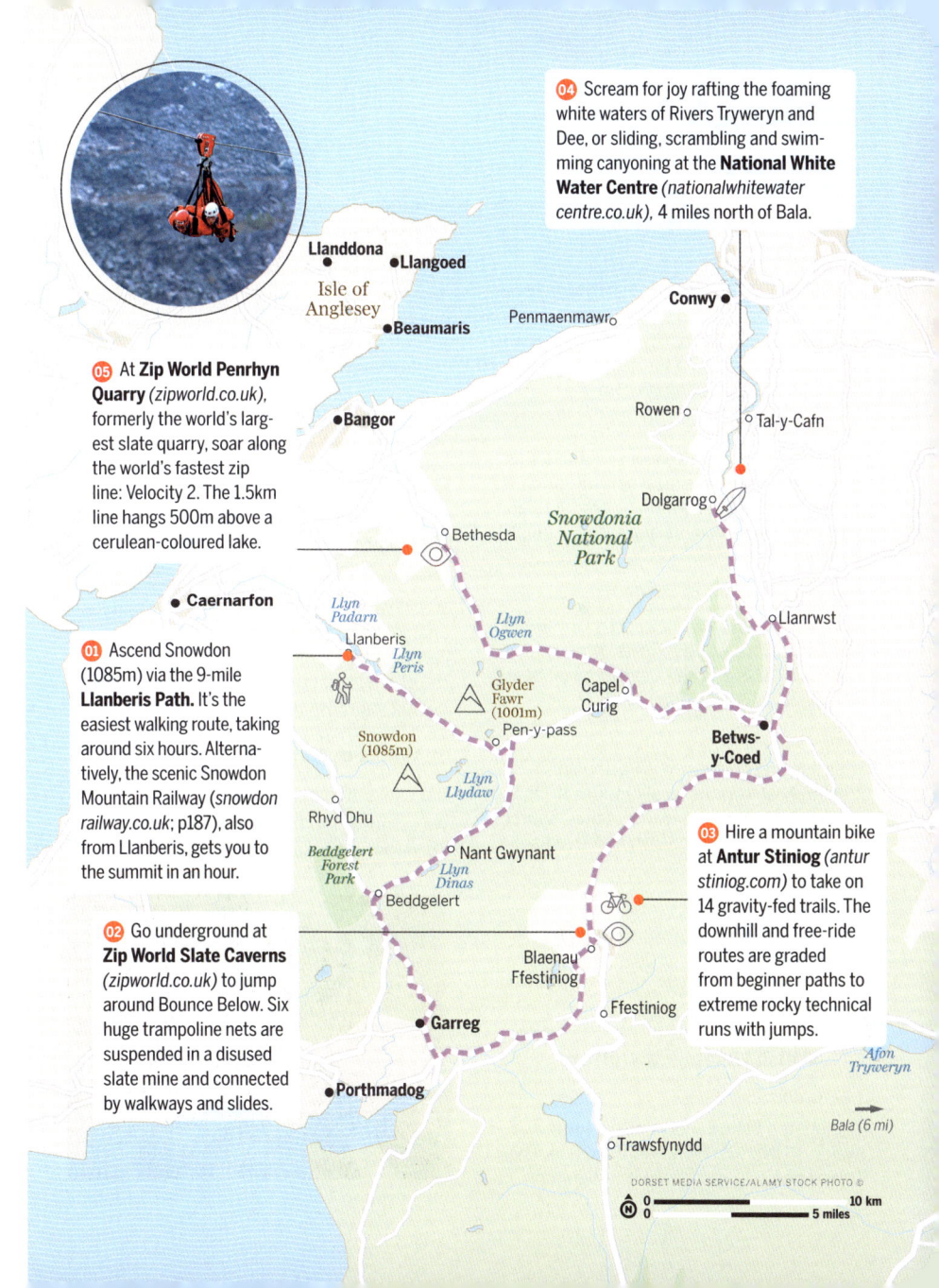

04 Scream for joy rafting the foaming white waters of Rivers Tryweryn and Dee, or sliding, scrambling and swimming canyoning at the **National White Water Centre** (nationalwhitewatercentre.co.uk), 4 miles north of Bala.

05 At **Zip World Penrhyn Quarry** (zipworld.co.uk), formerly the world's largest slate quarry, soar along the world's fastest zip line: Velocity 2. The 1.5km line hangs 500m above a cerulean-coloured lake.

01 Ascend Snowdon (1085m) via the 9-mile **Llanberis Path.** It's the easiest walking route, taking around six hours. Alternatively, the scenic Snowdon Mountain Railway (snowdonrailway.co.uk; p187), also from Llanberis, gets you to the summit in an hour.

02 Go underground at **Zip World Slate Caverns** (zipworld.co.uk) to jump around Bounce Below. Six huge trampoline nets are suspended in a disused slate mine and connected by walkways and slides.

03 Hire a mountain bike at **Antur Stiniog** (antur stiniog.com) to take on 14 gravity-fed trails. The downhill and free-ride routes are graded from beginner paths to extreme rocky technical runs with jumps.

Listings

BEST OF THE REST

🍴 Local Food Experiences

Halen Môn
On the Menai Strait banks, Halen Môn converts charcoal-filtered seawater into premium salt flakes. Tour the facility to discover the story and process behind the seasoning, followed by a salt tasting. *halenmon.com*

Penderyn Distillery
Based in the Brecon Beacons foothills, this whisky distillery uses local natural spring water to make its award-winning products. Join a tour for facts, insights and whisky sampling. *penderyn.wales*

Tiny Rebel Cardiff
The original bar from Newport's Tiny Rebel Brewery, with around 10 of its own beers on tap from casks and kegs, lots of guest beers and a bar menu. *tinyrebel.co.uk*

The Shed
This fish and chip bistro in Porthgain, Pembrokeshire, puts local produce front and centre. Every day, the team catches, sources and serves its own local fish and shellfish. *theshedporthgain.co.uk*

Welsh Venison Centre
Watch deer and sheep graze the fields from the cafe terrace, while munching on a gourmet venison burger topped with Welsh cheddar. *beaconsfarmshop.co.uk*

📖 Welsh Heritage & Culture

Llechwedd Slate Mines
Explore the Slate Landscape of Northwest Wales, a UNESCO World Heritage Site. The Deep Mine Tour guides you through the cavernous belly of the world's former slate capital. *zipworld.co.uk*

Dylan Thomas' Laugharne
Trace the story of one of Wales' greatest poets, Dylan Thomas. Stroll from his Boathouse to his writing shed, his old watering hole (Brown's Hotel), his statue and his grave.

St Fagans National History Museum
Wander through time at this open-air museum of Welsh life. Over 40 reconstructed buildings tell Wales' history brick-by-brick, from a terrace of miners' houses to a grand manor house. *museum.wales/stfagans*

Melin Tregwynt
Welsh wool is woven into traditional blankets, cushions and more in this centuries-old Pembrokeshire mill. Watch workers create the characteristic patterns on looms before buying your own piece. *melintregwynt.co.uk*

⛰ Walks in Nature

National Botanic Garden of Wales
Wales' answer to the Eden Project (p110) in Cornwall has millions of plants across nearly

Melin Tregwynt

243 hectares. Lord Foster's glasshouse, the British Bird of Prey Centre and themed gardens punctuate Carmarthenshire's wild vistas. *botanicgarden.wales*

Merthyr Mawr National Nature Reserve

This extensive dune system has over 324 hectares of sand-covered limestone cliffs, grasslands, marshlands, woods and a beach. Walk the Big Dipper dune, the second largest of its kind in Europe.

Roath Park

Shut out the capital's sounds with a peaceful walk around Roath's rose gardens, botanical conservatory, wooded river and large lake, complete with a brighter-than-white lighthouse and ice-cream kiosks.

Welsh Wildlife Centre

Nature flourishes at the Wildlife Trust's Welsh HQ. Four trails loop around the Teifi Marsh Nature Reserve, dotted with bird hides and riverside otter-spotting areas. Hire binoculars from the shop. *welshwildlife.org*

Noteworthy Towns

Hay-on-Wye

A haven for bookworms and culture-obsessed bargain hunters, this pretty bookshop-lined border town is known as the Town of Books. It's busiest during the annual Hay Festival of literature in late May/early June.

Penarth

Across Cardiff Bay Barrage lies this elegant seaside town, with a fossil-housing pebble beach, pastel-toned esplanade buildings, Victorian pier and blooming parks.

Llandudno

The largest seaside resort in Wales, Llandudno has lured staycationers for decades. Highlights include Wales' longest pier (jutting 700m into the sea) and epic views from the Great Orme headland.

Merthyr Mawr National Nature Reserve

Aberystwyth

'Aber', as it's known, is a university town on the coast of west Wales. Independent shops and delis sit behind the mile-long Victorian promenade and the country's oldest pier, where starlings nest.

Scenic Train Rides

Ffestiniog and Welsh Highland Railways

The world's oldest independent railway company runs a 13.5-mile journey from Porthmadog harbour to Blaenau Ffestiniog, travelling alongside mountains, fields, forests, lakes, waterfalls and slate mines. Allow three hours. *festrail.co.uk*

Snowdon Mountain Railway

With no roads to the summit, this glorious route is the only transport up Snowdon unless you hoof it. The scenery as you ascend is spectacular: ancient forests, a waterfall, lakes and mountains. *snowdonrailway.co.uk*

Bala Lake Railway

This hour-long round trip through Snowdonia National Park begins in Llanuwchllyn village. It passes through other charming little villages, with the expansive Bala Lake in view most of the time. *bala-lake-railway.co.uk*

Brecon Mountain Railway

Let the train do the trekking through Brecon Beacons National Park. It passes quarries and ruins, runs along the entire length of Taf Fechan Reservoir then climbs up to Torpantau. *bmr.wales*

Welshpool and Llanfair Light Railway

Connecting the market town of Welshpool to Llanfair Caereinion, this narrow-gauge steam railway has carriages with open balconies so passengers can watch the rolling hills of Mid-Wales unfold. *wllr.org.uk*

Back to Nature Experiences

Jacob Sheep Trekking

Take a woolly friend for a walk at this organic farm slung high in the hills of the Brecon Beacons. Tip: treats work! *sheeptrekking.co.uk*

St Brides Spa Hotel

The treatment rooms and infinity pool at this clifftop hotel overlook Saundersfoot harbour and long beach. Float away as masseurs use organic marine-sourced products that echo the seaside location. *stbridesspahotel.com*

Wye Valley Forest Bathing

Be led by a trained forest guide for a three- to four-hour Shinrin Yoku (forest bathing) session in the magical Wye Valley. Walking mindfully through the lush, rain-washed woodland of Hill Farm in Tintern helps you reconnect with nature and find calm. *forestretreats.co.uk*

Really Wild

Feel the cold sea slap your ankles as you comb rock pools for edible (and delicious) seaweeds and more on a guided foraging walk with Really Wild in St Davids. *reallywildemporium.co.uk*

By the Wye

On the banks of the River Wye, this eco-minded escape takes glamping to a whole new luxury level, with treetop safari tents, fire pits and river-facing decks. *bythewye.uk*

Coffee, Bakes & Sweet Treats

Coaltown Coffee Roastery £

One of Wales' biggest coffee producers, Coaltown has its roastery in Ammanford, a former mining town. Watch coffee being prepped and packed while sampling roasts in the bustling on-site cafe. *coaltowncoffee.co.uk*

Bakestones £

Watch a team of bakers mix, knead, roll and griddle-cook traditional Welsh cakes at this Cardiff Market stall. If you like sweet raisin treats, satisfaction is guaranteed. *bakestoneswales.co.uk*

Crwst £

With its original cafe in Cardigan and a smaller set-up at Poppit Sands, Crwst serves hearty brunches, fresh loaves and moreish doughnuts including lemon meringue, apple crumble and salted caramel specials. *crwst.cymru*

MamGu Welshcakes £

This cafe in Solva serves traditional and alternative Welsh cakes hot off the griddle. Order a selection of sweet, savoury, vegan or gluten-free Welsh cakes to dine in or to go. *mamguwelshcakes.com*

Snowdon Mountain Railway (p187)

Providero £

There are two branches of this Llandudno coffee shop, affectionately known as BigProv and LittleProv. Both pull brilliant espressos and serve nourishing savoury light bites and sweet bakes. *providero.co.uk*

Alex Gooch £

Expert plant-based baker Alex Gooch's flagship Cardiff cafe is packed with delicious baked treats. Expect loaded focaccia, pizza slices, berry-topped French toast and amazing pastries. *alexgoochbaker.com*

🌱 Green Living

Vegetarian Food Studio £

Family-owned Indian and pan-Asian restaurant cooking up the best curries in Cardiff, all of which are vegetarian or vegan. The menu is huge, with everything from dosas to *kulfi* (Indian ice cream). *vegetarianfoodstudio.uk*

Crumbs £

Cardiff's longest-running vegetarian cafe is a landmark in the city's arcades. Heaped wooden bowls of wholesome salads are the speciality, along with freshly prepared quiches, chilli and soups. *crumbskitchencardiff.co.uk*

The Bug Farm & Grub Kitchen £

Marvel at bugs in the museum and gardens at this eco-minded St Davids farm surrounded by wildflower meadows, then feast on the food of the future (organic grub spiced up with edible insects). *thebugfarm.co.uk*

Annwn £££

From wild garlic preserved in its life cycle to fermented crab apple ice, forager Matt Powell revives ancient Welsh recipes in a 10-course feast at his Michelin green-starred restaurant in Narberth. *annwnrestaurant.co.uk*

Caws Cenarth

Little Green Refills

This treasure trove is run by two women encouraging Abergavenny to reduce plastic waste. It's divided into homeware, toiletry refills, food refills and a cafe, with locally made gifts scattered throughout.

💎 Upmarket Souvenirs

Welsh Lavender

Thousands of lavender plants purple the hillsides at this converted sheep farm in Builth Wells. In summer see how the distillery extracts essential oils from them to create lavender products, then go for a picnic and wild swim.

The Lovespoon Gallery

This specialist shop and gallery in the Mumbles has the largest selection of hand-carved Welsh lovespoons (p183), with over 300 designs. Learn about the symbolism and craft behind this traditional item. *welshlovespoon.com*

Caws Cenarth

Stick your nose into the world of Welsh artisanal cheese at Caws Cenarth Dairy in Lancych, Carmarthenshire. Watch the cheese-making process before tasting the traditional and modern cheeses on sale. *cawscenarth.co.uk*

SOUTH SCOTLAND

HISTORY | CULTURE | FOOD

- **Trip Builder** (p192)
- **Practicalities** (p194)
- **Green Glasgow** (p196)
- **Witches & Wizards** (p198)
- **The Festival City** (p200)
- **Secret Kintyre** (p202)
- **South West Coastal 300** (p204)
- **Biking the 7Stanes** (p206)
- **Seeking Walter Scott** (p208)
- **Mackintosh's Glasgow** (p210)
- **Listings** (p212)

SOUTH SCOTLAND
Trip Builder

Road trip Kintyre, Scotland's next big food and drink destination (p202)
🚗 3 hr from Glasgow

Applaud the genius of design godfather Charles Rennie Mackintosh in Glasgow (p210)
🚶 1 day on foot

Explore national bard Robert Burns' backyard in Ayrshire (p204)
🚆 1 hr from Glasgow

This is Scotland in all its show-stopping 21st-century glory. From crumpled hills to the cove-nibbled coastline, the south hides the country's most underrated adventures and is home to evocative castles, spirit-raising distilleries, once-in-a-lifetime beaches and unforgettable cities.

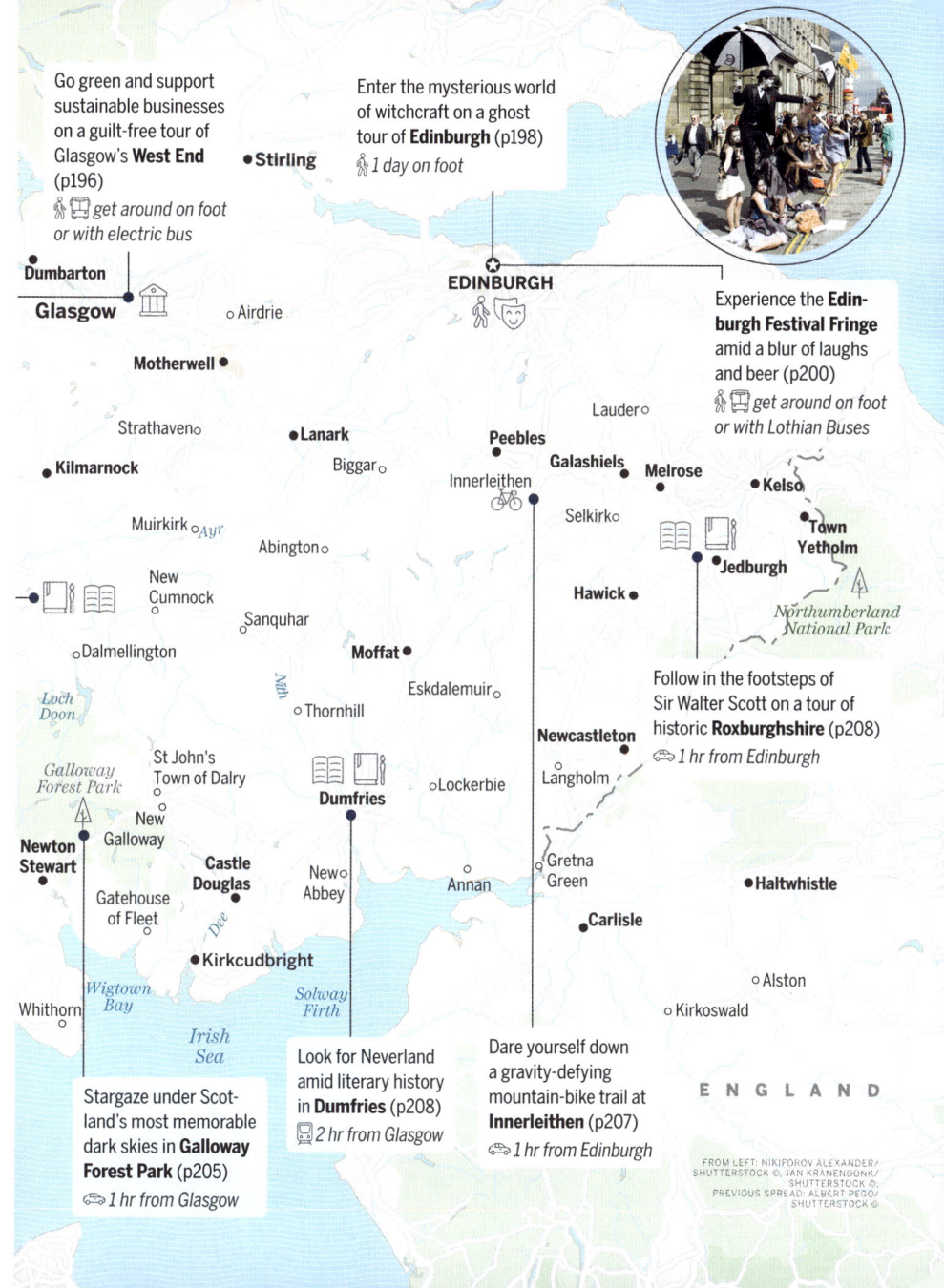

Go green and support sustainable businesses on a guilt-free tour of Glasgow's **West End** (p196)
🚶🚌 *get around on foot or with electric bus*

Enter the mysterious world of witchcraft on a ghost tour of **Edinburgh** (p198)
🚶 *1 day on foot*

Experience the **Edinburgh Festival Fringe** amid a blur of laughs and beer (p200)
🚶🚌 *get around on foot or with Lothian Buses*

Follow in the footsteps of Sir Walter Scott on a tour of historic **Roxburghshire** (p208)
🚗 *1 hr from Edinburgh*

Stargaze under Scotland's most memorable dark skies in **Galloway Forest Park** (p205)
🚗 *1 hr from Glasgow*

Look for Neverland amid literary history in **Dumfries** (p208)
🚆 *2 hr from Glasgow*

Dare yourself down a gravity-defying mountain-bike trail at **Innerleithen** (p207)
🚗 *1 hr from Edinburgh*

FROM LEFT: NIKIFOROV ALEXANDER/SHUTTERSTOCK ©, JAN KRANENDONK/SHUTTERSTOCK ©, PREVIOUS SPREAD: ALBERT PEGO/SHUTTERSTOCK ©

Practicalities

ARRIVING

Edinburgh and Glasgow Home to the country's largest international airports, Scotland's two largest cities are your most likely entry points. Both have centrally located train stations, plus bus connections covering onward travel across the south.

Ayrshire The south's only other airport is Prestwick Airport. The towns of Ardrossan, Largs, Wemyss Bay and Gourock offer ferry connections to the southern islands and Cowal Peninsula.

WHEN TO GO

JAN–MAR
Darker days, cold and often snowy. Highlights are Burns Night (25 Jan) and Glasgow's Celtic Connections folk festival.

APR–JUN
Ideal for walking, birdwatching and bikepacking. May is often the sunniest month. Midge-free.

JUL–SEP
The height of tourist season. Edinburgh packs out in August.

OCT–DEC
Ideal for leaf-peeping in the Borders. Galloway's dark skies are at their clearest.

HOW MUCH FOR A

Edinburgh bus ticket £2

Pint of craft lager £5

Burns Night haggis £15

GETTING AROUND

Car Barring the Central Belt of Edinburgh and Glasgow, this is the realm of narrow, quiet roads, making south Scotland ripe for a slow-paced road trip. These are popular cycling roads, so proper driving etiquette is mandatory.

Public transport ScotRail (scotrail.co.uk) runs trains from Glasgow and Edinburgh to all main towns and cities, including Ayr, Stranraer, Dumfries and Dunbar. Travel by bus with **Citylink** (citylink.co.uk), **Lothian Buses** (lothianbuses.com), **First Bus** (firstbus.co.uk), **Stagecoach** (stagecoachbus.com) and smaller local operators. Use route planner **Traveline** (travelinescotland.co.uk) to plot journeys.

Ferry CalMac (calmac.co.uk) runs car and passenger ferries from the west coast to the islands of Cumbrae and Arran and for onward connections to Kintyre and the Southern Hebrides. Foot passengers and vehicles should book in advance.

EATING & DRINKING

Edinburgh and Glasgow are the most memorable places to eat in the country, with the lion's share of Michelin-star restaurants and thriving food and drink scenes for vegetarians, vegans, coffee addicts and craft beer drinkers. Try haggis (pictured top), on its own, as a burger or pakora, or one that is entirely plant-based; sample artisanal cheese, a speciality in Ayrshire and Galloway; or go global at a farmers market. Southern Scotland is the home of the berry, so in summer go strawberry (pictured bottom) and raspberry picking in the Borders. Drinks-wise, the Lowland distilleries are often overlooked – don't make the same mistake.

Best for pub grub
The Bonnie Badger, Gullane (p213)

Must-try gin
Beinn an Tuirc Distillers, Kintyre (p203)

CONNECT & FIND YOUR WAY

Wi-fi Widespread in cities with free hot spots. Found in all accommodation, most pubs, restaurants and attractions. In rural southern Scotland, particularly around Galloway's interior, connection speed can be nonexistent.

Navigation Both Edinburgh and Glasgow are perfect for wandering, while the south is well served by road signs and public transport route maps.

DISCOUNT SIGHTSEEING

Save money when exploring the Scottish capital with the **Edinburgh City Pass** (edinburgh citypass.com). Valid for one, two or three days, including airport transfers, bus travel and admission to some attractions. Prices from £55.

WHERE TO STAY

The south of Scotland has accommodation for all tastes and budgets, from the country's swankiest five-star boutiques to refurbished lighthouses and golf resorts.

Place	Pros/Cons
Edinburgh	Castle stays, Gothic guesthouses, hilltop perches, golf hotels and other memorable accommodation options; can be expensive, particularly in August and around Hogmanay (New Year).
Glasgow	Chock-full of branded hotels and boutique boltholes, with the West End the preferred option for a like-a-local experience.
North Berwick	Seaside outpost with great seafood, golf, beaches, bike routes and seafront holiday cottages.
Ayrshire Coast	Atlantic beaches and world-class golf resorts give Ayr and its surrounding towns a Scottish riviera feel in summer.

MONEY

Cards are widely accepted, but it's wise to carry cash when away from tourist centres. Tips of 10% to 15% are customary and often included on the bill in the big cities. Edinburgh is noticeably more expensive than the rest of the country.

40 Green GLASGOW

CULTURE | FOOD | SUSTAINABILITY

Glasgow's nickname 'Dear Green Place' is the first clue that Scotland's largest city means business when it comes to sustainability and guilt-free ecotourism. Leaving its once post-industrial image in the distant past, the host city of COP26 – the 2021 UN Climate Change Conference – is now home to vegan cafes, electric buses, walking tours and parklands galore.

How to

Getting around Glasgow is served by electric bus. Local operator First Bus has installed 160 charging points – the UK's largest electric vehicle charging hub – and replaced half its fleet with green machines.

When to go Visit between October and April to support businesses outside of summer. Avoid public holidays and weekends.

Top tip For a green night out, visit **SWG3** (*swg3.tv*). Its latest trick is to power the nightclub and venue using body heat from clubbers and gig-goers.

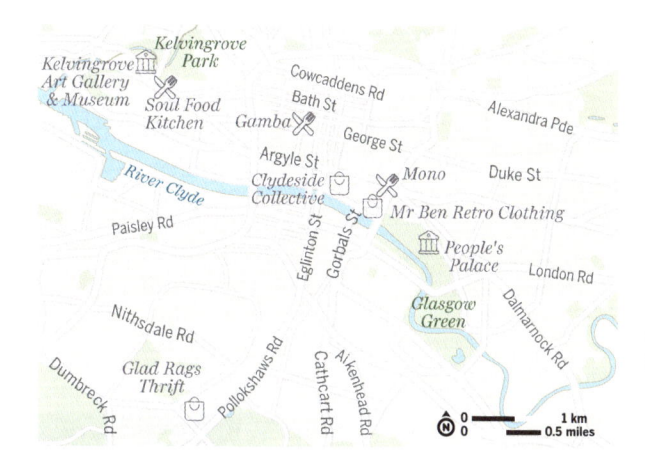

Park life Green spaces of all shapes and sizes provide urban lungs for Glaswegians and there are more than 90 parks scattered around the city. Most visitors will savour a stroll through the West End's **Kelvingrove Park**, with its Victorian-era bandstand and the world-class **Kelvingrove Art Gallery & Museum**. East of the centre there is also beloved Glasgow Green, home to the historic **People's Palace** glasshouse (currently closed for renovation and expected to reopen in 2027).

Walk this way Glaswegians take everything in their stride and there is no better way to explore the city than on a walking tour. **Glasgow Music City Tours** (glasgowmusiccitytours.com) is run by Scotland's leading music critics and the tours reveal the city's musical secrets step by step, while the **City Centre Mural Trail** (citycentremuraltrail.co.uk) shows how decaying industrial lots, underpasses and gable end walls have been repurposed with new meaning. Delving further into the West End and Southside, the **Green Route** maps a trail to 12 sustainable businesses.

Eat better Glasgow is regularly dubbed the vegan capital of the UK and with good reason. There are dozens of places to delve into the plant-based food scene and memorable kitchens include **Soul Food Kitchen** (soulfoodkitchen.co.uk) in trendsetting Finnieston, with its 'soul bowls' and vegan raw cakes. Another top stop is **Mono** (monocafebar.com), a hybrid of vegan cafe, record store and gig venue. Alternatively, for a sustainable seafood feast of local-sourced, non-endangered species, head to the award-winning **Gamba** (gamba.co.uk).

Top left Kelvingrove Park
Bottom left Mr Ben Retro Clothing

Forever Fashion

Going the extra mile to be green in Glasgow is easy if you're a dedicated follower of fashion. There are dozens of thrift stores and vintage shops where yesterday's high street must-haves are given a second lease of life.

Start by browsing the vintage wares at **Mr Ben Retro Clothing** (mrbenretroclothing.com) on Kings Ct in the Merchant City, then head to the St Enoch Centre to support local artists and designers at the **Clydeside Collective**.

Afterwards, bus south across the Clyde to Queen's Park to check out indie shops selling recycled, upcycled and vintage garb, including not-for-profit **Glad Rags Thrift** (thegladcafe.co.uk), and have lunch in its nicely chilled cafe.

41 Witches & WIZARDS

CULTURE | HISTORY | TOURS

Picture a city with a fairy-tale castle, crooked tollbooths, hair-raising graveyards and spooky subterranean alleyways where tales of witchcraft are rife and it's not hard to think of Edinburgh. This is Britain at its most fantastic – and far-fetched – and as you discover its stories you'll understand why the city was designated the world's first UNESCO City of Literature.

How to

Getting around Invest in some comfy shoes. Edinburgh is born for wandering by foot and there is a world of streets, steps and alleys to discover. Or invest in a Lothian Buses day ticket (£5).

When to go To avoid the worst of the crowds come between February and May or after the **Edinburgh Festival Fringe** *(edfringe.com)* in September.

Take a break Follow the Royal Mile from the Esplanade to lunch at **The Witchery** *(thewitchery.com)*, an atmospheric restaurant at the castle gates with the candlelit romance of a Gothic novel.

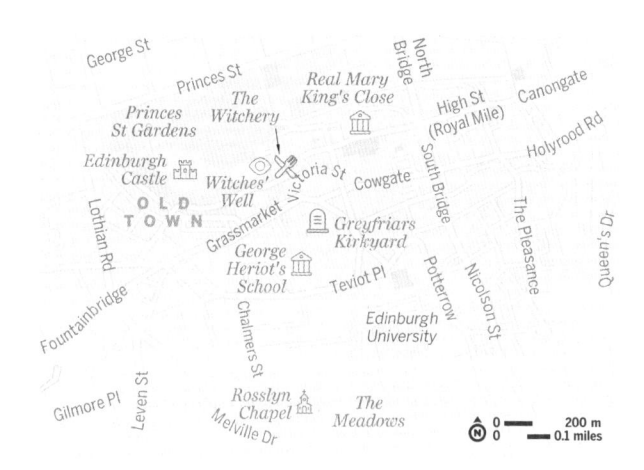

Top left Real Mary King's Close
Bottom left Witches' Well

Dark magic Start the day at **Edinburgh Castle** (edinburgh castle.scot), which has played a pivotal role in Scottish history, both as a royal residence and as a military stronghold. It was also here that hundreds of women were convicted of witchcraft and burnt at the stake in one of the capital's darkest chapters. Make a point of seeking out the **Witches' Well**, a fountain that pays tribute to those executed between the 15th and 18th centuries.

Fact or fiction? Harry Potter author and local resident JK Rowling took inspiration for many of the places in her wizard world from her adopted home and it's not hard to see Hogwarts when looking at the 17th-century **George Heriot's School** or Diagon Alley when window-shopping on cobblestoned **Victoria Street**.

Night frights Another place intrinsically connected to the Harry Potter myth is **Greyfriars Kirkyard** (greyfriarskirk.com), where grave-spotting is serious business. Look for the headstones of the books' most memorable characters – the Potter family, Moody, McGonagall and Riddle – then scare yourself learning the story of the cemetery's supposed Mackenzie Poltergeist.

Go underground While the Edinburgh Dungeon offers up touristy kitsch, far better are tours of **Real Mary King's Close** (realmarykingsclose.com), a dimly lit subterranean warren of once-plagued streets. The preserved 17th-century attraction is a time capsule of Edinburgh and its visceral history will grab you more than anything that goes bump in the night.

Celebrity Chapel

Few places of worship are as mysterious as **Rosslyn Chapel** (rosslynchapel. com), located 45 minutes south of Edinburgh by bus. A sanctuary for the faithful since 1446, the chapel took on a second life as a 'celebrity' church following its climactic role in Dan Brown's The Da Vinci Code. Try and unpick the meaning of the 200-plus keystone carvings that cover the nave, apse and altar, then head down into the crypt to see the supposed final resting place of Mary Magdalene.

The Festival City

THE WORLD'S LARGEST ARTS FESTIVAL

Festivals don't get bigger – or more bizarre – than the Edinburgh Festival Fringe. Held every year in August and with a mind-boggling number of shows, the monthlong carnival infiltrates every aspect of city life. From theatres and comedy clubs to mountain summits and public toilets, it maximises every space to turn the city upside down for art's sake.

Left Half Price Hut on the Mound
Centre Gilded Balloon
Right Assembly

The first thing you need to know about the Edinburgh Festival Fringe is you'll never understand it. Don't even try. In 2019, before the COVID-19 pandemic hit, the programme delivered more than 3800 shows, the most in its 75-year history, including some 1900 premieres and 55,000-odd performances across more than 320 venues. The numbers don't stop there: in excess of three million tickets were sold, underlining the Fringe's position as the world's largest celebration of the arts. More than this, it was also the catalyst for other festivals around the world, namely the Adelaide and Edmonton fringes. Phew, it's a lot to take in.

The Beginning

When it started back in 1947, the festival was little more than a ragbag collective of eight theatre companies hoping to impress Edinburgh's typically hard-to-please audience. The inaugural programme pitched the event as 'a platform for the flowering of the human spirit', and that thread still runs through the festival's philosophy today. But by anyone's measure, the size and scale of it is something else entirely. Don't be surprised to see genre-bending acts such as swearing puppets or zombified drag queens. There might be a performance staged in a chicken pen, or a rereading of Dostoyevsky in a circus big top.

Making a Plan

To feel in tune with the festival vibe, it's important to stay longer than you think you'll need. One day is lunacy, two days not enough, three days a good start. Plus, if you've never been to Edinburgh before, you'll want to marry time at the festival with a couple of guidebook must-dos. And then there are the potential parties and subsequent hangovers to consider. All venues serve alcohol from before midday and the city extends its licensing laws to let venues sell locally produced beer and whisky late into the night.

With so much to consider, knowing the correct strategy is essential. Buy all your tickets in advance *(tickets.edfringe.com)* and you'll miss the freedom of spontaneity. Don't and you'll find everything you want to see has sold out; by the second and third week, tickets for the critics' picks are gold dust. Instead, do as locals do and tackle your days with a half-baked plan: line up a brief schedule of shows at some of the big four venues – Assembly, Pleasance, Gilded Balloon and Udderbelly – then see how the mood takes you during the rest of your time, aided by word of mouth and reviews in the newspapers. Also, bear in mind the Half Price Hut on The Mound for last-minute seats and on-the-spot recommendations.

> To feel in tune with the festival vibe, it's important to stay longer than you think you'll need. One day is lunacy, two days not enough, three days a good start.

A Perfect Day

For the quintessential Fringe day, turn up by lunchtime, consider a few drinks in a beer garden on George Sq or at the Pleasance Courtyard, then gamble on the unknown. In previous years, you could have seen the unheard-of Stephen Fry, Alan Rickman, Robin Williams, Trevor Noah, Emma Thompson or Billy Connolly before they were famous – and for less than £5.

An Actor's Guide

The festival is incredible and a world-renowned experience. Everywhere turns into a theatre. It could be someone's car, a telephone box or the back of the pub. You can see shows nearly 24 hours a day, meet friends, grab drinks, see more shows. It makes for a long day of seeing performances that you'd never imagine seeing, but it's a real discovery. I once saw an eight-hour German version of *Hamlet* with a female lead and subtitles. The first play I did was at the Traverse and that kickstarted my career. Today the Traverse Bar is still the place to go for performers.

■ **By Sam Heughan,** *actor and star of* Outlander, *@SamHeughan*

42 Secret KINTYRE

FOOD | TRADITIONS | ROAD TRIP

Kintyre – so often dubbed Scotland's longest cul-de-sac – remains a secret to most Scots: your satnav won't bring you, the locals say. A road trip here is a slow jaunt through the Scotland you never knew existed, offering the best of the country in microcosm, with 66 miles of sandy beaches, seafood huts and seductive distilleries.

How to

Getting here and around Kintyre is 130 miles from Glasgow and has one looping circuit road that sticks to the coast. With public transport a rarity, touring by car or bike are both wonderful options.

When to go Accommodation is limited, so avoid the peninsula's peak season by visiting in late spring or early autumn.

Top tip Music lovers shouldn't miss Saddell Bay, where former Campbeltown resident Paul McCartney was inspired to write megahit 'Mull of Kintyre'.

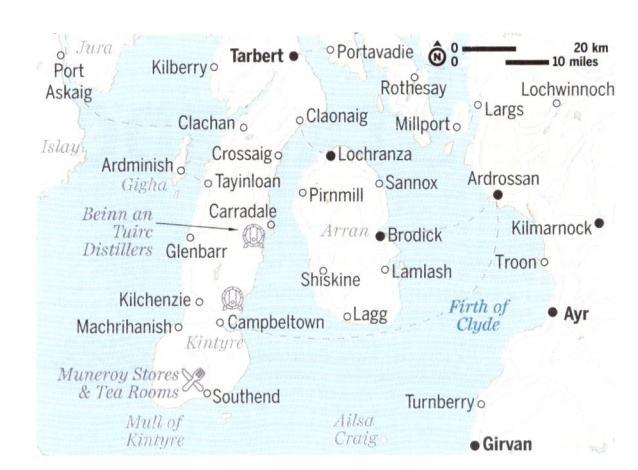

Top left Machrihanish
Bottom left Whisky barrels, Springbank

Local spirit Overlooking the peninsula's eastern shore near **Carradale**, **Beinn an Tuirc Distillers** (kintyregin.com) occupies a former piggery next to Torrisdale Castle and produces world-class spirits. Kintyre Gin is made here using Iceland moss and sheep's sorrel, both of which flourish on the surrounding estate, and there's a gin school with superlative views out to Arran's granite mountains. Further south, **Campbeltown** is home to **Glen Scotia** (glenscotia.com) and **Springbank** (springbank.scot), two creaky distilleries in the heart of what was once the world's whisky capital. Afterwards, visit the dedicated whisky bar at **Ardshiel Hotel** for a mind-boggling selection of drams.

Seafood heaven Watch sides of salmon, mussels and halibut being smoked at the **Kintyre Smokehouse** (kintyresmokehouse.com), a traditional smokery in Campbeltown, before stocking up on goodies for a picnic on an Atlantic beach in nearby **Machrihanish**. Further north, take the 20-minute ferry from Tayinloan to the **Isle of Gigha** for lunch with a pinch-yourself view at **The Boathouse** (boathouseongigha.com). Tables are set amid the beach's machair (low-lying grasslands) and the menu is a shuck-fest of oysters and scallops just off the boat.

Sweet treats For guilt-free vegan salted caramels, keep an eye out for Fetcha Chocolates in Campbeltown's cafes, or continue towards the Mull of Kintyre lighthouse for a cake stop at the art deco **Muneroy Stores & Tea Rooms**, where meringues are a speciality.

♫ It's Only Rock 'n' Roll

The song 'Mull of Kintyre' isn't the peninsula's only footnote in musical history. Paul McCartney moved to the peninsula after The Beatles disbanded and wrote 'The Long and Winding Road' while driving the curving east coast road to his High Park Farm in Campbeltown. He was a resident for years here and this was where he brought up his family; the town created the **Lady Linda McCartney Memorial Garden** in tribute to his late partner and Wings bandmate. Elsewhere, Mick Jagger once failed in an attempt to buy the Isle of Gigha. Strange but true.

43 South West COASTAL 300

ROAD TRIP | CULTURE | HISTORY

A 300-mile road trip around the southwest regions of Ayrshire and Galloway reveals countryside, lighthouses and island adventures that most overlook. As you journey around the coast, you'll discover parks, palatial castles and poems that help define the nation.

How to

Getting here and around It's a quick one hour by train or bus from Glasgow to the starting point in Ayr. The road heads south along the coast to the Mull of Galloway, before turning east to Dumfries. A car is recommended.

When to go For quieter roads and clear skies, visit in May, June or September.

Top tip Walks in the south of Scotland don't get much more atmospheric than the hilltop trail connecting Portpatrick with Killantringan Lighthouse and Bay (three hours return).

Read This

Wigtown, south of Newton Stewart, is Scotland's national book town. While it's home to a 10-day literary festival every September and October, the real draw is a dozen bookshops to discover. To immerse yourself in the life of a bookworm, rent **The Open Book**, an apartment with a bookshop that guests need to run during their stay.

01 With its ploughmans' cottages and barley fields, **Alloway** was a fitting birthplace for Scotland's national bard, Robert Burns. There are six sites to visit that bring his story to life, including the **Robert Burns Birthplace Museum**.

02 Overlooking a lovely sandy beach, **Culzean Castle** (nts.org.uk) is a Scottish castle with secrets aplenty. Count hidden follies, secluded coves and a walled garden. Oh, and supposedly seven ghosts – but who's counting?

03 Join a terrific boat trip to the seabird colony of **Ailsa Craig** off the coast of Girvan to see what feels like a million puffins, gannets (pictured), guillemots and razorbills.

04 The road ends abruptly at the almost-mythic **Mull of Galloway**, where lighthouse-topped cliffs (pictured far left) look over to Ireland. Hike the crags, or picnic below on one of the sandy bays of South Rhins.

05 Veer east and inland to explore the wilds of **Galloway Forest Park**, Scotland's largest swathe of forestry and the UK's first designated Dark Sky Park. Book a stargazing night with a ranger.

FROM LEFT: AGEFOTOSTOCK/ALAMY STOCK PHOTO ©; CAROLE MACDONALD/SHUTTERSTOCK ©

Biking the
7STANES

CYCLING | NATURE | ACTIVITIES

Tighten your helmet strap and let gravity set your wheels in motion as you mountain-bike downhill through pine thickets and over log pile obstacles, before jackknifing around chicanes with adrenaline flowing through your veins. This is an everyday feeling when riding at Scotland's seven world-class mountain-biking centres, nicknamed the 7Stanes for short.

How to

Getting here and around The 7Stanes are around one to two hours south of central Scotland by car. The easiest for day trips are Glentress and Innerleithen, which are both one hour from Edinburgh. Advice, info and maps can be found at *forestryandland.gov.scot*.

When to go All year round, but keep an eye on the calendar for mountain-biking championships, including the Enduro World Series in June.

Did you know? 'Stane' is the colloquial Scots word for stone and each of the trail centres is marked by a rock sculpture reflecting a local legend.

Top left Kirroughtree Forest, 7Stanes
Bottom left Biking, near Innerleithen

South Scotland's Best Rides

Besides the 7Stanes, there are many other exhilarating trails in southern Scotland to hit with two wheels.

Go East Lothian Trail (39 miles) A great loop for riders who want to get into adventure cycling, featuring the wonderful coastline of East Lothian and loads of opportunities to stop for local produce.

Raiders' Road Forest Drive (10 miles) An easy way to see more of the Galloway Forest Park's woods and wildlife. Only open to cars from Easter to October, but to cyclists all year.

Capital Trail (153 miles) An award-winning, mostly off-road bikepacking loop into the hills of the Borders and back. Suitable for experienced cyclists, but can be also broken up in shorter legs by using the Borders Railway.

■ Recommended by
Markus Stitz, founder of Bikepacking Scotland, @bikepackingscot

For beginners Hidden away near Peebles in the Borders, **Glentress** is the flagship centre of the 7stanes network and is criss-crossed by both easy-on-the-heart trails for beginners and white-knuckle trails for those with experience. Test your skills on the **Blue Route**, a 10-mile thigh-burner with two life-affirming loops through pine forest. For something harder, try the 18-mile **Black Route**, with climbs, descents and all manner of jack-in-the-box surprises.

For families Glentrool might be one of the smaller centres, but it is the gateway to the drama of **Galloway Forest Park**. Those after a slower pace can try **The Glen**, a 4-mile green route around postcard-pretty **Palnagashel Glen**. Elsewhere, bigger kids will be tempted by the **Big Country Route**, a 36-mile full-day journey around sculpted lochs, hills and crowd-free spaces.

For experts You'll need to metaphorically shift up a gear at **Innerleithen**, a leading contender as the best downhill mountain-biking centre in southern Scotland. Pick from five mettle-testing, ultra-black routes, a red-graded cross-country trail and extreme descents only for those who've had their porridge. For somewhere quieter, head to **Newcastleton** – it's the 7Stanes' word-of-mouth secret.

Fuel up Cyclists have as much of an affinity for coffee and cake as they do single-track slopes. Try **Ae Forest Bike Shop & Cafe** north of Dumfries or **Kirroughtree Cafe** near Newton Stewart. Both are a cupcake's throw from the nearest mountain-bike trail.

45 Seeking Walter SCOTT

CULTURE | HISTORY | ACTIVITIES

Sir Walter Scott, author of *Rob Roy* and *Ivanhoe,* was a historical novelist, poet and treasure hunter, but he was also the 'father' of Scottish tourism, inspiring the first travellers to tour his home region, Roxburghshire in the Borders, in the early 19th century. Come for the stories but stay for the baronial mansions, abbeys and heathery hills.

How to

Getting here and around The Borders is 25 to 50 miles south of Edinburgh and a delight to explore on two wheels. Alternatively, ride the scenic Borders Railway from Edinburgh to Tweedbank and take local bus connections from there.

When to go Gardens, forests and riverbanks are a showstopping blaze of red and gold in autumn.

Have a dram The Borders is hardly renowned for whisky production, but Hawick's newfangled **Borders Distillery** *(thebordersdistillery.com)* is the first single malt distiller in the southeast since 1837.

Finding Neverland

Like Walter Scott, *Peter Pan* author JM Barrie also plumbed his early life in southern Scotland for inspiration for his most famous works. One particular location of note is Moat Brae in **Dumfries**, which has been reimagined as the **National Centre for Children's Literature & Storytelling** (pictured). The author credited the house and garden as the inspiration for Neverland and it's not hard to picture the Lost Boys causing mischief amid the thickets of trees and on the pirate ship.

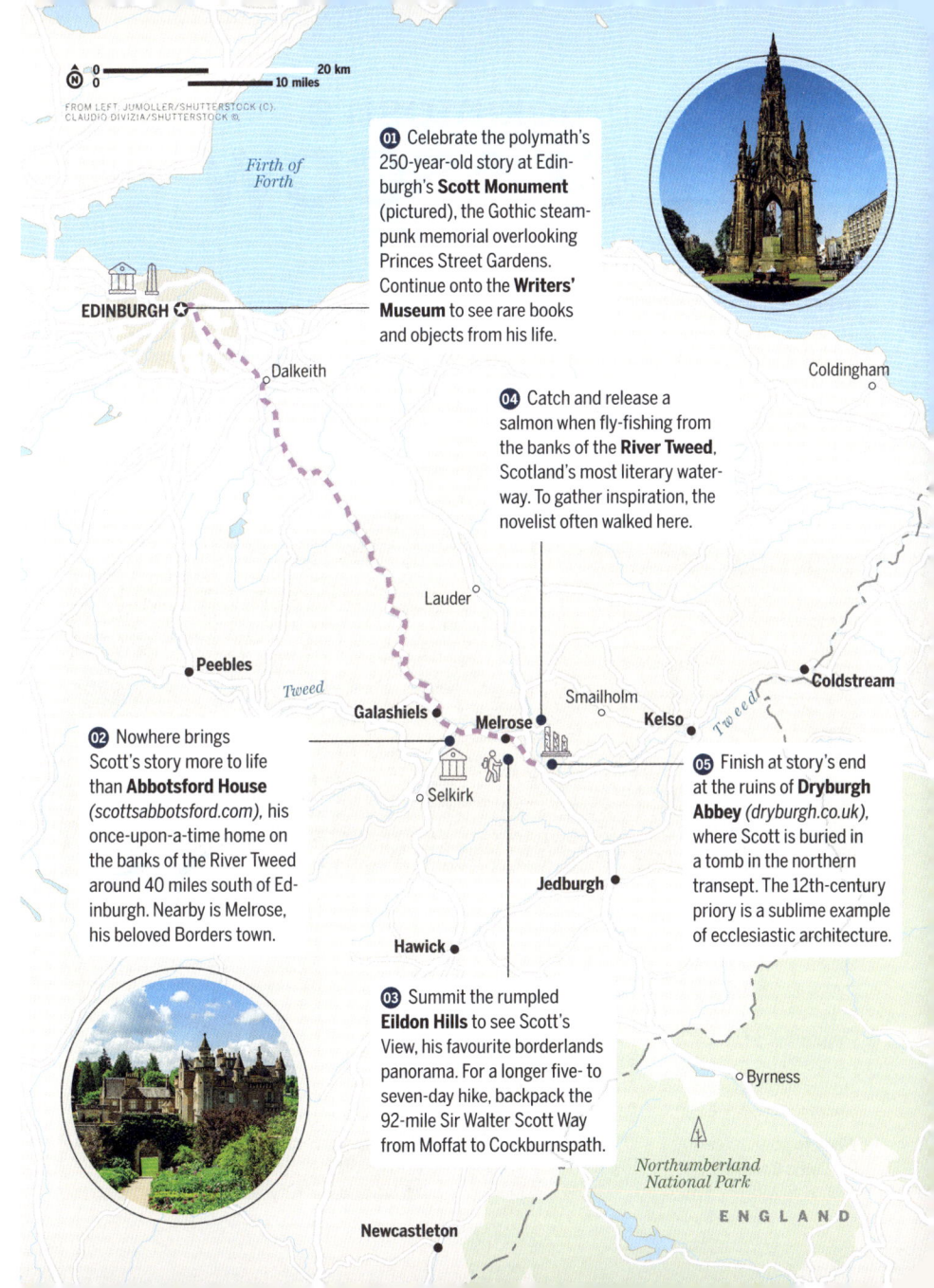

EDINBURGH

01 Celebrate the polymath's 250-year-old story at Edinburgh's **Scott Monument** (pictured), the Gothic steampunk memorial overlooking Princes Street Gardens. Continue onto the **Writers' Museum** to see rare books and objects from his life.

04 Catch and release a salmon when fly-fishing from the banks of the **River Tweed**, Scotland's most literary waterway. To gather inspiration, the novelist often walked here.

02 Nowhere brings Scott's story more to life than **Abbotsford House** (scottsabbotsford.com), his once-upon-a-time home on the banks of the River Tweed around 40 miles south of Edinburgh. Nearby is Melrose, his beloved Borders town.

05 Finish at story's end at the ruins of **Dryburgh Abbey** (dryburgh.co.uk), where Scott is buried in a tomb in the northern transept. The 12th-century priory is a sublime example of ecclesiastic architecture.

03 Summit the rumpled **Eildon Hills** to see Scott's View, his favourite borderlands panorama. For a longer five- to seven-day hike, backpack the 92-mile Sir Walter Scott Way from Moffat to Cockburnspath.

46 Mackintosh's GLASGOW

ARCHITECTURE | ART | HISTORY

Glasgow is rife with the work of Charles Rennie Mackintosh (1868–1928), an architect and designer whose ambition changed the city forever, and his architectural masterpieces can be discovered across its mercantile centre. Equally inspiring is how the designer moved from student to genius architect, becoming a father to the international art nouveau movement.

How to

Getting around Mackintosh's greatest hits are spread across the city, so buy a ticket for the Glasgow Subway, the world's third-oldest underground metro system. An all-day ticket costs £4.30.

When to go Mid-January. For **Celtic Connections** (celticconnections.com), Britain's largest celebration of Celtic music, and to see a rare live performance inside The Mackintosh Church (Mackintosh Queen's Cross).

Top tip The House for an Art Lover in Bellahouston Park is a beloved arts centre and cafe, built on original, if unrealised, Mackintosh designs.

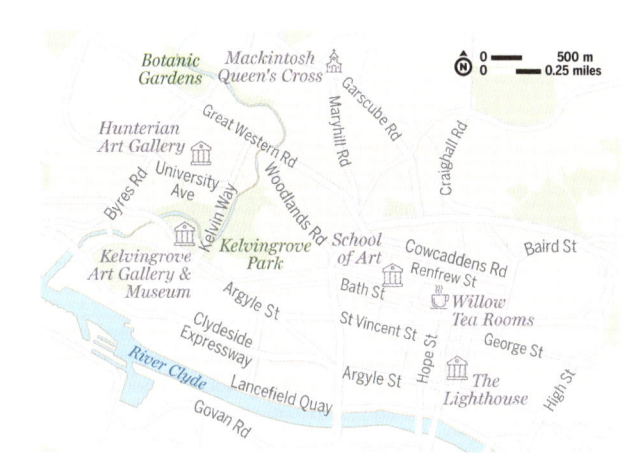

Top left The Lighthouse
Bottom left Hunterian Art Gallery

School days Mackintosh's architectural experiments redrew the map of Glasgow and have since become hallmarks of the city. His most famous creation is the **School of Art**, sadly ravaged by a fire in 2018. It is being faithfully restored, with an eye on reopening around 2030.

Museum life Ask a Glaswegian to name their favourite building in the city and many will say the **Kelvingrove Art Gallery & Museum** in the West End. Though not designed by Mackintosh, it's home to the world's largest permanent display dedicated to his work. Likewise, the nearby **Hunterian Art Gallery** features a brick-by-brick recreation of the designer's home from 1906 to 1914.

City views Ground zero for Mackintosh, **The Lighthouse** (aka Scotland's Centre for Design and Architecture) was the architect's first public commission to be completed. It has a superb helter-skelter tower and an observation gallery with views across Glasgow's rooftops. Closed at the time of writing, it is expected to reopen in the not-too-distant future. For now, grab a cuppa and cream scone at the nearby **Willow Tea Rooms** (willowtearooms.co.uk), originally designed by Mackintosh in 1903.

Religious art Mackintosh excelled when designing houses, mansions and schools, but only ever attempted one church. **Mackintosh Queen's Cross** (mackintoshchurch.com), renowned for its stained glass and stonework, is now an arts venue and the HQ of the Charles Rennie Mackintosh Society, which offers all sorts of guided tours from March/April until autumn.

V&A Dundee

Charles Rennie Mackintosh's **Oak Room**, a Glasgow tearoom first designed in 1907 and lost to view for nearly half a century, can now be seen at the Scottish Design Galleries at **V&A Dundee**. It has been restored piece-by-piece by conservationists and allows visitors to time-travel back to the early 20th century when Glasgow was alive with imperial grandeur. The industry on display here and elsewhere provides a shot of inspiration, but the overarching mission of V&A Dundee is far grander. The hope is the ship-shaped museum masterminded by Japanese architect Kengo Kuma will help transform Dundee's waterfront into a global design hot spot.

Listings

BEST OF THE REST

☼ Beautiful Beaches

Yellowcraig Beach
Swim, stand-up paddleboard (SUP), snorkel or sunbathe in front of the spectacular Fidra Island lighthouse, a supposed inspiration for Scottish author Robert Louis Stevenson's *Treasure Island* (1883) in East Lothian.

Rockcliffe Beach
Search for an ancient citadel on the beach hilltop or bask on the windswept sands of this terrific spot near Dalbeattie in Galloway. Nearby, Rough Island is home to a bird sanctuary and reachable at low tide.

Coldingham Bay
North of the English border in St Abbs, this pristine slice of holiday perfection is popular for surfing and rock-pooling for crabs.

Saddell Bay
Kintyre's most splendid sandy spot, with a prime view of the Isle of Arran and an incongruous cast-iron sculpture by Antony Gormley jutting out of the wave-bashed rocks.

🐟 Seafood Suppers

Lobster Shack £
Crustaceans and just-landed fish served in takeaway boxes on North Berwick's beautiful quayside. There's a heated outdoor dining area to protect diners from East Lothian's unpredictable elements. *lobstershack.co.uk*

Crabshakk ££
This poky Argyll St restaurant in Glasgow's Finnieston excels with scallops, mussels, langoustines and – naturally – whole brown crab. Get cracking! *crabshakk.co.uk*

White Horse Oyster & Seafood Bar ££
Located on the Royal Mile, this is Edinburgh's premiere counter seafood bar, with a menu of iced shellfish towers and weekly oyster happy hours. *whitehorseoysterbar.co.uk*

Fish Works £
Award-winning family-run fish-and-chip shop on the Largs promenade, but one that comes with a side serving of made-to-order langoustines and squid. *thefishworks.co.uk*

◎ Weird & Wonderful

Jupiter Artland
Edinburgh's forest-set sculpture park for those in the know, with a terrific cafe, shop and more than a tip of the hat to Alice's Wonderland. *(jupiterartland.org)*

Glasgow Necropolis
Slip back in time amid the ivy-covered confines of Glasgow's 'city of the dead' to stroll around one of the world's finest Victorian-era cemeteries. *glasgownecropolis.org*

Glasgow Necropolis

Museum of Lead Mining
Experience the Caledonian gold rush and try your hand at gold panning on the Mennock Pass, the precious-metal capital of Britain. *leadminingmuseum.co.uk*

Inchcolm Abbey
Sail from South Queensferry to a time-stopped monastic priory and seal-inhabited beaches on this island adrift in the Firth of Forth.

Caerlaverock Castle
This 13th-century oddity with swampy moat and pink sandstone aesthetic is the only triangular castle in the country. Castle-hunting heaven!

Campbeltown Picture House
A work of art in its own right and the only surviving example of an atmospheric cinema in the country. *campbeltownpicturehouse.co.uk*

🛏 Sophisticated Stays

Glenapp Castle £££
A contender for the most fabulous five-star hotel in Scotland, with fairy-tale suites and located on a private estate in the Ayrshire countryside. Expect sublime service, plus marine biologist-led sea safaris along the coastline. *glenappcastle.com*

Knockinaam Lodge £££
A delightful hideaway on a private Galloway beach and where Sir Winston Churchill supposedly plotted D-Day with US President Dwight Eisenhower during WWII. The guestbook shows the former wartime prime minister was a regular. *knockinaamlodge.com*

Bonnie Badger ££
Nestled between East Lothian's championship golf courses in Gullane and run by Michelin-star chef Tom Kitchin. There are two restaurants to choose from, both serving exquisite local produce. *bonniebadger.com*

Campbeltown Picture House

🥃 Undiscovered Distilleries

Clydeside Distillery
The first whisky producer on the banks of the Clyde in Glasgow for more than a century. Explore the dockside story with a dram, or try a distillery tour with paired whiskies and artisan chocolates. *theclydeside.com*

Glenkinchie Distillery
This Victorian-era distillery in East Lothian is one of the four pillars of the world-famous Johnnie Walker blend. It's an easy 30-minute drive from Edinburgh, and malthouse tours offer fruity samples and a look around the orchard gardens.

Annandale Distillery
A champion of Lowland spirit and the closest whisky produced to the English border. Extend a visit with an insightful tour of the historic Globe Inn in Dumfries, a former coaching inn known as Robert Burns' favourite howff (pub). *annandaledistillery.com*

Bladnoch Distillery
More than 200 years old and still going strong on a 20-hectare estate in Wigtownshire. Highly recommended bespoke hands-on tours. *bladnoch.com*

NORTH SCOTLAND

ADVENTURE | CULTURE | SCENERY

- **Trip Builder** (p216)
- **Practicalities** (p218)
- **Remote Tearooms** (p220)
- **Follow the Jacobite Trail** (p222)
- **The Sunshine Coast** (p226)
- **West Highland Wild Swimming** (p228)
- **Mini Archipelago Adventure** (p230)
- **Eco-Distillery Hop** (p232)
- **Wind & Fire** (p234)
- **Up Helly Aa** (p236)
- **Listings** (p238)

NORTH SCOTLAND
Trip Builder

Escape to the north, Scotland's wild side: a vast, diverse and intensely dramatic playground of small cities, unspoiled isles and ancient landscapes. Feel the sudden shift in pace, rewind through the centuries and revel in the freedom of the outdoors.

Take a day trip to **Knoydart** (p221) peninsula, Britain's last wilderness
⛴ *30 min from Mallaig*

Go cycling, kayaking and puffin-spotting on the **Small Isles** (p230)
⛴ *2–4 hr from the mainland*

Book a guided wild swim in Loch Sunart in the **West Highland Peninsulas** (p228)
🚗 *1 hr from Fort William*

Tour the award-winning, ecofriendly **Oban Distillery** (p232) in the Gateway to the Isles
🚆 *3 hr from Glasgow*

ATLANTIC OCEAN

Butt of Lewis
Stornoway
Harris
The Minch
Tarbert
Outer Hebrides
Gairloch
Lochmaddy
North Uist
Uig
Dunvegan
Skye
Portree
Kyle of Lochalsh
Canna
Rum
Mallaig
Sea of the Hebrides
Eigg
Lochailort
Tobermory
Salen
Mull
Iona
Kilmartin
Jura
Kintyre
Islay
Portnahaven

ATLANTIC OCEAN

0   50 km
0   25 miles

IAIN MACLEAN/GETTY IMAGES ©;
PREVIOUS SPREAD: ESSEVU/SHUTTERSTOCK ©

Shetland

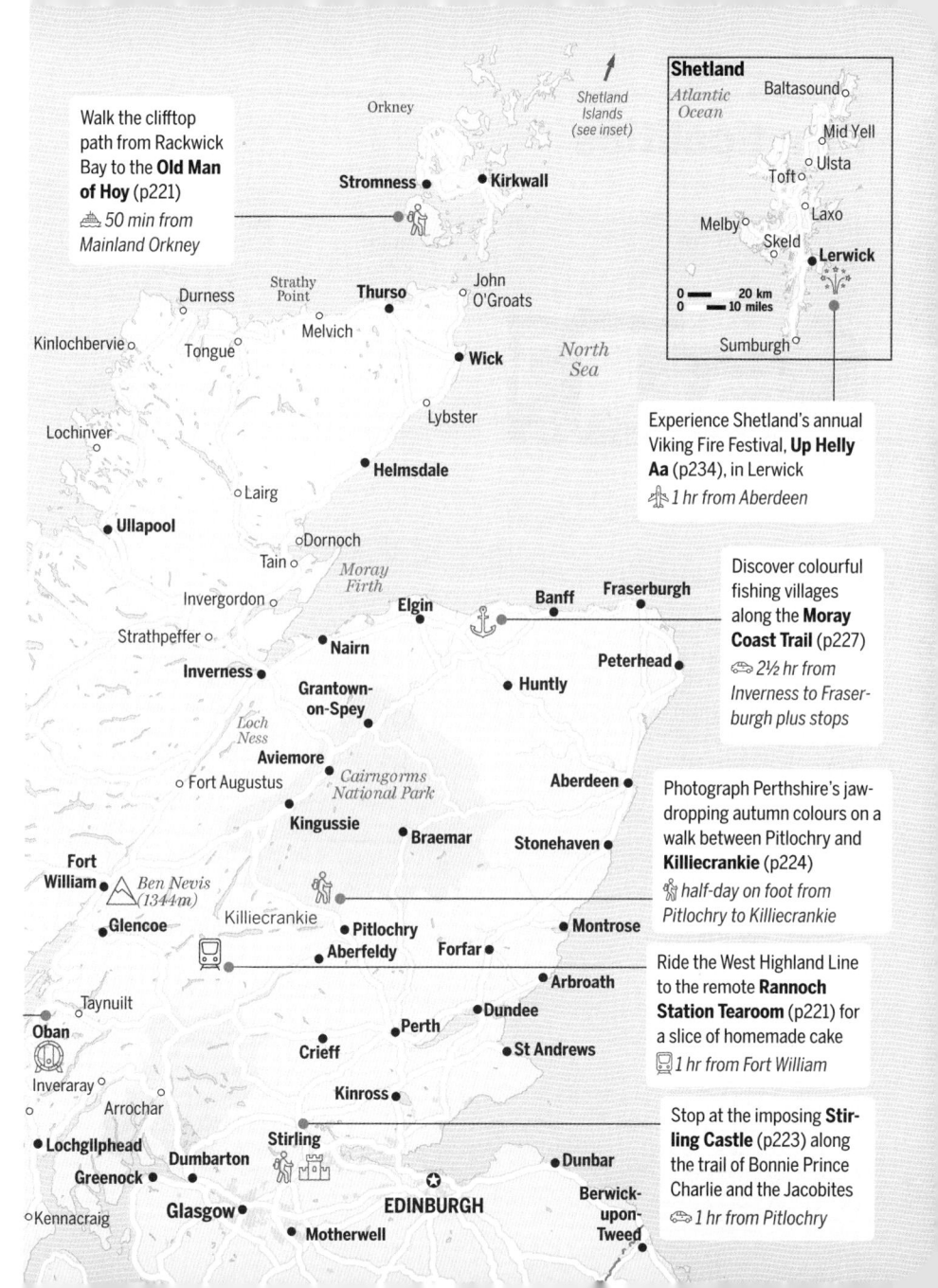

- Baltasound
- Mid Yell
- Ulsta
- Toft
- Laxo
- Melby
- Skeld
- Lerwick
- Sumburgh

Atlantic Ocean

0 20 km
0 10 miles

Walk the clifftop path from Rackwick Bay to the **Old Man of Hoy** (p221)
⚓ *50 min from Mainland Orkney*

Experience Shetland's annual Viking Fire Festival, **Up Helly Aa** (p234), in Lerwick
✈ *1 hr from Aberdeen*

Discover colourful fishing villages along the **Moray Coast Trail** (p227)
🚗 *2½ hr from Inverness to Fraserburgh plus stops*

Photograph Perthshire's jaw-dropping autumn colours on a walk between Pitlochry and **Killiecrankie** (p224)
🚶 *half-day on foot from Pitlochry to Killiecrankie*

Ride the West Highland Line to the remote **Rannoch Station Tearoom** (p221) for a slice of homemade cake
🚆 *1 hr from Fort William*

Stop at the imposing **Stirling Castle** (p223) along the trail of Bonnie Prince Charlie and the Jacobites
🚗 *1 hr from Pitlochry*

Orkney: Stromness, Kirkwall
Shetland Islands (see inset)
Durness, Strathy Point, Thurso, John O'Groats
Kinlochbervie, Tongue, Melvich, Wick
Lochinver, Lairg, Helmsdale, Lybster
Ullapool, Dornoch, Tain, Invergordon, Elgin, Banff, Fraserburgh
Strathpeffer, Nairn, Moray Firth, Peterhead
Inverness, Grantown-on-Spey, Huntly
Loch Ness, Fort Augustus, Aviemore, Cairngorms National Park, Aberdeen
Kingussie, Braemar, Stonehaven
Fort William, Ben Nevis (1344m), Killiecrankie, Pitlochry, Montrose
Glencoe, Aberfeldy, Forfar, Arbroath
Taynuilt, Dundee
Oban, Perth
Inveraray, Crieff, St Andrews
Arrochar, Kinross
Lochgilphead, Stirling, Dunbar
Dumbarton, Berwick-upon-Tweed
Greenock, Glasgow, EDINBURGH
Kennacraig, Motherwell

North Sea

Practicalities

ARRIVING

Bus and train The main transport hubs of Aberdeen, Inverness, Fort William and Oban all have centrally located train stations and bus connections covering onward travel across the Highlands and the north, west and east coasts.

Air Inverness and Aberdeen have regional airports with routes to the islands. The port town of Oban, known as the Gateway to the Isles, has frequent ferries to the Inner and Outer Hebrides, as well as a small airport with flights to the islands.

WHEN TO GO

JAN–MAR
Cold and quiet; snow on the mountains. Not many tourists around.

APR–JUN
Spring flowers and pleasant weather, lovely for island-hopping and walking.

JUL–SEP
Busy peak season. Sunshine for beach days, puffins. Heather in bloom.

OCT–DEC
Stunning autumn colours and dark skies for northern lights.

HOW MUCH FOR A

Tea and cake £6

Cullen Skink £7

Distillery tour £15–35

GETTING AROUND

Car North Scotland is prime road-trip territory: every route is the scenic route here. Narrow single-track roads, sharp bends and steep inclines are likely, so allow extra time for caution. Research the driving etiquette and use of 'passing places' on single-track roads.

Public transport For a slower, more local experience. **ScotRail** (scotrail.co.uk) has trains to the main hubs. Bus travel with **Citylink** (citylink.co.uk), **Stagecoach** (stagecoachbus.com), **West Coast Motors** (westcoastmotors.co.uk) and smaller local operators. Use **Traveline** (travelinescotland.co.uk) to plan your route by bus, train and ferry. Alternatively, explore on foot (walkhighlands.co.uk) or hire a bike.

Ferry CalMac (calmac.co.uk) ferries for the West Coast; **NorthLink** (northlinkferries.co.uk) ferries for Shetland and Orkney. Foot passengers and vehicles should book in advance.

EATING & DRINKING

The west coast and islands are famed for fresh seafood served up at salty sea shacks, cosy inns and high-end restaurants. In the Highlands, try venison stew, burgers and wild venison salami (pictured top). In rural areas, pull over at roadside honesty boxes for fresh eggs and homemade sweet treats like Scottish Tablet. Cullen Skink (pictured bottom), from the Moray Coast, is a creamy soup with smoked haddock.

Purchase single malt whisky, craft gin and fine ales directly from distilleries and independent breweries or enjoy by the fire in a local pub.

Best for fresh shellfish
Lochleven Seafood Café, Onich (p239)

Must-try fudge doughnut
Fisher & Donaldson, St Andrews (p238)

CONNECT & FIND YOUR WAY

Wi-fi Available at most pubs, cafes, restaurants, accommodation and ferry ports, though connection speed is hit and miss. Remote areas with no signal are perfect for a digital detox.

Navigation It's generally easy to navigate using road signs, public transport route maps and Google Maps. Download routes and directions in advance: don't rely on internet connection when you're on the go.

WHERE TO STAY

Place	Pros/Cons
Oban	The Gateway to the Isles is a busy port and transport hub; accommodation can be pricey.
Cullen	Beautiful fishing village with holiday cottages on the Moray Coast Trail.
Lerwick	Arrival port and main town in Shetland. Traditional hotels, guesthouses and B&Bs.
Pitlochry	Perthshire tourist town with lots of shops, places to eat and accommodation options.
Isle of Eigg	Wonderful island and friendly community; stay in a pod, bothy or yurt.
Strontian	Scenic main village in Sunart. Well positioned to explore the West Highland Peninsulas.

TRAVEL PASS

Save money when travelling by bus, train and ferry with the Spirit of Scotland travel pass. Prices start from £150 for four days of unlimited travel across Scotland over eight consecutive days; see *scotrail.co.uk* for more info.

MONEY

Card payment is widely accepted but carry some cash for small businesses, honesty boxes and tipping. Tips are customary but not compulsory; aim for 10% of food bills and taxi fares.

47 Remote TEAROOMS

CAFES | TRAINS | WILDERNESS

Tearooms are the desert oasis of Scotland's great outdoors: quaint eateries where local hospitality is served with hot drinks, comfort food and home-baked treats. Whether you've walked through the wilderness, hopped across to a sparsely populated isle or simply stepped onto the platform of a remote railway station, tearooms can be found in the most unexpected places.

How to

Getting here Take the ScotRail train from Glasgow to Rannoch Station and to Mallaig for the ferry to Knoydart. The CalMac foot passenger ferry travels from Gallanach (Oban) to Kerrera, and Orkney Ferries from Orkney Mainland to Hoy.

When to go For the best chance of clear skies, go April to September. Some tearooms close in the winter.

Advanced rail fares Book 12 weeks ahead for the best fares to Oban, Rannoch Station and Mallaig.

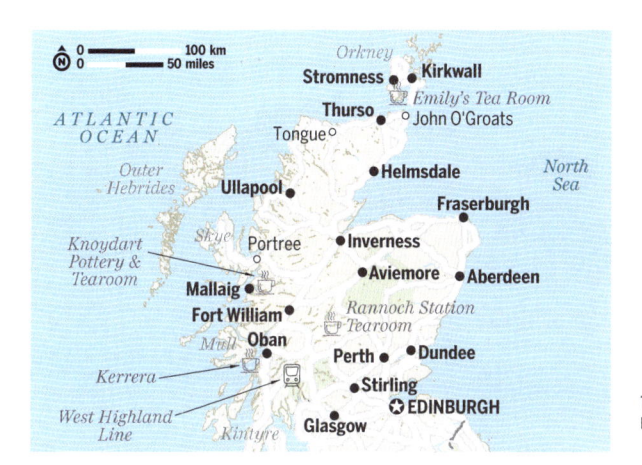

Top left Knoydart Pottery & Tea Room
Bottom left Kerrera Tea Garden

Off the rail The world-famous **West Highland Line** travels across the wild expanse of Rannoch Moor and stops directly outside **Rannoch Station Tearoom** (rannochstationtearoom.co.uk) at one of Britain's most remote railway stations. The cakes, freshly baked each morning, are legendary here. Stop for breakfast, lunch, afternoon tea or a hot toddy; there's occasional live music and quiz nights, too.

Edge of the wilderness Knoydart peninsula, known as Britain's last wilderness, is accessible only by boat from Mallaig (westernislescruises.co.uk) or a 14-mile hike from Kinloch Hourn. In **Inverie**, the main village here, **Knoydart Pottery & Tearoom** (visitknoydart.co.uk) serves breakfast rolls, light lunches and home baking (as well as attractive local pottery). Grab a table outside on the decking overlooking Loch Nevis.

The secret garden Painted teapots and signs lead south on the **Isle of Kerrera**, following a coastal dirt track until the charming **Kerrera Tea Garden** (kerrerabunkhouse.co.uk) comes into sight. Seasonal specials include potato and wild garlic soup, and blackberry, apple and custard cake. The homemade lentil soup is a best-seller, even on hot summer days.

Far north The mountains of Hoy rise up from the sea like no other Orkney island. **Hoy** is home to **Emily's Tea Room** (emilystearoomhoy.co.uk), a colourful cafe, craft shop and ice-cream parlour. Try the Westray smoked mackerel with Orkney oatcakes, or local fish and shellfish pie with creamy mash and peas. The hot Belgian waffles with Orkney fudge ice cream is delicious regardless of the weather.

Wild Walks

To the beach Discover an unexpected golden-sand beach against a backdrop of wilderness on the shores of **Loch Laidon** (0.7 miles from Rannoch Station Tearoom).

Munro bagging Climb two of Knoydart's three Munros – **Luinne Bheinn** and **Meall Bhuidhe** – in one day from Inverie. A challenging climb for experienced walkers (17 miles).

Ancient stronghold The 16th-century ruin of **Gylen Castle** blends into the rugged coastline just a five-minute walk from Kerrera Tea Garden.

The sea stack From Rackwick Bay, the clifftop walk to the **Old Man of Hoy** is nothing short of spectacular (5.75 miles).

48 Follow the Jacobite TRAIL

HISTORY | BATTLEFIELDS | CASTLE

Climb castle walls, stand on the front line of battle and immerse yourself in all-consuming scenery on the trail of Bonnie Prince Charlie and the Jacobites. One of the most turbulent and pivotal periods in Scottish history, inspiring American author Diana Gabaldon's *Outlander* stories, these iconic sites have strong connections to the Jacobites and the Highland way of life they fought to preserve.

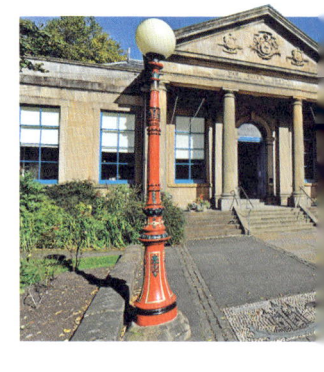

How to

Getting around Go by car for ease and speed. Alternatively, Stirling, Pitlochry and Inverness are served by bus and train with ScotRail, Citylink and Stagecoach.

When to visit All locations are accessible year-round but are very busy in peak summer. Autumn for stunning colours, winter for possible snowy scenes.

Explore Pitlochry makes a good base for day trips, as the Killiecrankie walk is accessible from here and you can take the train to both Stirling and Inverness. For more routes and inspiration, visit the **Jacobite Trail** (jacobitetrail.co.uk).

Royal Fortress

Playing a hugely significant role in Scotland's past, the impressive **Stirling Castle** is a must-visit for any history lover. Perched on volcanic rock, guarding the route between the Highlands and Lowlands, this highly sought-after castle was at the heart of the action throughout the centuries. In 1707 the Jacobites attempted to seize the castle from the government forces and Bonnie Prince Charlie tried again in 1746 during the Siege of Stirling Castle: neither were successful.

Join an hourly tour of the castle, roam the ramparts, then walk downhill to the **Stirling Smith Art Gallery & Museum** (smithartgalleryandmuseum.co.uk) to see the ancient key to Stirling Port Gate, delivered to Bonnie Prince Charlie in January 1746 to prevent an attack on the town.

The Beginning

In 1688 William of Orange deposed King James (Jacobus in Latin) VII & II of Scotland, England and Ireland. The Jacobites fought to restore the Stuart dynasty to these thrones in five armed uprisings between 1689 and 1746: motivations included religion, clan obligations and anti-Union sentiments. All were united by Stuart loyalty.

Above left and right Stirling Castle
Left Stirling Smith Art Gallery & Museum

NORTH SCOTLAND EXPERIENCES

Gorge Walk

Drive (58 miles) or take the train (one hour and 10 minutes) from Stirling to **Pitlochry** for a stunning half-day walk to **Killiecrankie** and back (12 miles). The Battle of Killiecrankie took place nearby in the summer of 1689, during the first Jacobite rebellion. The Jacobites were victorious, despite being outnumbered by over 1000 soldiers, largely driven by their execution of the deadly Highland charge.

Follow in the footsteps of the Jacobites on their march through the **Pass of Killiecrankie**, a wondrous tree-lined gorge on the River Garry. Look out for bungee jumpers on the Garry Bridge and see the Soldier's Leap, where a government redcoat soldier hurtled across the surging river to escape capture. **Killiecrankie Visitor Centre** *(nts.org.uk)* has a small cafe and interesting displays. In autumn the colours here are breathtaking.

Farewell Bonnie Prince

Bonnie Prince Charlie, full name Charles Edward Louis John Casimir Sylvester Severino Maria Stuart, was the grandson of the deposed King James VII & II. Raised in Italy, he rallied the Highland clans at Glenfinnan in August 1745 in a bid to restore the Stuarts to the thrones of the 'Three Kingdoms' – Scotland, England and Ireland.

After the Jacobite defeat at Culloden, Bonnie Prince Charlie sought refuge in the Outer Hebrides. Flora MacDonald famously disguised him as a female maid, 'Betty Burke', sneaking him 'over the sea to Skye' where he was rescued on 20 September 1746, never to return.

David C Weinczok, *author of* The History Behind Game of Thrones: The North Remembers *(2019),* castlehunter.scot

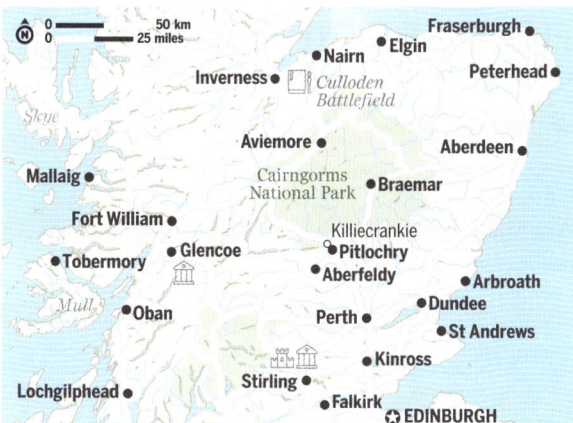

Left Soldier's Leap, Pass of Killiecrankie
Below Culloden Battlefield

The Final Clash

Head north to **Inverness** by road or rail (approximately one hour and 45 minutes), where the tale of the Jacobites comes to a brutal end. Less than 4 miles from the city centre lies the bleak expanse of **Culloden Battlefield**, the scene of the last battle fought on British soil. On 16 April 1746, led by Bonnie Prince Charlie, the Jacobites were defeated by the Hanoverian army in under one hour. The aftermath of the battle, and the subsequent Highland clearances, saw the systematic destruction of the clans, changing the Highland way of life forever.

Take time to browse the engaging, modern displays in **Culloden Visitor Centre** before exploring the battlefield with an audio guide. Culloden can be reached by bus (Stagecoach North Scotland) or taxi from Inverness.

The Weeping Glen

If travelling by car, go west to the atmospheric landscape of **Glencoe**, site of the infamous Massacre of Glencoe. In February 1692, 38 members of Clan MacDonald were murdered in their beds by government soldiers – punishment for the clan chief's late arrival to sign the oath of allegiance to King William of Orange and their loyalty to the Jacobite cause. Visit nearby **Glencoe Folk Museum** (glencoe museum.com) to learn more.

49 The Sunshine COAST

VILLAGES | COASTLINE | WALKING

Stroll, swim or cycle the Moray Coast for quaint fishing villages, historic harbours, sublime seaside scenery and pure relaxation in a warm and dry microclimate. While streams of cars and motorhomes follow the North Coast 500 on the other side of the Moray Firth, this southern stretch of coastline is blissfully unspoiled and surprisingly overlooked by the masses.

How to

Getting here and around Explore the North East 250 by car, or visit parts of the coast on the Stagecoach bus service 35 between Elgin and Aberdeen; Elgin is 40 minutes by train from Inverness.

When to go Spring and summer. Late June for the Glenglassaugh Scottish Traditional Boat Festival in Portsoy; October to April for dark skies and possible northern lights.

Cullen Skink Cullen is home of the famous fish soup; try it at Rockpool Café.

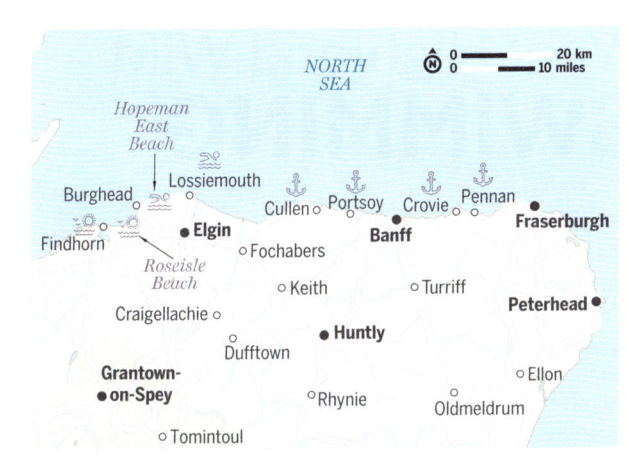

Village views From the 19th-century harbour, views of the fishers' cottages in the Seatown conservation area of **Cullen** are complemented by the old railway viaduct in the background; follow the path across the viaduct for a different perspective. On the Aberdeenshire section of the coast, a single row of picture-perfect cottages lines the foot of the cliffs in **Crovie**, beautifully and precariously close to the sea. The oft-photographed red phone box in nearby **Pennan** starred in the classic Scottish film *Local Hero* (1983), while the charming old harbour in **Portsoy** featured in the TV series *Peaky Blinders* and the 2016 remake of *Whisky Galore*.

Beach days A row of brightly painted beach huts provides a pop of colour on the flawless stretch of **Findhorn Beach**. Further east, the long curve of **Roseisle Beach** is concealed by a passageway of pine forest, where remnants of WWII defence blocks are found scattered along the base of the dunes. Similar structures can be found on **Lossiemouth West Beach** and **Sandend Beach**; book a surf lesson or hire a stand-up paddleboard (SUP) board from **Suds Surf School** (surfschoolscotland.co.uk).

Dive in Wild swimmers have the whole coast to play with. Try the sheltered bay at **Hopeman East Beach** or, for a long sweep of pristine golden sand, cross the new bridge to **Lossiemouth East Beach** – sometimes fighter jets fly overhead here from the nearby RAF Lossiemouth.

Top left Findhorn Beach
Bottom left Cullen

Trail Highlights

Choose a section or walk the full **Moray Coast Trail** from Findhorn to Cullen (50 miles). Alternatively, the **Moray Coastal Cycle Route** covers 29 miles from Burghead to Cullen.

Findhorn Foundation Explore the vibrant community of ecofriendly homes, including the whisky barrel house. *findhorn.org*

Burghead Pictish Fort Check out this settlement dating from around 400 CE. *burghead.com*

Spey Bay Keep an eye out for the Moray Firth's many resident dolphins, particularly around this bay. *dolphincentre. whales.org*

Findochty Stop for a pint at the Admirals Inn by the harbour.

Portknockie Head here for the striking Bow Fiddle Rock sea arch.

Findlater Castle Extend the walk from Cullen to these lonely ruins.

50 West Highland Wild SWIMMING

PENINSULAS | BEACHES | SWIMMING

Venture off the tourist trail and head to the far-flung west for a refreshing dip in epic surroundings. While the benefits of cold water exposure are well known, the West Highland Peninsulas are still under the radar to many. From Sunart to even more remote Ardnamurchan, paradise beaches and serene lochs await, and with no crowds in these parts, peaceful swims are guaranteed.

How to

Getting here A car is essential. Drive in on the A861 from 'Road to the Isles' or arrive via the turn-up-and-go ferry services from Corran to Ardgour; Fishnish (Mull) to Lochaline (Morvern); and Tobermory (Mull) to Kilchoan (Ardnamurchan).

When to go Summer for sunny weather and more daylight hours; September/October for warmer water temperature and stunning autumn colours.

Go with a pro Book a guided swim or hire equipment from **Swim Highlands** (westhighlandpeninsulas.com).

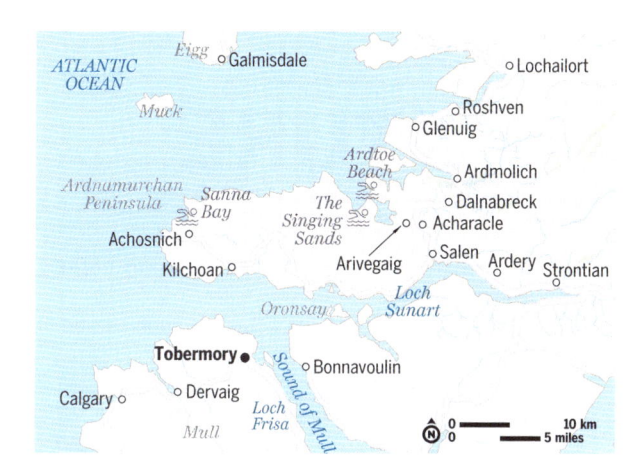

Top left Sanna Bay
Bottom left Loch Sunart

Bonnie beaches Take a long, lonely road from the village of **Kilchoan** through the crater of an extinct volcano to **Ardnamurchan**'s beach of dreams, **Sanna Bay**. White sand dunes and dazzling turquoise waters contrast the dark, rocky outline beyond. At the most westerly part of the UK mainland, facing straight into the Atlantic, both the sea and the surroundings will take your breath away here. For a more sheltered swim, head northeast to explore the sandy bays at **Ardtoe Beach**, particularly magical at sunset. The delightful drive here finishes on a narrow, tightly winding road to the car park; take coins for the small parking charge.

Walk to the Singing Sands Next leave the car at the road's end in **Arivegaig** for a beach mission by foot on the 6-mile, out-and-back route along a coastal and forestry track to the hidden haven of **The Singing Sands**. The size, shape and silica content of the sand grains 'sings' in the wind and under shuffling feet. Swim with views across to the Small Isles and back towards the secluded sands.

Into the loch Stretching 19 miles from Sunart to Ardnamurchan, **Loch Sunart** is the longest sea loch in the Highland region and a Marine Protected Area thanks to the outstanding natural environment of small islands and diverse marine life. Local wild swimmers set off from the stone jetty by the green shed in **Strontian**: easy access and panoramic views.

Local Tips

Ardery Wander through native oak woodland from Àrd-Àirigh car park for a swim around the small islands in Loch Sunart; the setting here feels far from civilisation, despite being close to the shore. Head above water, keep an eye out for white-tailed eagles and otters. Look below for the different colours of seaweed – it's like swimming through a tropical, underwater forest.

Safety advice Wear the necessary kit: wetsuit, tow float, swim shoes and gloves. Check the tides and ever-changing weather. And be prepared for after your swim with warm layers, a hat and a hot drink.

■ Tips by Laura McConnachie, *Open Water Swim Coach and Owner of Swim Highlands*, @swimhighlands

51 Mini Archipelago ADVENTURE

ISLANDS | WILDLIFE | ACTIVITIES

Castaway for a few days on the Small Isles, the less-trodden islands of the Inner Hebrides. These miniature isles are big on community spirit, beautiful beyond measure and completely unspoiled – no visitor vehicles are allowed and you'll see wildlife galore. Nature is the star attraction here.

How to

Getting here Take the ferry from Mallaig with **CalMac** *(calmac.co.uk)* or from **Arisaig Marina** *(arisaig.co.uk)*; the ScotRail train operates from Glasgow to Arisaig and Mallaig.

When and how long Spring for frequent ferries and less visitors; June or July for puffins. Spend two to three days on each island to relax and explore, or take day trips if you're short on time.

Shop local Stock up for your stay at the community shops on Eigg, Rum and Canna.

On Your Bike: Jurassic Park

Cycle from Eigg Pier to The Singing Sands (p229), where the jaw-dropping outline of the Isle of Rum dominates the horizon. Combine with a visit to the north shore of **Laig Bay** for striking Jurassic rock formations and internationally significant fossils. In 2019 the 166-million-year-old bone of a stegosaurian dinosaur was discovered here.

■ Recommended by Owain Wyn-Jones,
owner of Eigg Adventures, @eiggadventures

04 Pre-order the Canna bay platter for dinner at **Café Canna** (cafecanna.co.uk) – an epic feast of fresh, local shellfish. Sit outside and stick around to see Rum burst into colour at golden hour.

02 As menacing as the Norse who named them, the **Rum Cuillin** on Rum is a challenging pursuit for hardcore hillwalkers. Scramble the ridge to reach jagged peaks and reap visual rewards in every direction.

05 Walk the signposted **Puffin Trail** from St Edward's Church to the craggy cliffs and sea stacks on **Sanday** – a playground for puffins in their thousands (half a day from Canna).

01 Hire a kayak from Eigg Adventures and paddle to **Kildonan Bay** on the Isle of Eigg for a secluded cove beach picnic. The prominent pitchstone ridge of An Sgurr looks glorious from this angle.

03 **Gallanach Bay** on Muck is where seals frolic, Highland ponies roam, and eagles, otters and marine life like to make an appearance. It's a leisurely 30-minute stroll from Port Mòr.

FROM TOP: VINCENT LOWE/ALAMY STOCK PHOTO ©, STEVE LEWIS ARPS/ALAMY STOCK PHOTO ©

52

Eco-Distillery
HOP

WHISKY | DISTILLERIES | SUSTAINABILITY

Whether it warms your cockles or makes you wince, sampling the national drink on a whisky distillery tour is a rite of passage in Scotland. These west Scotland distilleries not only produce top-quality single malt in picturesque island and coastal locations, they are leading the way with their pioneering sustainability practices and initiatives. Grab a dram and *sláinte* to that!

How to

Getting around Visit all the distilleries on a multiday road trip; a car is essential for Morvern. ScotRail trains run from Glasgow to Oban. Take a Loganair flight or CalMac ferry to Islay and explore by bus.

When to go The distilleries are open year-round but operate on reduced hours in the colder months between November and February; always check in advance and prebook if necessary.

Distillery tours Prices start from £15; takeaway drams are available for drivers. Alcohol-free tours are also sometimes available.

Lonely peninsula Hidden away, 12 miles from the closest village on **Morvern**, **Nc'nean Distillery** *(ncnean. com)* is a small, special place you won't just stumble upon. Opened in 2017, Nc'nean has become the first whisky distillery in the UK to achieve net zero emissions (Scope 1 & 2). The distillery uses 100% Scottish organic barley, 100% recycled glass bottles and is powered by local biomass (all trees are replanted). Tours include spirit tastings and homemade cake; book in advance.

Port town One of Scotland's oldest and smallest distilleries, **Oban Distillery** *(obanwhisky.com)* combines tradition with innovation. Bio fuel is the primary fuel for the boiler, providing all the steam required for distillation. In 2020 the distillery launched a water-reduction initiative which saves approximately 80,000L of water per week.

The distillery received a Green Tourism Gold Award in recognition of its efforts. A Distillery Exclusive limited bottling is served on the tour.

Whisky island **Bruichladdich Distillery** (uk.bruichladdich. com), a Victorian distillery which was resurrected in 2001, is home to one of the world's peatiest whiskies, Octomore, and is the largest private employer on Islay, creating exciting career opportunities for the younger generation. To reduce greenhouse gas emissions, the distillery has secured funding to implement the use of hydrogen-power technology. Sample Bruichladdich's completely unpeated whisky, and more, on the Core Range Tasting.

Get to Know Nc'nean

Say it Nic-nee-an

Drink it As you like

Suggested serve The Whisky Six: 2 parts whisky, 4 parts soda, ice and garnish with a sprig of mint.

Eco facts The world's second-biggest carbon store is our soils, yet farming barley is the distillery's single biggest source of carbon emissions.

Carbon footprint Nc'nean's entire carbon footprint in 2021 (cradle to gate) was less than one return flight from London to New York!

For a good cause In 2020 the distillery's first-ever bottle of whisky sold for £41,000, breaking the world record for the most expensive bottle of three-year-old whisky sold. The proceeds were donated to charity.

■ Local insight by **Amy Stammers,** Visitor Manager at Nc'nean Distillery, @ncnean

Above Bruichladdich Distillery

53 Wind & FIRE

FESTIVALS | VIKINGS | ISLANDS

Flames, elaborate costumes and all-round madness prevail at Shetland's annual Viking Fire Festival, Up Helly Aa. In the dark depths of winter, quiet residential streets in these windswept northerly isles descend into a flurry of heat and noise, in celebration of the islands' Norse heritage. A community-wide effort, taking a whole year to prepare, Up Helly Aa is a cultural spectacle unlike any other.

How to

Getting here Take an overnight NorthLink ferry from Aberdeen to Lerwick, or a Loganair flight from Aberdeen to Sumburgh; flights from Edinburgh and Glasgow are expensive. Haggis Adventures and Highland Explorer Tours run organised tours.

Festival season January to March. The largest festival is held in Lerwick on the last Tuesday of January.

Plan ahead Tours, transport links and accommodation fill up months in advance, so book early in the year for the following year's event.

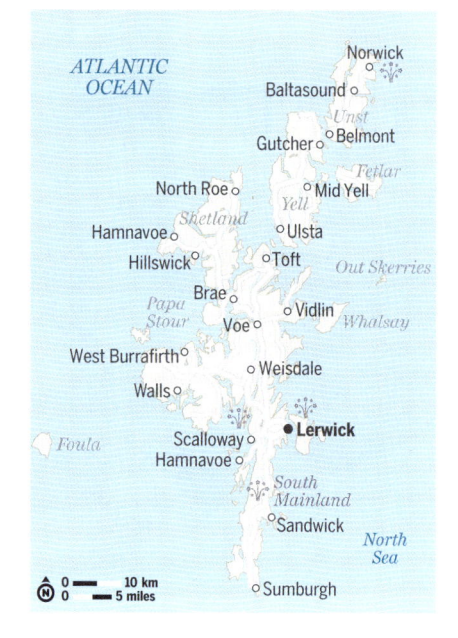

Squad life More than 1000 local men across 46 'squads' participate. The Guizer Jarl dresses as a figure from Norse legend and leads the Jarl Squad through 24 hours of parades, parties and Viking-clad shenanigans. Treated like a local celebrity for the whole year, the Guizer Jarl serves a 15-year apprenticeship on the Up Helly Aa Committee for the honour. Look out for the adorable Junior Jarl Squad and other squads kitted out in hilarious non-Viking costumes.

Festival highlights At 9am hang around the **Royal British Legion** in Lerwick to witness a surreal Viking sing-song inside, before the **Morning Parade** continues to Bressay Ferry Terminal for photos with the beautifully crafted replica Viking galley. Head to the **Shetland Museum** around 3pm to mingle with the Jarl Squad and get a clear view of the **Junior**

Galley burning in the early evening.

Rocket fire from the Town Hall signals the start of the **Torchlight Procession** at 7.30pm.

The squads march the streets wielding paraffin-soaked torches, culminating in the burning of the galley in a children's play park! The boat takes four months to build and less than 30 minutes to burn.

The after party Celebrations continue all night with performances from the squads in public buildings around Lerwick, known as **The Halls**. These are attended mainly by locals. Contact **Lerwick iCentre** (lerwick@visitscotland.com) in January to get on the waiting list.

Festival Season

From January to March, you'll find a small community somewhere in the isles burning a replica Viking longship. Rural Up Helly Aa celebrations are less formal, grittier and offer a greater opportunity to get involved than the more famous Lerwick festival.

Scalloway's Fire Festival (early January) Kicking off the fiery season, this festival weaves through the village's picturesque waterfront before burning the galley in the harbour.

Norwick Up Helly Aa (end of February) The most northerly celebration, set against the spectacular backdrop of Norwick Beach.

South Mainland Up Helly Aa (mid-March) The most recently established Up Helly Aa, with the first-ever female Jarl.

■ Recommended by Laurie Goodlad, *travel writer and tour guide at Shetland with Laurie, @shetlandwithlaurie*

Above Scalloway's Fire Festival

UP
Helly Aa

01 Replica longboat
The Viking galley crafted over four months by locals in the Up Helly Aa committee.

02 Viking dress
Jarl Squad Viking costumes designed by the squad and worn for the full day of the festival.

03 Morning parade
The Jarl Squad marching through Lerwick on the morning of Up Helly Aa.

04 Jarl Squad
The full squad with the Viking galley, pictured at Bressay Ferry Terminal at the end of the Morning Parade.

05 Up Helly Aa Bill
A satirical look at local events, people and politics displayed every year on the Market Cross in Lerwick.

06 Torchlight procession
A procession of around 1000 squad members carrying fire-lit torches through the residential streets of Lerwick.

07 Burning of the galley
The Viking galley is set alight, taking less than 30 minutes to burn. This is the grand finale of the torchlight procession.

08 Norse settlement
The remnants of a traditional 9th-century Viking longhouse at the Jarlshof site in Sumburgh.

09 Underhoull, Unst
Ruins of 30 Viking longhouses on Scotland's most northerly isle; there are more longhouses here than anywhere in the world.

10 NorthLink Ferry
The most popular transport route to Up Helly Aa, 'Hjaltland' is the Old Norse name for Shetland.

11 Viking brooch
Tortoise-shaped bronze brooch, uncovered from a Viking boat burial site on the island of Fetlar. It's displayed in the Shetland Museum.

01 ANDY BUCHANAN/AFP VIA GETTY IMAGES ©, 02 ANDREW J SHEARER/SHUTTERSTOCK ©, 03 KONSTANTIN BELOVTOV/SHUTTERSTOCK ©, 04 ANDREW J SHEARER/SHUTTERSTOCK ©, 05 ANDREW J SHEARER/SHUTTERSTOCK ©, 06 KONSTANTIN BELOVTOV/SHUTTERSTOCK ©, 07 ANDREW J SHEARER/SHUTTERSTOCK ©, 08 DORSTEFFEN/SHUTTERSTOCK ©, 09 ROBERTHARDING/ALAMY STOCK PHOTO ©, 10 MARCIN KADZIOLKA/SHUTTERSTOCK ©, 11 SHETLAND MUSEUM PHOTO ARCHIVE ©. BACKGROUND IMAGES MADDYZ/SHUTTERSTOCK © (ENVELOPE), JOINTSTAR/SHUTTERSTOCK © (AIRMAIL POSTCARD)

Listings

BEST OF THE REST

Woodland Walks & Waterfalls

Puck's Glen, Dunoon
A damp, dark trail of wooden bridges, waterfalls and rock pools. Named after the sprite in Shakespeare's *Midsummer Night's Dream*, this rocky, mossy gorge is the stuff of magic.

The Hermitage, Dunkeld
Wander through tall trees to Black Linn Waterfall; this enchanting spot is best viewed from the stone bridge or Ossian's Hall balcony. Popular during autumn.

Glen Affric
Home to one of Scotland's last and largest remaining native Caledonian pine forests, the whole area is wildly scenic and untouched. Check out Plodda Falls and Loch Affric.

Dollar Glen, Clackmannanshire
Ascend the deep gorges in a forest oasis, formed by the Burns of Care and Sorrow, from the pretty town of Dollar to the medieval ruins of Castle Campbell.

Baked Goods

Blackwater Bakehouse, Isle of Arran £
Artisan bread freshly baked with wild yeasts and sweet surprises displayed in the self-serve Bread Shed outside. Join the queue before opening time at 11am for first pick and fantastic coffee.

Fisher & Donaldson, St Andrews £
Five generations over 100 years have worked in this family bakery empire in Fife. There are sweet and savoury bakes, but it's the world-famous fudge doughnuts you need to try.

The Bakehouse, Mallaig £
Sourdough loaves, mouth-watering pastries, and hand-stretched, wood-fired pizzas (spring/summer weekends only) overlooking the bustling harbour in Mallaig.

Croft 36, Isle of Harris £
A roadside shed operating by honesty system. Everything from fresh bread and hot soup to homemade pies and tarts. Pre-order takeaway meals with local seafood and homegrown veg.

Wee Whistle Stop Cafe, Torridon £
On the shores of munro-capped Loch Torridon, this community cafe rustles up delicious home bakes, cakes, toasties and daily specials.

Historic Wonders

Gearrannan Blackhouse Village, Isle of Lewis
A restored traditional crofting village by the sea, capturing the island way of life in the 1800s. Watch a Harris Tweed weaving demonstration in one of the blackhouses.

Machrie Moor Standing Stones, Isle of Arran
A circle of mysterious stones stand tall in open moorland with distant mountain views;

Skara Brae, Orkney

smaller stones and cairns nearby. The site was used for burials and religious ceremonies over 4000 years ago.

Skara Brae, Orkney

Not to be missed on Orkney, this amazingly well-preserved neolithic village offers a glimpse into domestic life 5000 years ago; beds and furniture are still intact.

Calanais Standing Stones, Isle of Lewis

Feel the pulse of prehistory at one of Britain's most complete and impressive stone circles, on a wild, remote promontory.

Waterfront Seafood

Lochleven Seafood Café, Onich ££

West coast seafood heaven. Order a showstopper shellfish platter on ice, or if you prefer it hot, go for the roasted shellfish version with aioli. *lochlevenseafoodcafe.co.uk*

North Harbour Bistro, Scalpay £££

A short drive across the bridge from the Isle of Harris, this unassuming, unpretentious island eatery serves up modern, high-end cuisine with excellent fresh seafood options.

Shieldaig Bar & Coastal Kitchen, Shieldaig ££

Dazzling loch views await at this cheery waterside restaurant, serving boat-fresh fish and seafood. Go for blackboard specials or a superb seafood platter.

Café Kisimul, Isle of Barra ££

Named after the striking castle on the bay outside, this family-run island institution serves seafood with an Italian and Indian twist. Order the scallop pakora and a fish curry. *cafekisimul.co.uk*

Quirky Gifts

Island Blue, Tobermory

As colourful within as its bright facade on the iconic harbourfront, this small, friendly

Cairngorm Reindeer Centre, Aviemore

independent shop is filled with beautiful ethical gifts, homeware, clothing and toys. *islandbluetobermory.co.uk*

Coralbox Gift Shop, Isle of Berneray

A pretty little shop by the sea specialising in island-themed items, as well as Eilidh's own photography showcasing the natural beauty of the Outer Hebrides. *coralbox.ecwid.com*

Wildlife Experiences

Uist Sea Tours, Isle of Uist

Explore the Outer Hebrides from the water on a bottlenose dolphin cruise or see puffins on a Mingulay tour (April–September). Once-in-a-lifetime trips to St Kilda run during summer. *uistseatours.co.uk*

Mull Magic, Isle of Mull

Join a guided Otter Detective Walk along the scenic shoreline of Mull for the chance to spot some of the island's elusive otter population. Transport and a delicious packed lunch is included. *mullmagic.com*

Cairngorm Reindeer Centre, Aviemore

Get up close to Britain's only free-ranging herd of reindeer on a guided Hill Trip in the Cairngorms National Park: truly magical in winter. Tickets are released 30 days in advance. *cairngormreindeer.co.uk*

Practicalities

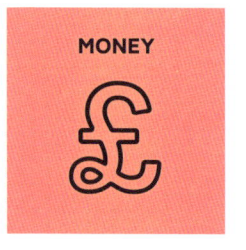

ARRIVING	GETTING AROUND	SAFE TRAVEL
242	**244**	**246**

MONEY	ACCOMMODATION	RESPONSIBLE TRAVEL
247	**248**	**250**

ESSENTIALS
252

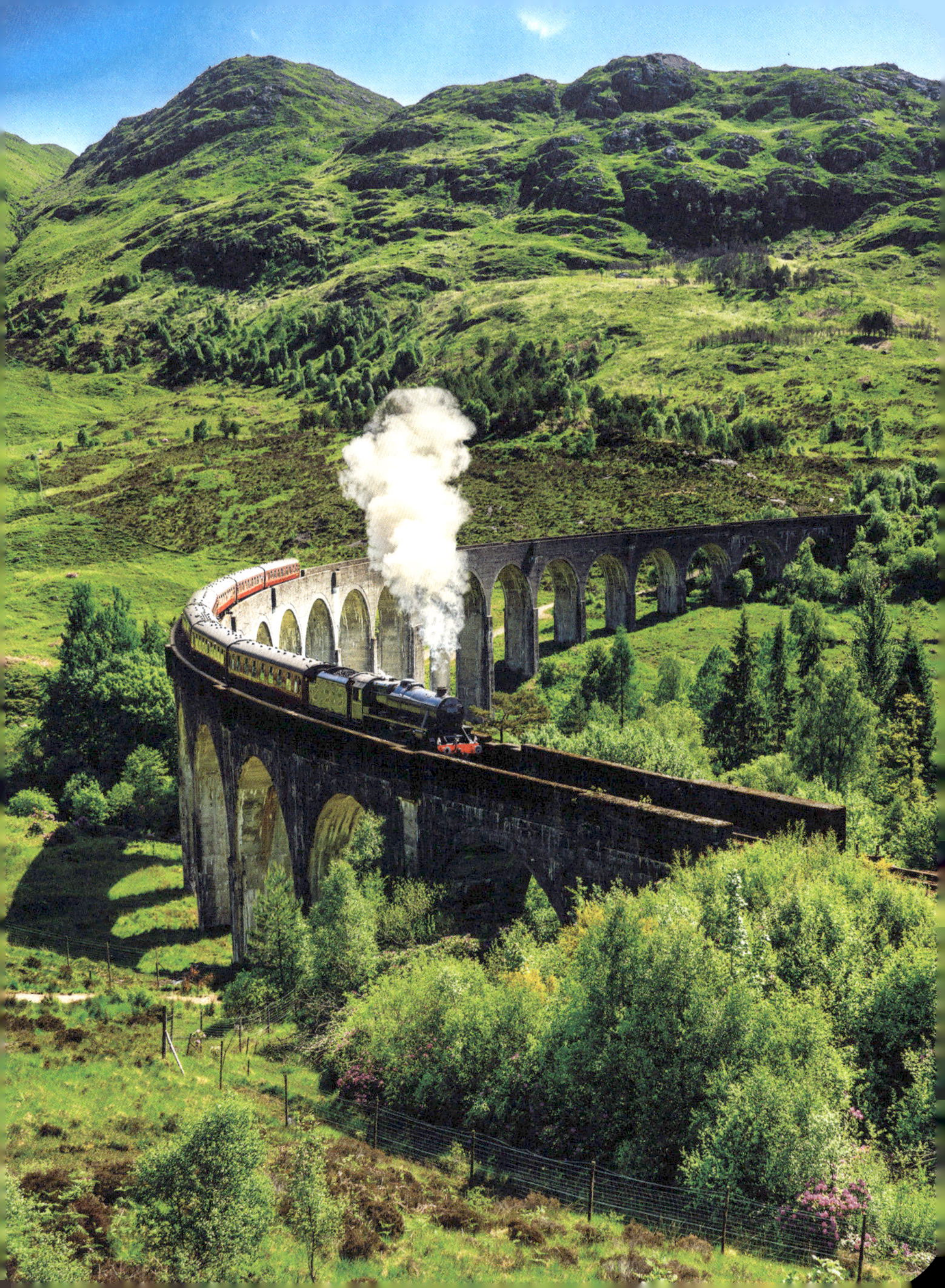

EASY STEPS FROM THE AIRPORT TO THE CITY CENTRE

Heathrow (pictured) is the main port of entry for visitors to Britain. Located 15 miles west of the city centre, it has four terminals (terminals 2–5). Terminal 5 is used exclusively by British Airways and Iberia; all other carriers use 2, 3 and 4. Heathrow is connected to London by the Underground, and has a range of pubs, restaurants, shops, money exchanges and car-hire options.

AT THE AIRPORT

SIM CARDS
SIM cards for unlocked phones can be bought in all of Heathrow's terminals, either at WHSmith (5am–11pm) or Sim Local (6am–10pm) stores, or from a SIM vending machine that is accessible 24/7.

CURRENCY EXCHANGE
Travelex currency exchange desks can be found in terminals 3, 4 and 5, after security near Departures. In Terminal 2, the Travelex desk is in the check-in area before security. Rates are always better at the post office or banks in the cities.

WI-FI Free wi-fi is available in every terminal. The network name is '_Heathrow Wi-Fi' and reaches all taxi ranks and car collection points.

ATMs There are ATMs that accept all major foreign cards before and after security in every Heathrow terminal.

CHARGING POINTS Every terminal has free Power Pole charging stations before and after security. These take European and UK plugs as well as USBs.

CUSTOMS REGULATIONS

Duty-free You can bring in up to 200 cigarettes, 18L of wine or 4L of spirits from outside the UK as part of your personal allowance.

GETTING TO LONDON CITY CENTRE

PUBLIC TRANSPORT Heathrow is served by the Underground (Piccadilly Line) and buses (5am–midnight) on the Transport for London (TfL) network. Grab an Oyster card at the Underground station or pay contactless for the best rates.

COACH National Express *(nationalexpress.co.uk)* runs a coach service from all Heathrow terminals to London Victoria from £8.40 one way.

TAXI There are taxi ranks at each terminal. If an accessible taxi is required, seek out Heathrow staff to arrange. Rideshare and taxi apps use the designated drop-off and pick-up zones for each terminal.

PLAN YOUR JOURNEY Use the TfL Go app to plan your journey to and from Heathrow and around London.

VISITOR OYSTER CARDS Topped-up Oyster cards can be purchased from the **British Tourist Board** *(visitbritainshop.com)* or at the Heathrow Underground station.

TRANSPORT FARES Single fares on the Underground to central London cost £6.70 (or £5.60 with an Oyster card/contactless) and are capped at £15.90 for the day.

TOP UP Oysters can be topped up at any station, ticket machines, local stores and online, or via the TfL Oyster app for those with a UK address.

OTHER POINTS OF ENTRY

Air London has five more airports carrying its name, with the furthest actually based in nearby Luton. Britain's busiest airport in each country after that is Edinburgh Airport (Scotland) and Cardiff Airport (Wales).

Eurostar The main international train entry port is London's St Pancras International train station, where Eurostar trains arrive from Paris, Brussels, Amsterdam and Marseilles. Fares vary greatly, from £39 for a one-way standard-class ticket to Paris to around £275 for a fully flexible business premier ticket.

Ferry The main international ferry ports into Britain from mainland Europe are Dover, Newhaven, Liverpool, Newcastle, Harwich, Hull and Portsmouth, while ferries to and from Ireland depart from Liverpool, Holyhead, Fishguard and Pembroke Dock.

Bus Britain is linked to other European countries by the long-distance bus and coach network Eurolines. Services to/from Britain are operated by National Express. Examples of journey times to/from London: Amsterdam (12 hours), Barcelona (24 hours), Dublin (12 hours) and Paris (eight hours). If you book early, and can be flexible with timings (ie travel off peak), you can get some very good deals.

TRANSPORT TIPS TO HELP YOU GET AROUND

Transport in Britain can be expensive, especially when going by train. Bus and rail services can also be sparse in the more remote areas. This is why Brits tend to drive, especially as distances are not great on this compact island nation and you get to see things at your own pace. But beware the eye-watering rising cost of fuel.

TRAIN
With extensive coverage and frequent departures, train travel around Britain is fast, comfortable and picturesque, but it is usually very expensive, can be crowded and services aren't as punctual as they should be given the cost. Where possible travel off peak as rates are lower and tickets more flexible.

CAR
The normal driving position on Britain's three-lane motorways is in the left lane; the other two are for overtaking. However, almost nobody except lorry drivers seems to follow these rules, so be prepared for drivers who just sit in the middle and right lane, oblivious to everyone else and forcing others to dangerously undertake them.

CAR RENTAL PER DAY
from £45

Petrol approx £1.44/L

Park and ride £6.80 per day return

HITCH-HIKING
Hitching is not common in Britain. While it is possible, as long as you don't mind long waits, it is never entirely safe and we don't recommend it. If you do hitch, remember it's illegal to hitch on motorways. It's very different in remote places like Mid-Wales or northwest Scotland, where hitching is how people get around. On some Scottish islands, local drivers might stop and offer a lift without you even asking.

BUS Cheaper and slower than trains, but useful in more remote regions that aren't serviced by rail.

BOAT As an island nation, there are ferry services all around Britain, which connect the mainland to smaller coastal islands, Ireland and Europe. In larger cities, there are also commuter boat services to get about.

DRIVING ESSENTIALS

A foreign driving licence is valid in Britain for up to 12 months.

Blood-alcohol limit is 80mg/100mL (0.08%) in England and Wales, and 50mg/100mL (0.05%) in Scotland.

Drive on the left; the steering wheel is on the right.

Speed limits are usually 30mph in built-up areas, 60mph on main roads and 70mph on motorways and most dual carriageways. In Wales, the speed limit is 20mph on restricted roads.

Give way to your right at junctions and roundabouts.

PARKING Many cities have short-stay and long-stay car parks, and offer 'Park & Ride' systems that allow you to park on the edge of the city then ride to the centre on frequent nonstop buses for an all-in-one price.

Single yellow lines on the road indicate parking restrictions; double yellow lines mean no parking or waiting at any time. In some cities there are also red lines, which mean no stopping at any time.

INSURANCE It's illegal to drive a car or motorbike in Britain without insurance. This will be included with all rental cars, but if you're bringing a car in from Europe, you'll need to arrange insurance.

BIKES ON TRAINS Bicycles can be taken free of charge on most local urban trains (although there are restrictions at peak travel times). Bikes can also be carried on long-distance train journeys free of charge, but advance booking is required for most services.

KNOW YOUR CARBON FOOTPRINT A domestic flight from London to Edinburgh emits about 140kg of carbon dioxide per passenger. For the same distance per passenger by car it is 72kg, by train it is 19kg and by bus it is 13kg.

There are a number of carbon calculators online. We use Resurgence at *resurgence.org/resources/carbon-calculator*.

ROAD DISTANCE CHART (MILES)

GREAT BRITAIN

	Birmingham	Brighton	Bristol	Cardiff	Dover	Edinburgh	Glasgow	London	Manchester
Brighton	176								
Bristol	97	157							
Cardiff	123	188	42						
Dover	203	104	194	225					
Edinburgh	291	464	373	398	470				
Glasgow	290	462	371	397	472	417			
London	126	64	118	149	77	403	412		
Manchester	86	259	168	193	295	216	214	208	
Oxford	78	106	85	116	142	366	364	56	161

SAFE TRAVEL

Britain is a very safe country for travellers but it is wise to keep your wits about you in busy, urban areas, such as in large shopping centres and on congested public transport, as you would at home.

PICKPOCKETS Britain's busy tourist areas, especially in London, are often patrolled by those with sticky fingers, so be on your guard.

ATMS Known as cash machines in Britain. Occasionally these are tampered with; if the machine looks unusual, avoid using it and stick to those belonging to large, established banks. Always cover the keypad with your hand when entering your PIN.

UNLICENSED TAXIS A common presence around town centres, especially late at night when many people are leaving clubs and bars. Do not use any taxi that doesn't have an official licence sticker clearly displayed. If pestering continues, threaten to call the police.

NON-EMERGENCY CARE If you are feeling unwell and it is not an emergency, you can call the NHS 111 service by dialling 111 and get free medical advice from trained professionals over the phone.

TAP WATER Unless otherwise stated, tap water is safe to drink everywhere in Britain and most establishments will happily provide a free jug with meals upon request.

DRUG POSSESSION Illegal drugs are widely available, especially in clubs. Carrying any quantity of drugs is a criminal offence and may lead to a fine and imprisonment. Marijuana is not legal in Britain. Those caught dealing face much stiffer penalties.

'FALLOUT TIME' Late on Friday and Saturday nights, when pubs and clubs are closing, British town centres can become intimidating and rowdy places where drunken behaviour is widespread.

QUICK TIPS TO HELP YOU MANAGE YOUR MONEY

CREDIT CARDS Visa and Mastercard credit and debit cards are widely accepted in Britain. Other credit cards, including Amex and Maestro, are not so widely accepted. Most businesses will assume your card is 'Chip and PIN' enabled (using a PIN instead of signing). Credit-card purchases over £100 are also subject to extra protection, which means if there is an issue with the purchase a refund can be requested.

CONTACTLESS If enabled, contactless cards can be used for payments up to £100 and for fares on many city transport systems.

MONEY EXCHANGE There are currency-exchange bureaux and banks in large towns and cities. For the best rates try post offices and large supermarkets, like Tesco.

CURRENCY
Pound sterling (£)

HOW MUCH FOR A...

Coffee £3.50

Pint of beer £5

Fish and chips for two £20

ATMS & CASHBACK ATMs are normally attached to a supermarket or bank; some charge fees. You can also request 'cashback' in some supermarkets, which is where you withdraw cash by adding an amount to the bill.

SCOTTISH BANKNOTES In Scotland, banks issue their own notes. These are interchangeable with Bank of England notes and, in theory, accepted across Britain; however, you may sometimes have problems outside of Scotland.

COINS In spite of the move to a cashless society, there are still some places in Britain where coins remain essential, such as when paying for parking in remote parts or simply grabbing a trolley at the supermarket.

TIPPING
Tipping is not usually expected in Britain.
Restaurants Some restaurants automatically add a service charge, so check before leaving a tip. If nothing is added, a tip around 10% is standard.
Pubs and bars There is no need to tip staff in bars and pubs unless you are having a sit-down meal.
Taxis Round up to the nearest pound, and in bigger cities like London add around 10%.

DISCOUNTS & SAVINGS
Most sights, activities and public transport services offer reduced rates to seniors, kids and families, and in many cities museums are free.

There is no countrywide discount card, but for those visiting London the **London Pass** *(visitbritain.com)* allows entry to numerous sights at a reduced rate.

UNIQUE AND LOCAL WAYS TO STAY

Accommodation in Britain is more than just about having a bed for the night. There are luxury experiences that range from staying in a medieval castle to five-star London hotels with award-winning restaurants, while the more quirky and quaint can mean sleeping on a houseboat or the excitement of shutting out the wilderness and bedding down in a bothy.

HOW MUCH FOR A...

Pub or inn £60

University room £80

Medieval castle £300

HOUSEBOATS Drift lazily down Britain's many picturesque waterways in your very own houseboat, combining the joys of travel with a quintessentially British accommodation. Numerous agencies offer beautifully dressed houseboats for rental for a few days or a week with no previous nautical experience required. Prices start from around £1200 for three nights.

LANDMARK STAYS Fancy a night in a 15th-century castle on the shores of Devon? What about an 18th-century chateau overlooking the lush greenery of Lincolnshire? Or maybe a Tudor manor house with an impressive great hall is more your style? Whatever grand, regal overnight stay your heart desires, in all likelihood you can rent it via the **Landmark Trust** *(landmarktrust.org.uk)*, which has restored stunning historic British landmark buildings, furnished in period style, available for your sleeping pleasure. Approximately £225 to £1370; minimum four-night stay.

BUNKHOUSES

An ultrabasic hostel that is essentially a communal sleeping area with a bathroom. You have to bring your own sleeping bag and there might be a kitchen area with stoves, but even then you'll need your own cooking gear. Basically pack everything as if you were camping, except the tent. Roughly £12 to £25 per person per night.

OVERNIGHTING IN A BOTHY

Bothies are basic mountain shelters, located in remote spots along hiking trails, and entirely free for short overnight stays, courtesy of the kind owners. They epitomise rural British hospitality. And until quite recently, these quaint, rustic little former shepherd's huts remained a local secret, carefully guarded by hikers and outdoor enthusiasts wandering through the wilderness and highlands of rural Scotland, northern England and Wales.

What to expect A bothy will have no more than one or two bedrooms where you might have a sleeping platform – no beds – and a communal area. There are no bathrooms (do your business outside and bury it) or kitchen facilities and you should bring a sleeping bag and pillow with you – the spartan offering is part of the charm.

The Bothy Code Most of the properties are looked after by the volunteer organisation **Mountain Bothies Association** *(mountain bothies.org.uk)*, but they also rely on communal care and respect. There is an expectation that everyone staying in a bothy abides by the Bothy Code: respecting others staying in the bothy; only using the bothy for very short stays; ensuring food and rubbish is taken away; respecting the immediate environment and the agreement with the landowner; and respecting the limit of six people per bothy. Bothy locations can be found on the website.

BOOKING

The best prices are always online, but in more remote parts, try local visitor centres to find accommodation if scarce. They can also book it for you. Reserve well in advance in peak tourist seasons: June through August, Christmas and Easter school holidays.

Lonely Planet *(lonelyplanet.com/hotels)* Find independent reviews, as well as recommendations on the best places to stay – and then book them online.
University Rooms *(universityrooms.co.uk)* A room in a university during the holidays.
ABC Boat Hire *(abcboathire.com)* Houseboat bookings in several popular spots.
Landmark Trust *(landmarktrust.org.uk)* Book a restored castle or a manor house.
Cottages & Castles *(cottages-and-castles.co.uk)* Castles and cottages across Scotland.
Cottages.com *(cottages.com)* Online platform to book cottages and lodges.
National Trust *(nationaltrust.org.uk/holidays)* Book interesting National Trust properties.
Sugar & Loaf *(sugarandloaf.com)* Great selection of luxurious self-catering stays in Wales.
Canopy & Stars *(canopyandstars.co.uk)* Quirky camping and glamping spots that include shepherd's huts and treetop cabins.
Welsh Rarebits *(rarebits.co.uk)* Fabulous hand-picked selection of boutique hotels, B&Bs and self-catering cottages across Wales.

UNIVERSITY STAYS

Spend a night on campus at the world-famous University of Oxford or University of Cambridge. During vacations, many British universities offer accommodation to visitors; these are usually a functional single bedroom or self-catering flat. From £55 to £120 for a single room.

POSITIVE-IMPACT TRAVEL

Positive, sustainable and feel-good experiences around Britain

ON THE ROAD

Reusable bags, cups and cutlery are increasingly welcomed by British shops, restaurants and cafes.

Plan sustainable stops to avoid reliance on large service stations and instead consider heading off motorways to shop at small independent and ecofriendly businesses that support the local economy around Britain.

Find a toilet. You can locate the nearest toilet with **Toilet Map** *(toiletmap.org.uk)*.

Lower your overall impact. Where possible, use the train and dramatically reduce your carbon footprint. When commuting and driving longer journeys try carpooling or driving an energy-efficient vehicle. **Collaborative Mobility UK** (CoMoUK; *como.org.uk*) is a charity dedicated to helping people move towards integrated low carbon transport solutions in the UK.

GIVE BACK

Visit wildlife reserves and protected areas and support organisations conserving wildlife and biodiversity. There are many all over Britain.

Support sustainable and low-impact enterprises. Seek out businesses across the country that are giving back to their community, from Celtic basket makers to wild food foragers. See *lowimpact.org/directory*.

Clean up the coastline. There are regular volunteer events across Britain. Check *mcsuk.org*.

Restore hedgerows and clean up green spaces as a volunteer with the countryside charity **CPRE** *(cpre.org.uk/get-involved/volunteering)*.

Make a donation. Contribute to tree planting and reducing the world's carbon by donating to the National Trust's tree-planting initiative *(nationaltrust.org.uk)*.

DOS & DON'TS

Do be polite Pleases, thank-yous and minding your Ps and Qs (manners) matter to Brits. Grumble discreetly and queue patiently!

Do be mindful of regional sensitivities The Welsh and Scots are proud of their country, culture and language. Never make the mistake of calling them English.

Do respect privacy That famous British reserve? It's more a question of respecting their privacy. Some people are happy to talk to strangers, others less so.

LEAVE A SMALL FOOTPRINT

Save some cash when you bring your own reuseable cup to cafes.

Leave nothing behind when walking or hiking. Many green areas no longer have litter bins so it is important you take everything away with you.

Recycle often – there are recycle stations across Britain, and many high street bins are now adapted to take litter and recyclables.

Buy ethically by typing what you are looking for into the **Ethical Consumer** (*ethicalconsumer.org*) search engine, which has been promoting ethical shopping since 1989.

SUPPORT LOCAL

Spread your tourist pound. Where you can, consider buying local and supporting small businesses, especially on high streets.

Eat locally. Buy fresh produce and meet locals at farmers markets. Find one via the **UK Farmers Market Directory** (*saturdayandsunday.co.uk*).

Buy gifts and souvenirs directly from artists and makers. The UK Craft Fairs (*ukcraftfairs.com*) website has a good list of craft fairs up and down the country.

CLIMATE CHANGE & TRAVEL

Lonely Planet urges all travellers to engage with their travel carbon footprint, which will mainly come from air travel. While there often isn't an alternative, travellers can look to minimise the number of flights they take, opt for newer aircrafts and use cleaner ground transport, such as trains.

One proposed solution—purchasing carbon offsets—unfortunately does not cancel out the impact of individual flights. While most destinations will depend on air travel for the foreseeable future, for now, pursuing ground-based travel where possible is the best course of action.

The UN Carbon Offset Calculator shows how flying impacts a household's emissions:

The ICAO's carbon emissions calculator allows visitors to analyse the CO2 generated by point-to-point journeys:

RESOURCES

ethicalconsumer.org
ukcraftfairs.com
lowimpact.org
cpre.org.uk

ESSENTIAL NUTS-AND-BOLTS

QUEUES
Queuing is a very serious matter in Britain. Always clearly establish where the queue starts and ends before joining it.

A ROUND
When drinking with Brits, everyone is expected to buy a 'round' once. This means buying a drink for everyone in the group.

SMOKING
Smoking is banned in all indoor spaces, and also near the entrance to buildings.

FAST FACTS

Time Zone GMT+0

Country Code +44

Electricity 230V/50Hz

GOOD TO KNOW

US, EU and several Commonwealth citizens can enter Britain visa-free and stay up to six months.

Free wi-fi is being rolled out on Britain's transport services.

Escalator etiquette: stand on the right, walk on the left.

The legal drinking age in Britain is 18 and it is legal to drink in public.

Brits drive on the left. This is clear on major roads but can be confusing on narrow lanes and single-tracks that see little traffic.

ACCESSIBLE TRAVEL

New buildings and larger hotels have wheelchair-accessible lifts and ramps, but smaller hotels and B&Bs in historic buildings are usually not great. Check before booking.

Most modern city buses and trams have low floors for easy access, although may require a ramp to be put out by the driver. Some taxis take wheelchairs, but they are not the norm outside of large cities.

For long-distance travel, opt for trains as most intercity services can be accessed by travellers with accessibility issues, although a ramp may be required. Always enquire at the time of booking or prior to travel and request assistance at stations, as many do not have step-free access to the street.

London's Underground is notoriously bad for accessibility. Plan your journeys carefully on the TfL Go app, where you can switch on the 'step free' mode.

Visit Britain (visitbritain.com) has an accessible guide that's a great resource for planning trips around the country.

GREETINGS
It's customary to shake hands when meeting for the first time.

CUTLERY
When in doubt, start by using the cutlery on the outside and then work your way inwards.

BAGGAGE LOCKERS
Most large train stations and ports have luggage-holding services that charge by the hour or day.

FAMILY TRAVEL
Family restaurant chains like Nandos, Giraffes and Harvester have kids' meals and high chairs, as do many family-friendly pubs and cafes.

Admission to sights is often reduced for under 16s (but the cut-off age might also be 12 or 14).

Prams do not have the same priority as wheelchair users on public transport.

Children aged four and under travel free on all trains.

Children aged five to 15 years pay reduced fares (usually 50%).

Child seats are generally not available in taxis.

TIME
Britain is on GMT/UTC with the clocks going forward one hour for 'summer time' at the end of March, and turning back again at the end of October. The 24-hour clock is used for timetables and tickets at stations and ports.

TOILETS
- Also referred to as the loo, bog, privy or khazi.
- Public toilets are becoming increasingly rare.
- Many pubs and restaurants will only allow customers to use their facilities.
- Use the **Toilet Map** (toiletmap.org.uk) to locate one on the road.

LGBTIQ+ TRAVELLERS
Britain's larger cities are easily the most welcoming to LGBTIQ+ travellers, and though the country is highly tolerant, discrimination does still happen in less metropolitan parts. British people remain quite conservative when it comes to public displays of affection. London, Manchester and Brighton have flourishing gay and lesbian scenes.

Gay Pride celebrations take place throughout the summer months, with large parades, outdoor parties and festivals planned in most big cities.

Follow **Gay Times** (@gaytimes) for the latest events, news and gigs across the UK.

Index

A
Aberystwyth 187
accessible travel 252
accommodation 248-9
Ailsa Craig 205
airports 242
Alloway 205
Alvechurch 123
Angel of the North 143
Anglesey 177
archaeology 92-3, 98, 238, 239
architecture 46-7, 210-11
Ardery 229
Arran 238
art galleries
  Albukhary Foundation Gallery 63
  BALTIC Centre 144
  Barber Institute of Fine Arts 123
  Birmingham Museum & Art Gallery (BMAG) 131
  Hepworth Wakefield 144
  Ikon 131
  Jameel Gallery 63
  Kelvingrove Art Gallery & Museum 211
  National Gallery 54
  Stirling Smith Art Gallery & Museum 223
  Tate Britain 54
  Walker Art Gallery 144
  Whitworth Art Gallery 144
art, public 142-5, 212
ATMs 247
Avebury Henge 93

B
balti 119
Bampton 75

000 Map pages

Banksy 101
Barrowford 147
Bath 110
bathrooms 253
beaches
  England 109, 138-9
  Scotland 212, 226-7
  Wales 175
Beachy Head 80
beer 8-9, 34, 71, 111, 130
birds 78, 172-3
Birmingham 112-31, **114**
  accommodation 115
  drinking 130
  food 118-19, 131
  itineraries 128-9, **129**
  planning 114
  travel seasons 115
  travel within 115
Black history 102-3
boat travel 244
boat trips 78-9, 81, 108-9, 159, **79**
books 36
bothies 249
Brecon Beacons 168-71
Brighton 61
Bristol 100-3, 110
Broadway 69, 80
bus travel 244

C
camping 99
canals 122-3
Cannock Chase 131
Canterbury 81
Cardiff 178-81, **179**
castles 15
  Beaumaris Castle 167
  Bodiam Castle 81
  Burghead Pictish Fort 227

Caerlaverock Castle 213
Caernarfon Castle 167
Caerphilly Castle 167
Cardiff Castle 167
Corfe Castle 89
Culzean Castle 205
Dover Castle 73, 74
Edinburgh Castle 199
Findlater Castle 227
Gylen Castle 221
Hever Castle 81
Kenilworth Castle 127
Oxford Castle 77
Pembroke Castle 167
Powis Castle 167
St Michael's Mount 110
Stirling Castle 223
Warwick Castle 123
cemeteries 60, 199, 212
Cerne Giant 93
cheese 11, 150-1
Cheltenham 81
children, travel with 253
Chipping Campden 69
chocolate 159
churches & cathedrals
  Birmingham Oratory 129
  Canterbury Cathedral 81
  Coventry Cathedral 127
  Ely Cathedral 75
  Holy Trinity Church 123
  Mackintosh Church 211
  Norwich Cathedral 81
  Rosslyn Chapel 199
  St Davids 175-6
  St Paul's Church 117
  University Church of St Mary the Virgin 77
  Westminster Abbey 51

cinemas 213
climate 18-25
Clitheroe 147
coasteering 95, 176
Cold Ashton 69
Cornwall 108-9
costs 244, 247, 248
Cotswolds 80
Coventry 127
credit cards 247
Crovie 227
Croyde 107
Cullen 227
Culloden Battlefield 225
cultural centres 48-9
currency 247
customs regulations 242

D
Dartmoor 96-9
deer 80
disabilities, travellers with 252
dolphins 173, 227, 239
Dover 73
drinking 8-9, 252, see also individual regions
driving 6-7, 12-13, 244-5
Dryburgh Abbey 209
Dundee 211
Durdle Door 95

E
Eastbourne 81
Eden Project 110
Edinburgh 198-201
Edinburgh Festival Fringe 19, 200-1
Eigg 231
electricity 34, 252
England, see southeast England, southwest England, Midlands, northern England
etiquette 251, 252-3
events, see festivals & events

Exford 107
Exmoor 106-7

F
Falmouth 108-9
family travel 253
festivals & events 18-25, 81, 182-3, 234-7
films 37, 74-5
food 10-11, 42-3, see also balti, cheese, chocolate, individual regions
football 156-7
fossils 95

G
galleries, see art galleries
gay travellers 56, 253
gin 159
Glasgow 196-7, 210-11
Glastonbury Festival 18
Glencoe 225
Glentress 207
Glentrool 207
Great Malvern 121
Gyllyngvase 109

H
Hadrian's Wall 152-5
Hay-On-Wye 187
healthcare 246
Heathrow Airport 242-3
hiking
  England 69, 81, 97-8,107, 120-1, 137, 147, 158
  Scotland 221, 224, 227, 238
  Wales 174-7
historic railways 81, 88-9, 159
history 14, 16, 50-1, 62-3 102-3, 222-5
hitch-hiking 244
Holy Island 139
Hoy 221

I
Inner Hebrides 230-1, **231**
Innerleithen 207
insurance 35, 245
Inverie 221
Inverness 225
Ironbridge Gorge 117
Islam 62-3
Isle of Purbeck 89
Isles of Scilly 104-5, **105**
itineraries 26-33, **26-7**, **28-9**, **30-1**, **32-3**, see also individual regions

J
Jacobites 222-5
Jurassic Coast 94-5

K
kayaking 95
Kildonan Bay 231
Killiecrankie 224
Kintyre 202-3

L
Lake District 141, 148-9, **149**
Lancashire 146-7
language 35, 165
Leamington Spa 123
Lerwick 234-7
LGBTIQ+ travellers 56, 253
libraries 77
Liverpool 60-1, 158, 159
Llandudno 187
Llechwedd Slate Mines 186
Loch Laidon 221
Loch Sunart 229
London 38-57, **40**
  accommodation 41
  drinking 41, 55
  food 41, 42-3
  itineraries 30-1, **30-1**
  navigation 41
  planning 40

shopping 55, 56
travel seasons 41
travel to 41, 242-3
travel within 41
walking tours 49, 52-3, **53**
Lyme Regis 95

M
Mackintosh, Charles Rennie 210-11
Maenporth 109
Malvern Hills 120-1
Manacles 109
Manchester 143, 145, 158
markets 11, 181
measures 35
Midlands 112-31, **114**
  accommodation 115
  planning 114
  travel seasons 115
  travel within 115
monasteries 213
money 247
monuments 50-1, 209
Morecambe 159
mosques 59, 60
mountain biking 99, 206-7
Mt Snowdon 184-5
Muck 231
museums 17
  Albukhary Foundation Gallery 63
  Beamish Living Museum of North 158
  Birmingham Museum & Art Gallery (BMAG) 131
  Black Country Living Museum 117
  British Museum 54
  Castlefield Urban Heritage Park 158
  Charmouth Heritage Coast Centre 95
  Chatham Dockyard 73, 74

000 Map pages

  Coalbrookdale Museum of Iron 117
  Coffin Works 117
  Georgian House Museum 103
  Glencoe Folk Museum 225
  Imperial War Museum (Duxford) 73
  International Slavery Museum 158
  Jameel Gallery 63
  Jorvik Viking Centre 158
  Kelvingrove Art Gallery & Museum 211
  Kent Battle of Britain Museum 73
  Lyme Regis Museum 95
  M Shed 100-1
  Museum of Lead Mining 213
  Museum of London Docklands 51
  Museum of the Gorge 117
  Museum of the Jewellery Quarter 117
  National Museum Cardiff 179
  Natural History Museum 54
  Pen Museum 117
  Pitt Rivers Museum 77
  St Fagans National History Museum 186
  Stirling Smith Art Gallery & Museum 223
  Story Museum 77
  Writers' Museum 209
music 36, 124-5
Muslim Britain 58-63

N
national parks 7, 184-5, **185**
New Forest 90-1
Newcastle 153, 156-7
Newcastleton 207
Norden 89
Norfolk 78-9, 80, **79**
northern England 132-59, **134-5**
  accommodation 137

  drinking 137
  food 137, 148-9, 150-1
  itineraries 28-9, 148-9, 150-1, **28-9**, **149**, **151**
  money 137
  navigation 137
  planning 134-5
  travel seasons 136
  travel to 136
  travel within 136
Northern Lights 139
Norwich 81

O
Orford Ness 73
Orkney 239
Oxford 76-7

P
Painswick 69
palaces 75
parking 245
parks & gardens 44-5
  England 44-5, 59-60, 77, 110, 130
  Wales 181, 187
  Scotland 197
Penarth 187
Pennan 227
Penzance 110
Pitlochry 224
Plymouth 110
podcasts 36
Port Lympne 80
Portknockie 227
Portsoy 227
pubs 246, 252

R
Remembrance Day 21
responsible travel 246, 250-1
Roman sites 110, 127
Royal Ascot 18
rugby 182

S

Sanday 231
Scarborough 141
scenic railways 221
Scotland 190-213, 214-39, **192-3, 216-17**
  accommodation 195, 219
  drinking 219
  food 212, 219, 238, 239
  itineraries 26-7, 204-5, 208-9, 230-1, **26-7, 205, 209, 231**
  money 195, 219
  navigation 195, 219
  planning 192-3, 216-17
  shopping 239
  travel seasons 194, 218
  travel to 194, 218
  travel within 194, 218, 219
Scott, Walter 208-9
Shakespeare, William 123
Shetland Islands 234-5
Skara Brae 239
Small Isles 230-1, **231**
smoking 252
Snowdonia National Park 184-5, **185**
Snowshill 69
social media 37
Solva 176
Somerset 106-7
southeast England 64-81, **66**
  accommodation 67
  itineraries 32-3, 78-9, **32-3, 79**
  money 67
  travel to 67
  travel within 67
South West Coastal 300 204-5
southwest England 82-111, **84-5**
  accommodation 87
  drinking 87, 111
  food 87, 111
  itineraries 32-3, 104-5, **32-3**
  money 87
  navigation 87
  planning 84-5
  shopping 111
  travel seasons 86
  travel to 86
  travel within 86, 87
Spey Bay 227
Spirit of Speyside 25
St Anthony 109
St Davids 175-176
St Mawes 109
St Michael's Mount 110
Stanton 69
stately homes 73, 75, 127
stone circles 14, 92-3
Stratford-upon-Avon 123
Suffolk 80
Sunderland 156-7
surfing 107, 141
sustainable travel 196-7
Swanage 88-9
swimming 95, 107, 109, 110, 141, 184

T

tearooms 220-1
Tenby 175
theatres 49, 53, 54-5, 103, 179
Thomas, Dylan 21, 183, 186
time 252, 253
tipping 247
toilets 253
Tolkien, JRR 128-9
Tower Bridge 53
train travel 244
travel seasons 18-25
travel to/from Great Britain 242-3
travel within Great Britain 244-5

U

Up Helly Aa 23

V

vegetarian & vegan travellers 189
Vikings 16, 234-7

W

Wales 160-89, **162-3**
  accommodation 165
  drinking 165
  food 165, 186, 188
  itineraries 178-9, 184-5, **179, 185**
  money 165
  navigation 165
  planning 162-3
  shopping 189
  travel seasons 164
  travel to 164
  travel within 164
  wi-fi 165
walking, see hiking
walking tours 49, 52-3, 109, 197, **53**
waterfalls 238
weather 18-25, 34
websites 37
West Bay 95
West Highlands 228-9
Westbury White Horse 93
whisky 8-9, 25, 130, 159, 186, 203, 213, 232-3
Whitby Abbey 158
Wigtown 204
wildlife 78, 80, 172-3, 187, 239
Wimbledon 18
Winchcombe 69
Winchester 81
wine & wineries 8-9, 70-1, 111
Woking 59-60
Worcestershire 120-1
Wotton-Under-Edge 69
WWI & II 17, 72-3

Y

York 158
Yorkshire 150-1, **151**

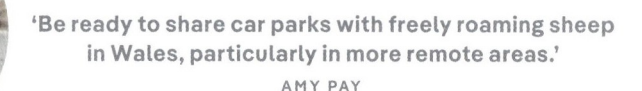

'Be ready to share car parks with freely roaming sheep in Wales, particularly in more remote areas.'
AMY PAY

'London is best at dawn. Grab an early coffee and head out while the city is still asleep for a sunrise stroll and photo session along South Bank before the crowds rock up.'
KERRY WALKER

'Even the car crossing to Holy Island is not for the faint-hearted, as we discovered one snowy day! Be extra sure to study the timetables or you may end up turning back in fright, as we did.'
RHONDA CARRIER

'I discovered that punting needs better balance than you think after getting stuck in a willow tree in Oxford.'
LUCY DODSWORTH

'Desperate for a photo of the roaring, fire-wielding squad of Vikings during Up Helly Aa, I slipped and landed backside first in a puddle of mud.'
KAY GILLESPIE

Although the authors and Lonely Planet have taken all reasonable care in preparing this book, we make no warranty about the accuracy or completeness of its content and, to the maximum extent permitted, disclaim all liability arising from its use.

All rights reserved. No part of this publication may be copied, stored in a retrieval system, or transmitted in any form by any means, electronic, mechanical, recording or otherwise, except brief extracts for the purpose of review, and no part of this publication may be sold or hired, without the written permission of the publisher. Lonely Planet and the Lonely Planet logo are trademarks of Lonely Planet and are registered in the US Patent and Trademark Office and in other countries. Lonely Planet does not allow its name or logo to be appropriated by commercial establishments, such as retailers, restaurants or hotels. Please let us know of any misuses: lonelyplanet.com/legal/intellectual-property.

THIS BOOK

Commissioning editor
Amy Lynch

Production editor
Sarah Farrell

Cartographer
Dorothy Davidson

Book designer
Jo-anne Riddell

Coordinating editors
Gabrielle Innes, Anne Mulvaney

Cover researcher
Hannah Blackie

Thanks
Gwen Cotter, Alison Killilea, Jenna Myers, Charlotte Orr, Claire Rourke